STRATEGIC ENVIRONMENTAL MANAGEMENT

▲▲▲ | **WILEY SERIES IN ENVIRONMENTAL QUALITY MANAGEMENT**

John T. Willig, Series Editor

AUDITING FOR ENVIRONMENTAL QUALITY LEADERSHIP: BEYOND COMPLIANCE TO ENVIRONMENTAL EXCELLENCE

John T. Willig, Editor

STRATEGIC ENVIRONMENTAL MANAGEMENT: USING TQEM AND ISO 14000 FOR COMPETITIVE ADVANTAGE

Grace Wever, Ph.D.

STRATEGIC ENVIRONMENTAL MANAGEMENT

Using TQEM and ISO 14000 for Competitive Advantage

Grace Wever, Ph.D.

John Wiley and Sons, Inc.
New York ■ Chichester ■ Brisbane ■ Toronto ■ Singapore

Library of Congress Cataloging-in-Publication Data:

Wever, Grace, 1939–
    Strategic environmental management : using TQEM and ISO 14000 for
  competitive advantage / Grace Wever.
      p. cm—(Wiley series in environmental quality management)
    Includes index.
    ISBN 0-471-14746-X (cloth : alk. paper)
    1. Industrial management—Environmental aspects. 2. Total quality
  management. 3. ISO 14000 Series Standards. 4. Environmental
  management. I. Title. II. Series.
  HD30.255.W48 1996
  658.4′08—dc20   95-52787

Printed in the United States of America

10 9 8 7 6 5 4 3 2 1

To the Wever clan:
Al, Dave, Lisa, Mike, Mary, and Ingrid

CONTENTS

PART I ■ BECOMING AN ENVIRONMENTAL QUALITY LEADER

CHAPTER 1 ■ THE GREENING OF QUALITY   3

CHAPTER 2 ■ MAKING TQEM WORK FOR YOU   13

CHAPTER 3 ■ LEADERSHIP   35

CHAPTER 9 ■ QUALITY TOOLS THAT WORK   125

CHAPTER 10 ■ DRIVING OUT SACRED COWS   139

CHAPTER 11 ■ PERFORMANCE—THE BOTTOM LINE   157

CHAPTER 12 ■ THE ART OF ACTIVE LISTENING   169

CHAPTER 13 ■ ENGAGING YOUR NETWORKS   179

CHAPTER 14 ■ USING BENCHMARKING TO IMPROVE YOUR PERFORMANCE   189

PART III ■ PRACTICAL TOOLS FOR IMPLEMENTING TQEM

ACKNOWLEDGMENTS

Most of us, myself included, will never become experts on Quality. Nonetheless, I thank George Vorhauer for illuminating the simplicity and elegance of its approach through the medium of the Baldrige framework. I similarly owe a debt of gratitude to Dr. Ronald Heidke, Kodak vice president and director of Corporate Quality, for his early and continuing support as we launched the Council of Great Lakes Industries' fledgling Total Quality Environmental Management (TQEM) program in 1990.

Members of the TQEM workgroup who collaborated to develop the original version of the TQEM Matrix and a model company case study included: John Grieve, Ontario Hydro; Ed Strauss, CN Rail; John Howard and John Kahabka, New York Power Authority; Paul Ireland and Bob Allen, Dow Chemical Canada; Tom Klein, Xerox; Rick McMullan, Canadian Pacific Forest Products Ltd.; Barbara Northan, DuPont; John Ogden, General Motors; Al Pasconis, Cleveland Advanced Manufacturing Program; Sheila Stacey, Dofasco; Lucius Williams, AT&T; Mel Wright, Bayer Rubber; Glenn Wygant, then with ERM; Dick Forbes, Sandra Walsh, George Vorhauer, and myself, Kodak. The TQEM Primer was published in 1993 with generous in-kind support from Al Monohan of Xerox.

I gratefully acknowledge a grant from the Great Lakes Protection Fund to the Council of Great Lakes Industries that supported industry workshops as well as case studies that inform the knowledge base behind this book. The latter project was enriched through the participation of Matthew Arnold, president of the Management Institute of Environment and Business, and Noellette Conway-Schempf, Arpad Horvath, and Lester Lave of Carnegie-Mellon University. We were pleased to have Curt Reimann's and Harry Hertz's assistance at the National Institute of Standards and Technology (NIST) in recruiting Baldrige

Examiners Nicholas Leifeld (Serigraph) and David Crowell (then of EG&G) to lend their expertise to the project.

Above all, I am deeply indebted to colleagues and friends, old and new, who shared their thoughts and experiences on many occasions. Not all can be mentioned here, but very special thanks to colleagues who provided input of various kinds on this manuscript, including Tom Briggs, Jim Blamphin, Neil Connon, Haines Lockhart, Jeff Mathews, Jeanne McDougall, Steve MacIntyre, Gary Katz, Dick Poduska, Deb Schoch, and Elliott Stern. Terry Johnston provided great insight into ISO 9000, ISO 14000, and Baldrige. Bill Chandler, Ron Morrison, Jeff Mathews, Peter Loberg, and Bob Gomperts actively supported the application of quality-based environmental management at Kodak Park.

Recognition is due to friends old and new (not all can be mentioned) who provided information through our TQEM benchmarking project and other avenues on their sector's approach to environmental management, such as Wally Vrooman at Avenor, Jim Kolanek at ITT Automotive, Tom Klein at Xerox, John Kahabka of New York Power, Dan Cuoco at EG&G, Frank Fedri at Occidental Chemical, Daryl Wilson and Andrew Connor at Dofasco, Lucius Williams at AT&T, Gerry Whitcombe at Dow, Jim D'Orazio at Inland Steel, Larry Green at Kodak Canada, Larry Chako at Brush Wellman, and Col. John Mogge, Bruce Stephens, Tim Blevins, and Rhonda Hayden, all of the Air Combat Command, Paula Kirk of BASF, Joe Marrone, Mary Ellen Burris, and Mike Lloyd at Wegmans Food Markets. Tom Davis of AT&T provided insights into the beginnings of GEMI. Bob Langert at McDonald's clarified the famous "foam versus paper" life-cycle controversy. Hart Swisher at Hammer Lithograph took time to educate me on the shopfloor about lithographic printing. Robert Dawson of Ryder Dedicated Logistics introduced me to the implications of logistics for environmental management strategies. Steve Thorp of the Great Lakes Commission thoroughly indoctrinated me on Great Lakes transportation issues and their environmental implications. David Smith of the Council of Ethics in Economics steered me through the growing literature on business ethics. Dan Sayre and John Willig of John Wiley & Sons provided encouragement and support from the concept stage to completion of the book.

For lending humor to this book through their inimitable artforms, I am happily indebted to Al, Harald, and Mike Wever. For review, special thanks to Dave Wever and Don Deliz, and to Don again, for prodigious indexing support. Patty Eastley's sunny disposition and efficiency helped me survive the rigors of this past year.

And finally, very special acknowledgments to George Kuper, CGLI president and CEO, for his comments and insight during the development of this manuscript—always with the best of humor—and to Robert Stempel, chair of CGLI, for his leadership and strong and continuing support of our environmental stewardship and policy programs.

ABOUT THE DISKETTE

DISK CONTENT

The enclosed disk for *Strategic Environmental Management* contains the following:

Filename	Description	Format
TQEMM.XLS	Matrix	Excel for Windows 5.0
SCORING.DOC	Blank Scoring Form	Word for Windows 2.0
TQEMLIST.DOC	Self-Assessment Checklist, Ch. 17	Word for Windows 6.0
TQEMLIST.TXT	Self-Assessment Checklist, Ch. 17 (text)	ASCII Text

COMPUTER REQUIREMENTS

To use the files on the disk, you will need an IBM PC or compatible computer with a 3.5" floppy drive, word processing software such as Microsoft Word and spreadsheet software such as Microsoft Excel. If you have different word processing or spreadsheet software, consult your user manual for information on loading files from other programs. *The Self-Assessment Checklist* is also provided in ASCII text so that you can reformat using different word processing or page layout software.

INSTALLING THE DISK

To install the files, do the following:

1. Insert the disk into drive A of your computer.

2. At the prompt **A:\>**, type **install** and press Return. If you are running Windows, choose <u>F</u>ile, <u>R</u>un in the Program Manager, type **a:Install** and press Return.

3. You will have the opportunity to name the subdirectory to store the data files. The default subdirectory is WEVER96. To accept this name, press Return.

The installation program copies the files to your hard disk. When all the copying is complete, you can press any key to exit the installation program. Remove the original disk from drive A and store it in a safe place.

USER ASSISTANCE AND INFORMATION

John Wiley & Sons, Inc. is pleased to answer questions regarding installation and use of the disk. If you have any problems please call our product support number at (212) 850-6194, weekdays between 9 A.M. and 4 P.M. Eastern Standard Time.

To place additional orders or to request general information about orders or other Wiley products, please call Wiley customer service at (800) 879-4539.

INTRODUCTION

This book was originally written *for* environmental managers *by* an environmental manager, but it should have broader appeal. It fills the gap between abstract management texts and anecdotal, topical accounts from industry practitioners who have learned the hard way how to manage. While it provides a conceptual framework for management, it also lends practical guidance on implementation. It relates the conceptual and real worlds through numerous case examples. But it also should help the academic community and students (however formally you define this term) understand the factors that influence and constrain decision-making in the business world, as well as value the efforts of those companies and individuals who have successfully mainstreamed environmental, health, and safety (EHS) management.

Parts I and II of the book introduce readers to environmental (or to EHS) management as visualized through Baldrige, Deming, and ISO 14001 frameworks. Part III of the book is crammed with tools for analysis, implementation, assessment, and study; thus it should be useful to novice as well as experienced managers.

The term "Total Quality Environmental Management" (TQEM) will, in time, become dated, for TQEM is not a stand-alone activity. Time and experience have shown that environmental issues, however critical to business, should not be managed separately, but should be integrated with other priorities addressed in business planning. That this integration has already occurred in many large companies supports this argument. For now, however, the term TQEM remains useful, highlighting as it does the marriage between the fields of Total Quality and environmental management that took place during the 1980s.

Numerous changes led to that union and to the ensuing and radical transformation in the way that we both regard and manage these issues. Today:

We know more about the environment, which helps us make better-informed decisions. Our investments in research and development (R&D) have broadened our knowledge base about the state, fate, and sources of contaminants, and their effects on public health and ecosystems. As a consequence, business has begun to recognize its own stake in behaving responsibly as a steward of the very resources it uses. Planners and decision-makers are becoming aware of the impacts of human encroachment on our natural resource base, habitat, biodiversity, and the underlying web of life. Policy-makers are more cognizant of the linkages between our natural resource base, and economic and social factors.

We move information around and manage it more effectively. Some of this movement and learning is focused and systematic, through training and education. Some is chaotic and unstructured—happenstance meetings, the browsing of technical or management journals, and "surfing the Net."

We recognize that the public has better access to information; thus business is increasingly held accountable. The media still has a powerful influence in broadcasting information. But access to electronic media is extending the public's individual reach in its search for and dissemination of information. These enabling tools remain, however, a two-edged sword—to minimize bias the public needs to be canny enough to search out and digest opposing views.

We are overwhelmed by the sheer volume of regulations; thus we have been forced to modify the way we manage compliance. Over the past few decades, the number of pages of U.S. regulation alone has grown to somewhere around 80,000. Compliance is complicated by the complexity of these rules; no one can be expected to be an expert in all areas, nor do all experts agree. New tools are still evolving to help organizations determine regulatory applicability, assess and report internally on compliance, as well as to report externally to regulators. Chapters 5 and 6 describe some information management approaches adopted by business to deal with these requirements, as well as the many gaps in existing tools.

We recognize that our public credibility depends in no small part on our ability to manage compliance. Regulators are increasingly funneling resources into enforcement activities. The number and magnitude of fines is increasing, as is the severity of penalties associated with existing and new laws. Senior managers and other employees may be subject to fines, as well as civil and criminal charges, if there is a breakdown of sound management practices. Public credibility is an exceedingly fragile commodity. The chemical industry's experience with its surveys of public confidence makes my point. Despite that sector's tangible progress in many areas, the results of its surveys demonstrate that it has not yet recaptured the public trust.

We are burdened by the soaring costs of compliance. Most estimates place environmental pollution control costs in the United States at around $200 billion, an underestimate when one considers the costs of documentation, record-keeping and other management systems and operating activities, along with the costs of product/process changes, lost sales, price and entry controls, remediation, and other liabilities. Superfund cleanup costs, for example, have soared as lawsuits, rather than technical or community-based solutions, were pursued. Business is obligated to shareholders and society alike to address these issues and burdens through responsible and proactive internal management strategies, as well as more effective input to the public policy process.

We need innovative new technologies that meet EHS improvement goals, while still meeting other business and financial goals. These new technologies should markedly improve not only our ability to control pollution, but also the way we manufacture and deliver products and services, and the way we manage our business. These improvements will come about through cycle time reduction and other productivity improvements. The new technologies we seek include, for example: (1) information technologies that transform the way we manage and integrate layers of data and the way we measure and communicate; (2) environmental technologies (one of the fastest growing of all industry segments today) whose diverse products and services include pollution control as well as treatment, testing, waste handling/recycling, and consulting/management services; (3) all other new technologies related to traditional product, process, service development, and design.

We increasingly involve those closest to the action in decision-making. Many of the most effective EHS improvement ideas come from those on the shopfloor. Organizations are increasingly recognizing the need to minimize the bureaucracy in implementing these ideas, as well as to value and recognize individuals and teams that contribute them.

We consider marketplace needs related to EHS. Businesses that ignore these issues may lose market share when competitors include "green design" features along with other customer-oriented factors in designing and marketing products. Senior managers need to relentlessly adapt the organization's culture, knowledge base, technologies, products, and response scenarios to the changing expectations of customers and stakeholders.

We respond to shareholder and board's concerns for responsible fiscal and EHS management. Senior managers, increasingly held accountable by both bodies, are recognizing the need to identify environmental costs and manage them. Proactively mainstreaming EHS management into planning and decision-making, rather than dealing with it as an afterthought, provides value-added and thus contributes to the bottom line.

We are faced with an increasingly internationalized climate. Many of our businesses will need to meet an increasing array of international and country-specific standards, and cope with broad issues related to the physical well-being of our planet and its peoples.

These, and other factors, have been instrumental in propelling forward-thinking EHS managers toward a more structured management approach. To those who are well on their way yet still asking the all-too-familiar "Are we there yet?" my answer is the equally familiar: "Not yet—we have a way to go." Unlike the family trip with a prescribed destination, however, our vision and end point are not fixed, but continue to evolve, directed by changing customer and stakeholder expectations. The process of adapting to change is, without question, a fundamental requirement of remaining in business, and may well be the *only* thing not likely to change.

Not all have moved from the start line. Some are stalled in place, or, worse, are unaware that the race is well underway. For these, the learning curve is steep, but not unclimbable. To them we say, "Come, take a hand up, network and learn with us, and through our shared learning, propel us all forward to our goal. "

PART I

BECOMING AN ENVIRONMENTAL QUALITY LEADER

CHAPTER I

THE GREENING OF QUALITY

CHAPTER OBJECTIVES

Presents a brief account of the development of Quality-based management

Illustrates how application of Quality-based management to EHS management provides value-added

QUALITY—MORE THAN THE SUM OF ITS PARTS

As an environmental manager with an interest in TQEM, you should find the story of Quality worth exploring for several reasons. First, it will acquaint you with the principles of Quality, why its application was such a success in Japan, and how to make it work for you. You will also learn how some companies have gone wrong in adopting Quality piecemeal rather than using a systematic approach, and how to avoid their pitfalls in your own business. In putting together this narrative, I found that no two versions were identical. The truth lies somewhere between insights offered by U.S. and Japanese writers, and opinions contributed by the devotees and detractors of W. Edwards Deming, surely the most controversial of U. S. Quality gurus.

Undisputed credit for the earliest work on the statistical Quality-based tools goes to Walter Shewart, a physicist at AT&T's Bell Laboratories. Shewart's work in the 1920s and 30s laid the foundation for process control methods and standards later used in production during World War II to remarkably increase the reliability of military equipment. Through these techniques, quality was "inspected into" products; the strictness of Quality Control (QC) standards determined how much waste and how much product came out of the process. A "think tank" was created at Stanford University by the War Department to educate defense contractors and others on these tools; during its heyday, Edwards Deming became a Shewhart disciple. In time, the Stanford center was shut down. Deming himself moved on to the U.S. Census Bureau.

As the war drew to a close, domestic production resumed. The U.S. economy was booming, and the high profits associated with mass production supported complacency. Producers could afford waste; they had little incentive to change. Although some continued to use QC tools to separate out defective parts, the field of Quality in the United States was otherwise at a standstill. Japan, however, was ripe for a Quality revolution. Only 40 percent of its production was running, and product quality was generally poor. The necessity of rapid economic recovery forced change. Through an ironic twist of fate, the U.S. military would again play a role in introducing Quality tools. In 1945, U.S. occupation forces dispatched engineers to help Japanese manufacturers introduce statistical methods into the manufacture of telecommunications equipment vital to postwar activities. The Japanese were receptive; their first QC circles were formed in 1949. Many influential members of the Union of Japanese Scientists and Engineers (JUSE) became Quality champions, including Kaoru Ishikawa and Taiichi Ohno.

Deming first appeared on the scene in Japan in 1946, assisting in postwar census activities in his capacity as a statistician with the U.S. Census Bureau. In time, his statistical expertise became known to those interested in Quality, and in 1950, he was invited to participate in a lecture series arranged by the JUSE, which brought Quality to the attention of senior managers. Deming's message was simple and direct: the responsibility for Quality is yours. The message fell on receptive ears. Training programs for business were created. Deming introduced the use of control charts, as well as the concept of continuous improvement of operations (today called the Deming cycle). Over the next few years, Ohno, Ishikawa, and other Japanese Quality experts continued to add to the edifice that would become Japan's "house of Quality." Ishikawa himself commented that a turning point came when producers recognized the need to "design-in" customer needs from the beginning in order to avoid costly waste at later stages.

In time, an extensive arsenal of tools evolved, including customer focus, worker training, self-directed teams (or Quality Circles, for problem-solving), production line stop (used when defects appeared), and root-cause analysis. Japanese producers, to their credit, did not discard older concepts, but built on what had already been proven. Eventually, Quality was recognized as more than a collection of tools; it became a systematic and pervasive approach. Productivity in Japan grew 400% the rate in the United States during postwar years. U.S. manufacturers, one by one, were outcompeted in the marketplace.

"Many so-called management techniques were imported to Japan after the Second World War. Of these, only quality control was fully naturalized to become Japan's very own, experienced great success, and was transformed into a new product to be widely exported to nations overseas." *Kaoru Ishikawa*

The success of Japanese producers in reducing waste and improving Quality and productivity initially went unnoticed. During the 1960s, however, teams from the United States and other countries began to visit Japan to dissect their methods, and Ishikawa himself traveled worldwide, lecturing on QC techniques. The Japanese economy continued to grow, and by 1980, it made up 10 percent of world gross product. An NBC special in 1980 that included a brief interview with Deming (who was all but unknown in the United States) stunned listeners. Its poignant question: "If Japan Can, Why Can't We?" would continue to go unanswered for some time.

U.S. producers were slow to recognize that success in the marketplace required more than simply "inspecting-in" Quality. Their earliest attempts to imitate the Japanese miracle were largely unsuccessful. Performance, in turn, continued to fall short of expectations. Manufacturers scrambled from one Quality tool to the next, rather than recognizing that Quality was a system with many elements. Some adopted statistical process control tools to guide decision-making on the shopfloor. Others incorporated the continuous improvement cycle into operations to make incremental improvements. Quality Circles came, and for the most part, went, without a whimper. Quality also tended to be sequestered or compartmentalized with specialists in a Quality department, unlike the Japanese model where everyone had expertise. Where changes were made superficially, piecemeal, and unsupported by high level management commitment or culture change, they tended to fail.

Despite setbacks, the belief that Quality was at least one of the keys to Japanese success persisted. By the late 1980s, the term Total Quality Management (TQM) took hold in the United States as a descriptor for a comprehensive management approach. Its proponents generally agreed on its key elements: a high level of senior management commitment; a strong customer and stakeholder focus, employee involvement, teamwork, and empowerment; data-driven decision-making; prevention; continuous improvement; a systematic approach; and a long-term focus. During the 1980s, a number of U.S. companies began to achieve success, and today, there is a growing demand for their high quality goods and services. But a long road still lies ahead for those slow to learn that Quality truly is more than just the sum of its parts.

Quality . . . more than just some of the parts.

In Japan, TQM was like a fine feathered fowl, whose creation began with very soul of the bird. Meat was added to the bone; it was feathered, given a voice, and when complete, the bird strutted about in all its glory. In the United States, one began with the fine feathered fowl, and dissected it bite by bite. And when each morsel was sampled and the meal was at an end, those who had come to dinner wondered why the bird no longer could strut, scratch, or crow. Which way was best? Fortunately, in the latter case, the bird did not die, but was miraculously revived, when producers recognized that the whole was truly more than the sum of its parts.

MAKING QUALITY A NATIONAL GOAL

The visibility of Quality received a strong boost in the United States in 1988 when the Malcolm Baldrige National Quality Award was created to recognize excellence in both management and performance. The Baldrige Award is housed in the National Institute of Standards and Technology (NIST) and administered by a consortium that includes the American Society for Quality Control. Annually, up to six companies are eligible to win, two each in the categories of manufacturing, service, and small business. Since the award's creation, over a million copies of the application book have been requested. Although only a few companies submit applications, many request the application to study, as well as apply, the criteria. The award categories are expected to be expanded to the education and health-care fields in the near future.

Other national and state-level Quality awards have also been created. U.S. federal agencies are eligible to compete for the prestigious President's Award for Quality, administered by the Federal Institute for Quality. Other countries, such as Australia and Mexico, have also created national-level awards. More than half the states in the United States have awards modeled after the Baldrige, recognizing the tie to economic productivity (e.g., manufacturers, service companies, and organizations within the public and education sectors can apply for New York State's Excelsior Awards). By design, state awards are not as rigorous as Baldrige, but prepare applicants for a higher level of competition.

DOES QUALITY PAY?

Members of the House of Representatives asked this question of the U.S. General Accounting Office (GAO) (1991). Their request triggered a study examining the impact of formal TQM practices; the performance of twenty Baldrige finalists (applying for award during 1988 and 1989) was evaluated. The GAO found an annual average improvement in a number of areas: quality improved, operating costs decreased, customer satisfaction and market share increased, as did profitability. The GAO report cited other studies that confirmed the link between quality, profitability, market share, and return on investment (1-1). For example, a Conference Board survey of 800 large U.S. corporations also showed that Total Quality is the "strategy of choice" for assuring the economic position of U.S. firms in the global marketplace.

Does Quality pay? When applied in the right way, it does.

QUALITY AND ENVIRONMENTAL MANAGEMENT

During the mid 1960s, public awareness of environmental issues began to surface in the United States, western Europe, and Japan. Environmentalists had discovered pollution and its consequences, and the response of the public, the media, and governments, in turn, was to restrict and control those consequences through legal remedies. Over the next two decades, a flood of regulations and attendant costs would wash over corporate America. New laws and regulations forced government and industry to face the consequences of cleanup requirements for polluted air, waterways, and soil (1-2).

The process of change during the 1980s was also accelerated by catastrophic accidents and emotional public response. The public became convinced that disasters were likely even in their own backyard when a release of toxic gas from a Union Carbide facility in Institute, Virginia, followed on the heels of the Bhopal crisis. Concern was further elevated by media attention on the *Valdez* oil spill. The media also played a role in alerting the public to action on less newsworthy, but admittedly contentious issues, such as overflowing landfills, incineration, endangered species, and climate change. The public soon came to believe in its ability to effect change. Whether the threats associated with such issues were real or perceived, their impacts, nonetheless, were felt in the halls of government and in the marketplace in terms of greater restrictions on producers, and greater costs to consumers.

Business woke up abruptly, but late. At least initially, managers were reactive; they often responded locally, and not very systematically, to public pressures. Held accountable by shareholders, consumers, and the public, many recognized the need for a more systematic approach to environmental issues. In many respects, they were ready for the Quality movement, and began to apply its principles and tools proactively to all aspects of business, including environmental management.

Over the next decade, Quality-based programs in the most progressive companies grew to include an environmental vision and principles, as well as performance standards that were translated into plans and action. The position of the environmental manager was formalized. Responsibility began to move into line management and away from centralized service or staff areas. Pollution prevention programs were initiated. The value of workers as contributors to these and other environmental improvement programs was recognized, and employee training on compliance and pollution prevention was initiated.

In time, proactive programs started to pay off. Some companies began to track waste and cost savings. They also identified product features that were important to consumers, hence would potentially affect market share. Recyclability was designed into autos, computers, copiers, cameras, and many other products. Formal "Design for Environment" (DFE) and other life-cycle-based approaches were introduced. Partnerships were created among once strange bedfellows to identify environmentally friendly materials, develop better tools for life-cycle analysis, improve accounting methods for environmental costs, and take a global view of environmental management.

Figure 1-1 illustrates the stages that many of these companies went through in implementing a Quality-based management system. Many of the leaders are now in the mature phase of management, and are actively engaged in the process of developing new Quality-based tools. For many others, the passage from reactive to proactive engagement has recently begun, and should be

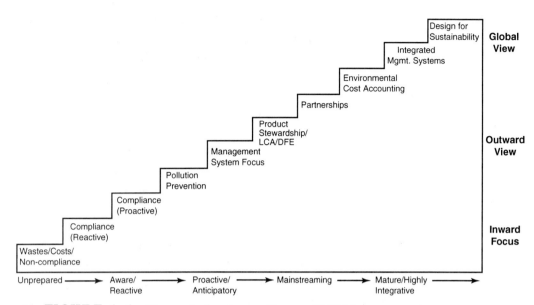

■ FIGURE 1-1. Stages in implementing an EHS Management System.

accelerated as the International Organization for Standardization (ISO) 14000 series of standards emerges.

Today, in retrospect, the proactive response of leaders in the field of TQEM tends to be taken for granted; yet it is worth the attention of those who have not yet adjusted to changing times. While EHS issues were once afterthoughts in the business plans of most corporate and government installations, today, it is rare to find a major institution that fails to consider such issues and plan for change, rather than respond reactively to circumstances. The marriage between Total Quality and environmental management, or TQEM, was an agent for cultural change, a vehicle through which companies learned to become more sensitive to customer and stakeholder needs and to measure success in those terms. A number of CEOs and senior managers became vocal supporters of environmental stewardship, participating in the development of sustainable development principles presented on behalf of business at the Rio Summit on the Environment in 1990.

Much of this progress was won in larger companies with extensive resources, although smaller ones have used their advantages in flexibility and rapid turnaround to advantage in marketing "green" products to a new customer base. However, the gap in management systems between large and smaller companies continues to widen, at a time when new regulatory and trade requirements are expanding, further placing smaller firms at a disadvantage.

ISO 9000's 1994 revision clearly requires that companies' Quality management systems address "the needs of both society and the environment" (clause 4.4.4 c of ISO 9000), and that they take a life-cycle approach in managing the design, production, and disposition (or recycling/reuse) of its products. ISO 14000 standards on environmental management, auditing, and product attributes are expected to be released beginning in late 1996, continuing through the late 1990s.

New challenges come from a public that recognizes product and service quality and registers its preference at the point of sale, where price, service, and value become the common denominators of choice.

Large companies that have already adopted a Quality framework should be well positioned for the future, whether consumer choice or new standards are the challenge, yet they too will need to adapt to change. Small and midsized companies, the traditional sources of new products and services, will be increasingly at risk, given their more limited resources. The success of other institutions within the education, health-care, and government sectors also hangs in the balance, as competition for customers intensifies and costs escalate.

For organizations of all kinds to succeed into the 21st century, Quality needs to become the goal as well as the preferred management strategy.

The Origins of TQEM Tools

Industry leaders in the field have not only been quick to adopt new tools, they are in fact driving and participating in their creation. The term TQEM was coined in 1991 by a business group, the Global Environmental Management Initiative (GEMI), formally merging the concepts of environmental management with Total Quality.

GEMI subsequently published a number of reference guides on topics such as benchmarking, cost-effective pollution prevention, and training. Its Environmental Self-Assessment Program (ESAP) (GEMI, 1992) was developed to assess conformance with the International Chamber of Commerce's "Business Charter for Sustainable Development Principles for Environmental Management."

Other organizations have also been active. The Council of Great Lakes Industries (CGLI) began to develop Quality-based implementation tools in 1991, responding to a challenge from the Council of Great Lakes Governors to create self-assessment criteria for environmental management (Wever and Vorhauer, 1991). In 1992, CGLI published its TQEM Matrix, based on the Baldrige categories and criteria. Its TQEM Primer (Council of Great Lakes Industries, 1993), which elaborates on the use of the Matrix, was published the following year.

Case studies evaluating the use of the Matrix and Primer were initiated by the Management Institute for Environment and Business and Carnegie-Mellon University, funded by the Great Lakes Protection Fund. Business participants in these cases included Occidental Chemical's Niagara Falls facility and Kodak Park's Utilities Division. NIST also provided project assistance through its recruitment of two Baldrige Examiners as participants.

A Quality-based framework was also developed and used to analyze the public policy process (Wever, 1994a, 1995a, 1995b).

Trade associations and several *ad hoc* groups have also contributed actively to the field of Quality-based environmental management in areas such as the development of environmental principles, LCA tools, and auditing and reporting guidelines. The efforts of these groups are referenced in various chapters of this book.

There is every indication that a ready audience exists for solidly founded materials that guide implementation of TQEM.

The writings of Ishikawa foreshadowed the Quality-based approach to global environmental stewardship: "As I look back on my life . . .the following becomes my hope and prayer: 'That . . .quality all over the world be improved, that cost be lowered, that productivity be increased, that raw materials and energy be saved, that peoples all over the world be happy, and that the world prosper and be peaceful.' "

ADDITIONAL READINGS

Abegglen, James C. and George Stalk, Jr. 1985. *Kaisha, the Japanese Corporation.* New York: Basic Books.

Bowles, Jerry and Joshue Hammond. 1991. *Beyond Quality.* New York: Berkley Books.

Geiser, K. 1991. "The Greening of Industry." *Technology Review* (August/September), pp. 64—72.

Halberstam, David. 1986. T*he Reckoning. New York*: William Morrison and Co.

Jablonski, Joseph R. 1994. *Implementing TQM: Competing in the Nineties through Total Quality Management.* Technical Management Consortium. Albuquerque, NM.

Ouchi, William G. 1981. *Theory Z: How American Business Can Meet the Japanese Challenge.* New York: Addison-Wesley Publishing Co.

Stead, W. Edward and J. G. Stead. 1992. *Management for a Small Planet: Strategic Decision-Making and the Environment.* Newbury Park: Sage.

Walton, Mary. 1986. *The Deming Management Method.* New York: Perigee.

CHAPTER 2

MAKING TQEM WORK FOR YOU

CHAPTER OBJECTIVES

Presents a Quality-based framework for environment, health, and safety (EHS) management

Introduces the ISO 14000 environmental management standards

Outlines commonalities and differences in approach among the Baldrige Quality framework, ISO 14000, and ISO 9000

TQEM AND THE BOTTOM LINE

Few in business have measured the full extent to which EHS costs affect their business. Revenue streams and market share can be lost when customers switch to greener competitors' products, when product introductions are stalled due to changing regulations, or when manufacturing sites are shut down by agency action. Operating costs can rise substantially when regulations require major changes in products, services, or facilities, when heavy penalties are imposed, or when other unexpected liabilities are uncovered.

Thomas Hopkins' study (1995) estimates current annual EHS costs in the United States at $500 billion. Less than half of this is for pollution control. The remainder pertains to documentation, record-keeping and price and entry costs. EHS expenses for an individual business are highly variable, depending on the extent of its risks and compliance burden, and its ability to respond.

A survey by the Conference Board (1995) documented that many respondents realized significant savings by proactively managing waste, material and energy inputs, packaging, incidents, accidents, and other such EHS issues. Baxter's "cost of Quality" approach led, by 1993, to cumulative cost savings for compliance alone of nearly $25 million. Its avoided costs totaled more than $48 million in areas like recycling revenues, hazardous waste reduction (disposal and material costs), and packaging. Xerox's pollution prevention initiatives have saved the company $10 million in materials and waste management costs. Many other respondents also reported they used a Quality-based management approach to address future liabilities and avoid both litigation and remediation costs.

How can companies with gaps in their Quality program improve? The first step in this process is to take a hard but systematic look at strengths and weaknesses. This type of assessment will reveal where gaps exist: Whether, for instance, you need to increase your focus on customers and stakeholders, or gain a better understanding of the costs and risks associated with your current operations. Perhaps, instead, you need to improve the extent to which your workforce is aware of and proactively involved in EHS management. You may be reactive in your approach to day-to-day and long-term EHS issues, rather than proactive. Or perhaps, EHS management is a stranded activity, rather than being mainstreamed into your business strategies and planning.

The simultaneous introduction to Total Quality and to environmental management can be made more cost-effective through the use of the systematic tools presented in this book.

Parts I and II These first two parts relate the seven Baldrige categories to EHS management, and provide illustrations drawn from real-world examples:

Chapters 1 and 2 Here we introduce the concepts of Quality management and its application to environmental or EHS management. We also introduce the ISO 14000 international environmental management standards, and relate these to the Baldrige and ISO 9000 systems.

Chapters 3 through 14 These chapters lead readers through the seven Baldrige categories step-by-step, and also introduce readers to benchmarking.

Chapter 15 This chapter provides practical case "vignettes" that illustrate a Quality-based approach to EHS management.

Part III The last section of the book introduces the TQEM Matrix, which serves as a building block system to implement Quality-based EHS management.

Chapter 16 Here we introduce the Matrix and its use.

Chapter 17 Self-assessment questions designed to complement individual Matrix elements are provided; they cover both Baldrige and ISO 14000 criteria.

Chapter 18 A model company case study, derived from real-world examples, is presented.

In summary, EHS managers can use the assessment tools, illustrations, and case studies to:

Systematically implement a Quality-based management system

Identify gaps and improvement opportunities

Develop a quantitative score to track progress and drive improvement

Identify areas for benchmarking

THE QUALITY FRAMEWORK

The framework for Quality presented in this book is based on the seven Baldrige categories. As you read the description here of how the categories relate to each other, refer to Figure 2-1 for visual reinforcement of what you are

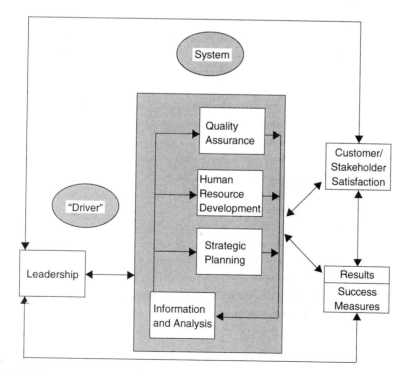

■ **FIGURE 2-1.** A Quality-based framework based on Baldrige Framework.

reading. The basic elements of Quality-based management include a strong customer and stakeholder focus, a high level of senior management commitment to meeting their needs and expectations, and a "tool kit" that includes teamwork, empowerment, continuous improvement, root-cause analysis, and a prevention approach. Each of these elements is highly relevant to environmental managers faced with formidable regulatory challenges, as well as increasing expectations of stakeholder groups.

- TQM begins and ends with a commitment to satisfying customers and stakeholders. Knowing what they need and expect drives the development of systems that improve performance and better satisfy their needs.
- The first step in this process requires high-level commitment from members of senior management. Commitment is essential if the organization is to commit the resources needed for excellent performance, and create consistency throughout the organization.
- Once commitment has been obtained, the organization then begins to gather and analyze comprehensive information pertinent to its environmental needs.
- Priorities are then channeled into strategic planning, where plans and objectives are created, and measures for success based on customer and stakeholder needs are selected.
- None of this can be done without the involvement of people, whose knowledge, skill, commitment, and teamwork are needed to implement successful improvement programs.
- A system of checks and balances, or Quality Assurance systems, provides the review and feedback loops needed to continuously improve the overall system.
- These activities, as well as benchmarking, move the organization ever closer to its ultimate goal of achieving a high level of performance, thereby satisfying the expectations of its customers and stakeholders. This, in effect, closes the loop and brings the organization full circle for another round of improvement.

DEFINITION OF CATEGORIES

A definition of each of seven Baldrige categories is provided below, adapted from the Baldrige definitions (National Institute of Standards, 1995), to create greater relevance to EHS management.

EHS Leadership: Looks at senior managers' personal leadership and involvement in creating the unit's EHS expectations and a leadership system that promotes EHS excellence in the areas of public responsibilities and corporate stewardship of natural resources.

EHS Information and Analysis: Looks at the effectiveness of management and use of EHS data and information to support customer/stakeholder-driven EHS performance excellence and marketplace success.

Strategic EHS Planning: Defines how the unit incorporates EHS needs and priorities into its strategic directions, and how it effectively implements plans that include EHS improvements.

Human Resource Development: Defines how an organization's workforce is enabled to use its full potential in attaining the unit's EHS objectives. It also defines how an organization encourages EHS responsibility, and fosters individual and team behavior that lead to EHS and overall business improvements.

Process Management: Defines key processes that ensure the unit's regulatory and customer/stakeholder-driven needs will be effectively met for the development and functioning of its operational processes, products, and services.

EHS Results: Looks at the organization's EHS performance in key areas associated with its products, processes, services, and EHS management systems, as well as financial performance indicators linked to these areas.

Customer/Stakeholder Focus and Satisfaction: Defines the unit's systems for customer focus, learning, and relationship-building. It also looks at key measures such as customer/stakeholder satisfaction with the unit's EHS performance, competitors' performance in this area, as well as impacts of EHS considerations on the unit's market share.

In the following chapters, you will learn more about individual Baldrige categories. Each chapter has case study material as well as practical guidance on implementation. Each also includes relevant material on the ISO 14000 series of international environmental management standards, since many companies are debating whether to seek ISO 14001 registration.

If your organization already has a TQM framework in place, you may be well along the path to registration, for ISO 14001 has overlaps with certain Baldrige quality system as well as ISO 9000 requirements. ISO 14001 is compatible as well as complementary with both. However, you will need to do a gap analysis since ISO 14000 has a number of specific environmental requirements that you may not have addressed in detail in your existing management system.

The next sections will introduce you to ISO 14000 as well as provide some insights into the relationships among these quality systems.

INTERNATIONAL ENVIRONMENTAL MANAGEMENT STANDARDS

The Origin and Intent of ISO 14000

The International Organization for Standardization (generally referred to as ISO) was chartered in 1946 to create harmonized, uniform world standards for the manufacturing, communications, and trade sectors in technical and safety areas. Its entrée into the management area began with ISO 9000 series of standards addressing business' needs for Quality management tools.

In 1993, the ISO turned its attention to environmental management to stem a growing tide of disparate country or regional standards that had the potential of hindering trade. Strong pressure to develop such standards also came from environmental advocacy groups and "green parties" in Europe.

The Aims of the ISO 14000 Series of Standards

■ Minimize trade barriers due to disparate national standards
■ Promote a common approach and language for environmental management similar to the broader Quality management standards
■ Enhance companies' ability to attain and measure improvements in environmental performance
■ Place a uniform registration requirement on companies that need to meet the standard
■ Reduce duplicative audits carried out by customers, regulators, companies, and registrars

---

The ISO 14000 series does not dictate performance. In most cases, its requirements will complement existing management systems, and direct attention to areas that are particularly critical for sound environmental management.

ISO 14000 Documents

The ISO 14000 series is expected to include the list of documents in Table 2-1. Only ISO 14001 is an auditable specification; the remainder are guidance documents, that is, they are not auditable for registration purposes. Within ISO, responsibility for ISO 14000 is shared by several subcommittees under the direction of Technical Committee (TC) 207 on Environmental Management (Figure 2-2).

Several standards are systems-related, including 14001 (environmental management systems—EMS), 14031 (performance evaluation), and the auditing series (Table 2-1). These deal with issues such as senior management commitment, policies, planning and objectives, measurement of environmental performance, and audits. The remaining standards deal with product attributes, design, and evaluation (life-cycle assessments and product standards), as well as marketing claims. These latter product-based standards are expected to have the most far-reaching impact on business, demanding data that is often difficult to generate and interpret. They will most likely also be the last of this series to be created, due to the lack of consensus on both approach and methodologies.

■ **TABLE 2-1** The ISO 14000 Series of Environmental
Management Standards

ISO Designation	Subject of Document
14001	Environmental management systems (EMS)
14004	Guidance on EMS
	Environmental auditing
14010	Principles
14011	Procedures
14012	Auditor qualifications
14031	Environmental performance evaluation
	Life-cycle assessment
14041	Guiding principles and practices
14042	Inventory analysis
14043	Impact assessment
14044	Improvement assessment
	Environmental labeling (marketing claims)
14021	Principles of all environmental claims
14024	Eco-label/seal of approval programs
14025	Manufacturer self-declaration claims
14060	Environmental aspects in product standards

What Are the Drivers for ISO 14001 Registration?

The ISO 9000 "Halo Effect" It is likely that requirements for ISO 14001 registration will follow the same pattern observed with ISO 9000. Over 100,000 ISO 9000 registration certificates had been issued by the end of 1994. A growing number of companies are requiring that their suppliers earn ISO 9000 registration, presumably driven by their desire for products of consistent quality. There is also a trickle-down effect as registered companies begin to require this of their own supply chain.

A Requirement for International Trade Some countries may require conformance with the ISO 14000 standards, in effect creating a trade barrier for companies that choose not to seek registration. An "eco-label," one of ISO 14000's proposed standards, is already mandated in a number of countries.

Government Contractor Requirements In the United States, the Department of Energy (DOE) has taken the lead in creating a draft requirement for ISO 14001 registration for its suppliers and contractors. Other departments, such as the Department of Defense, also have interest in the standard. Thus, in time, a large number of U.S. government contractors may be affected.

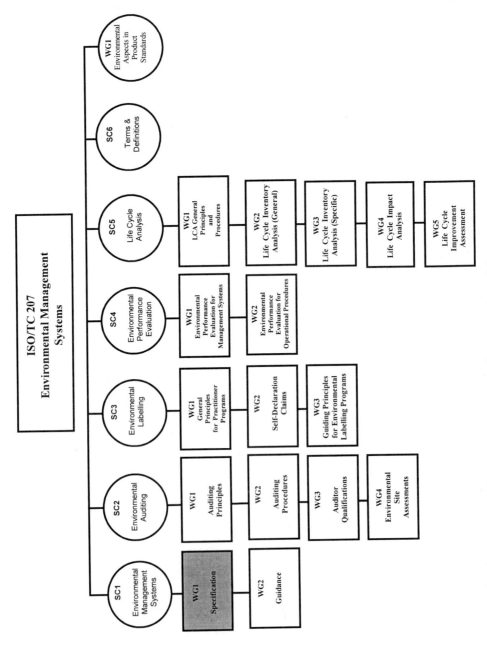

■ **FIGURE 2-2.** ISO/TC 207 subcommittees and working groups.

Regulatory/Enforcement Agency Interest Companies in the United States that adopt voluntary environmental management standards may have an advantage if current regulatory reforms move ahead that reward companies for voluntary adoption of exemplary management systems. The U.S. Environmental Protection Agency (EPA), for example, is considering incorporating ISO 14001 as a future qualification criterion for participating in some of its voluntary initiatives. The standard may also be used in actions by the Department of Justice and U.S. Sentencing Guidelines Commission in conjunction with enforcement policies and directives.

Benefits of Eliminating Duplicative Audits Companies with ISO 14001 registration may be more acceptable to customers and others, and thus may not have to undergo duplicative audits.

Benefits of Improved Cost and Compliance Many companies have recognized that the adoption of a Quality-based management system approach will, in the long term, reduce compliance costs and improve performance. Companies with ISO 9000 registration, for example, appreciate the greater level of management control that exists within their operations despite the rather high costs of implementation.

Greater Public Confidence. Companies with ISO 14001 registration may find greater public confidence in their ability to manage risks.

Marketing Advantage ISO 14001 registration may become an integral part of some organizations' marketing strategies, particularly if it differentiates them from competitors.

The Relationship of ISO 14001 to Other Management System Standards

ISO 14001 is an auditable conformance standard for environmental management. It has roots in ISO 9000, and was patterned after the Deming cycle (Plan–Do–Check), rather than the broader Baldrige framework (Figure 2-3). However many of its elements are also consistent and aligned with Baldrige (Table 2-2). The following discussion will help you understand the major differences in approach between the ISO standards and the Baldrige approach. (Robert Peach's 1994 publication on ISO 9000 is a useful reference source, for those desiring an introduction to the topic.)

Terry Johnston, a manager in Kodak's Corporate Quality Organization, recently described to me the differences between the Baldrige, ISO 9000, and ISO 14000 approaches:

> Apples, oranges, and Chevrolets. They're all so different it's hard to find a good way to show their alignment in a way that means something. Baldrige's aim is to drive competitiveness and world-class performance in all aspects of an organization's

Continual Improvement

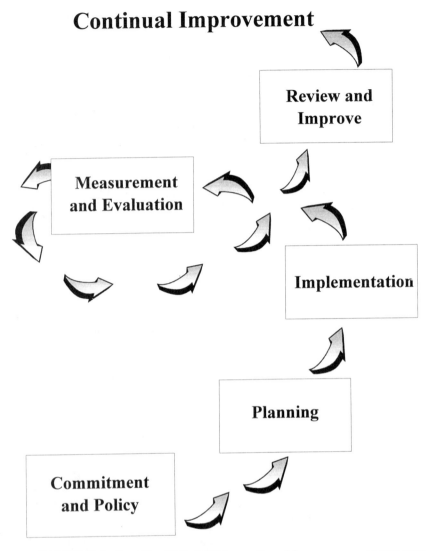

■ **FIGURE 2-3.** The ISO 14001 continual improvement process.

activities. Its foundation is continuous improvement. ISO 9001 is a conformance standard; it's designed specifically for product and service conformance with defined, customer-contracted requirements. Continuous improvement, although mentioned in ISO 9004 (Guidelines for Quality Management and Quality Systems) is not addressed directly in 9001. The focus of 9001 is the contractual relationship that assures customers that you make what you say you make.

We talked about ISO 14001, which is also a conformance standard that focuses narrowly on environmental activities. Its aim is to enable companies to comply with environmental legislation and address environmental impacts, including prevention of pollution.

■ TABLE 2-2 Alignment of Requirements in ISO 9000, ISO 14000, and 1995 Baldrige Criteria

Requirement	ISO 9000	ISO 14001	Baldrige[a]
Management System Aspects			
Leadership			
Senior management commitment	4.1.1	4.1	1.1
Policy	4.1.1	4.1	1.1
Values, ethics			1.1
Public responsibility	(3.3[b])	4.1	1.3
Roles/responsibilities	4.1.2.1	4.3.1	1.2
Policy/objectives relevant to customer/stakeholder needs	4.3	4.2.3	1.1
Commitment to resources	4.1.2.2	X	1.1
Management representative	4.1.2.3	4.3.1	1.1
Effective organization			1.1, 1.2
Management review	4.1.3	4.5	1.1, 1.2
Commitment to meet customer/stakeholder needs	(9004- 0.3)		1.1, 1.3
Commitment to prevention	4.1.2.1	4.1	5.2
Commitment to continuous improvement		4.1	
Commitment to compliance/conformance with legal/regulatory and other requirements		4.1	
Information and Analysis			
Legal and regulatory requirements	4.4.4 (also 3.3)	4.2.1	1.3
Risks, hazards, environmental impacts	(3.3)[b]	4.2.1	1.3
Competitor data			2.2
Information management, technology			2.1

■ TABLE 2-2 (Continued)

Requirement	ISO 9000	ISO 14001	Baldrige[a]
Quality of data			2.1
Use of data/information in planning, decision-making		4.2.1	2.3
Strategic Planning			
Planning process	4.2.3	4.2.3	3.1
Plans, including action plans	4.2.3	4.2.4	3.2
Objectives set using business, environmental, technological, customer/stakeholder considerations		4.2.3	
Resources	4.1.2.2	4.3.1	3.2
Consistency, alignment through organization		4.2.4	3.2
Human Resource Development/Utilization			
Education and training	4.18	4.3.2	4.1/3
Effectiveness of training, competence, awareness		4.3.2	4.3
Recognition, performance measures			4.2
Well-being, satisfaction, attitude			4.4
Linkage with strategic/business planning			4.1
Effective job/work design			4.2
Process Management/Quality Assurance			
Communication systems		4.3.3	
Documentation			
Management system		4.3.4	
Manual	4.2.1	4.3.4	
Procedures		4.3.6	5.2; etc.

Document/data control	4.5	4.3.5	
Records control	4.16	4.4.3	5.1, 5.2
Continuous improvement	(0.4, 5.6)[b]	4.1	5.1, 5.2
Corrective and preventive action	4.14	4.4.1, 4.4.2	5.1, 5.2
Statistical techniques	4.20		
Internal and external audits	4.17	4.4.4	5.4
Operational Aspects			
Contracts			
Contract review procedures	4.3		5.4
Purchasing			
Purchasing procedures	4.6.1		5.4
Conformance with requirements			5.4
Partnership relationships with suppliers			5.4
Design control	4.4		
Input of customer/stakeholder requirements, including legal/regulatory into design	4.4.4	4.2.1, 4.2.4	5.1
Validation of design conformance	4.4.8		5.1
Production and distribution			
Product identification and traceability	4.8		
Process control	4.9	4.3.6	5.1, 5.2
Measurement, monitoring	4.10	4.4.1	5.2
Inspection and testing	4.11	4.4.1	5.2
Control of inspection./measurement/ test equipment	4.12	4.4.1	5.2
Inspection and test status of product	4.12		

■ **TABLE 2-2** (*Continued*)

Requirement	ISO 9000	ISO 14001	Baldrige[a]
Control of nonconformance	4.13	4.4.2	
Handling, storage, packaging, preservation, and delivery	4.15	4.3.6	5.2
Servicing			
Conforms with customer requirements	4.19		5.2
Performance			
Results		(ISO 14031)	
Product/service			6.1
Correlation with customer indicators			6.1
Operational, financial results			6.2
Supplier		(ISO 14031)	6.3
Validation that product/service meets requirements	4.4.8		
Customer satisfaction			
Communications with customers/stakeholders		4.3.3	7.1
Contracts (customer requirements)	4.3, note 9		
Determining customer/stakeholder requirements	(7.1, 7.2)[b]	4.2.3	7.1
Response to customer/stakeholder questions, concerns	(7.3)[b]	4.3.3	7.2
Measuring customer satisfaction			7.3
Customer satisfaction results			7.4
Benchmarking			7.5

[a]From Malcolm Baldrige National Quality Award 1995 Criteria.
[b]Found only in ISO 9004, the guidance standard; number in parenthesis refers to clause.

Picking the Quality Tree.

There are a number of similarities among all three. Each deals with management activities; none gives absolute performance requirements. Each requires top management commitment, and a statement of policy (the Baldrige award application criteria today ask for values and ethics). Each requires planning, corrective and preventive action, audits, and management review. ISO 9001 and 14001 are narrower in focus and far less demanding than Baldrige in most areas. However, they specify greater detail in areas like documentation, document control, and calibration, as might be expected from a more traditional process control-based approach. In a nutshell, ISO 9000 provides a solid foundation to manage product and service quality, and Baldrige builds on the baseline that the ISO 9000 approach represents.

Continuous Improvement Let's look at some areas where there are differences, starting with continuous improvement—one of the Baldrige goals. The 1995 Baldrige criteria revisit the phrase, calling it "ever-improving value to customers." ISO 14001 requires continuous improvement of the organization's management system, including, for example, its policy and implementation processes. ISO 14001 also includes a requirement for preventive action, as well as management review of the effectiveness of the management system and its results. Both of these requirements support a continuous improvement mind-set. In addition, the standard requires that environmental priorities be considered during planning, along with financial, technological, and other business priorities. This ensures that continuous improvement, if applied to objectives, will relate broadly to the organization's overall needs (rather than blindly driving environmental performance beyond the point of demonstrable cost/risk/benefit considerations). ISO 9001 does not address continuous improvement, simply because customers typically do not contract for continuously improved products (or services).

In practice, however, companies have found that, in order to *remain* competitive, they need to apply the concept of continuous improvement across the board to all activities. Recognizing this need, the concept was included in a generic guidance standard (ISO 9004), as follows:

> To be competitive and to maintain good economic performance, organizations/suppliers need to employ increasingly effective and efficient systems. Such systems should result in continual improvements in quality and increased satisfaction of the organization's customers and other stakeholders (employees, owners, subsuppliers, society). *ISO 9000-1-1994*

Customer Needs. What about customer needs? Here again there are some significant differences. Baldrige's centerpiece is customer and, more recently, broad societal needs. Many of its criteria deal specifically with customer interactions, measures, and satisfaction. ISO 14001 simply requires that the views of "interested parties" be considered in setting objectives and targets, and asks for communication vehicles to receive and respond to input. How does ISO 9001 deal with customers? Primarily by creating documented customer requirements (e.g., a contract) and validating that product actually conforms to those requirements. The nature, extent, and involvement of customers is not dealt with in the standard (although more emphasis on meeting customer needs is addressed in the guidance standard ISO 9004). Robert Peach (1990) described gaps in ISO 9000 as follows:

> Notably absent in the ISO Standard are specific references to quality results and customer satisfaction. The ISO Standard specifies elements of a quality system, but does not discuss whether products resulting from that system actually meet customer requirements . . . . *The ISO Standard also omits reference to continuous quality improvement.*

Preventive Action. While the 1994 version of ISO 9001 includes a requirement for preventive and corrective action, this requirement essentially is fulfilled at the point where a process is capable of delivering product that conforms to contract requirements. Again, in practice, companies that are high performers use preventive action at a higher level in their organization (à la Baldrige) to go beyond what is required, defining changes that improve competitiveness by reducing waste levels, improving productivity by preventing incidents and accidents, and reducing risks throughout operations. The ISO 14001 conformance standard also requires preventive action in the context of reducing environmental risks.

Results   The ISO 14000 standard on environmental performance evaluation is still in the draft stage; however, it is likely that it will define generic performance indicators in a guidance format, leaving organizations the flexibility to choose those most relevant to their needs. ISO 9001 has little to say about performance. It requires validation that product actually conforms with defined user needs, for example, through testing, but this results- or performance-based requirement is much narrower than is defined in the Baldrige criteria. ISO 9000 also does not determine whether products are of "good quality," nor does registration force companies to continuously improve their product quality. ISO 9000 does not drive objectives such as productivity improvement and waste reduction. Thus a manufacturer could have very high waste levels; however, if it handled its wastes in accordance with procedures and followed its corrective action plans, it could still be ISO 9000 accredited.

Social Responsibility   ISO 14001 requires the identification of the environmental aspects of its products, service, and operations. It also requires that the views of interested parties be obtained in setting objectives. Baldrige now has a much stronger focus on corporate responsibility and citizenship, including both a prevention and life-cycle approach to EHS considerations. It also addreses the use of company resources for "public important purposes," such as environmental excellence and resource conservation. Clause 4.9.c of ISO 9001 requires "compliance with reference standards, codes. . . ," and this is often interpreted to mean safety codes and other legal requirements.

Financial and Competitive Position   ISO 14001 requires that organizations consider business issues such as cost when setting priorities and selecting from among alternative solutions. Baldrige considers competitor information, financial performance, as well as cycle time reduction and its relation to productivity and product quality. (This explicit recognition of competitive and financial benefits is critical to environmental management, where it is important to create priorities for planning based on cost, benefit, and risk determinations across a broad range of inputs.) While ISO 9001 does not address specifically address these areas, they are included in ISO 9004, the guidance standard.

Human Resource Development   ISO 9001 recognizes a need for training, education, and experience in qualifying personnel for activities affecting Quality. It also requires that responsibility, authority, and interrelations of personnel be defined and documented. ISO 14001 has similar requirements in the area of environmental management, but it also requires that employees be competent and aware of the environmental implications of individual action (including potential benefits and adverse outcomes of behavior). The Baldrige criteria are much broader, addressing employee empowerment, recognition, attitudes and well-being, work design, career opportunities, partnerships, and other factors (many of which are also important to effective environmental management). It also links human resource planning to strategic and business planning.

Alignment and Consistency In order to implement ISO 9001, organizations need both consistency and alignment if they are to meet their Quality policy and objectives. However, ISO 9001 does not require that the Quality system be aligned or consistent with overall business goals (although in practice, some organizations choose to do this). Baldrige, however, specifies overall alignment and consistency for the organization's goals, plans, and communications. Such alignment and consistency is also key to achieving success in environmental programs.

Comparison of Key Management Elements Table 2-2 cross-references a number of elements of ISO 9000, ISO 14000, and Baldrige by individual clause or criterion (note that this comparison is not all inclusive; only key clauses that illustrate alignment of requirements are identified).

Because it is difficult to appreciate the differences in approach using alignment matrices, whatever their type, readers are directed to the original standards as well as to the Baldrige criteria. These documents are not very long, nor are they very difficult to understand; reading them directly (rather than about them) will give you a better sense of the differences in approach and focus between the standards and the Baldrige criteria.

How Do You Stack Up?

If you have already implemented ISO 9000, and are considering implementing ISO 14001, which has many overlaps with 9000's requirements, you will find many strengths in your existing systems, including management commitment, documentation capabilities, definition of policy and responsibility, corrective action, planning, process control, and auditing. You will also be familiar with the registration process.

If you have a TQM system (like Baldrige) in place, you will also be at an advantage, due to the broad framework associated with this approach. Baldrige, for example, emphasizes customer-driven Quality, leadership, continuous improvement and learning, employee participation and development, fast response, design quality, prevention, a long-term view of the future, management by fact, partnership development, corporate responsibility, and a results orientation. Although the ISO 14001 conformance standard is modeled after ISO 9000 and the Deming cycle (Plan–Do–Check), it also has elements that can be easily aligned with Baldrige (Table 2-3).

ISO 14001's requirements for senior management commitment and a statement of policy can be aligned with the Baldrige category of Leadership. The 14001 category of Planning aligns with some elements in the two Baldrige categories of Information and Analysis and Strategic Planning. The 14001 category of Implementation has many overlaps with the Baldrige category of Quality Assurance (called Process Management in Baldrige 1995 criteria). It also overlaps the training requirement in the Baldrige category of Human Resource Development. (However, the broader Baldrige framework intends that the

■ **TABLE 2-3** Alignment of Elements of ISO 14001 with Baldrige Framework Criteria

Baldrige Element	ISO 14001 Element
Leadership	Environmental Policy
Information and Analysis	Planning
	Environmental aspects
	Legal and other requirements
Strategic Planning	Objectives and targets
	Environmental management programmes
Process Management	Implementation and Operation
	Environmental management system documentation
	Document control
	Operational control
	Emergency preparedness and response
	Checking and corrective action
	Monitoring and measurement
	Nonconformance and corrective and preventive action
	Records
	Environmental management system audit
	Management review
	Communication
Human Resource Development	Structure and responsibility
	Training, awareness and competence
Results	(ISO 14031 partially covers this category)
Customer/Stakeholder Satisfaction	No corresponding section

criteria for these two categories should apply systems-wide, not just to the implementation phase.) The ISO 14001 conformance standard does not have a Results category; this will be covered in ISO 14031, a guidance document on Environmental Performance Evaluation, which deals with selection and use of measures. Neither 14001 nor 14031 cover benchmarking or impacts on competitiveness, which are important Baldrige criteria. ISO 14001 also has large gaps in the area of Customer/Stakeholder Satisfaction.

ISO 14001 has a number of defined environmental requirements that Baldrige does not specifically address, such as environmental auditing, tracking of environmental requirements and issues, emergency planning and response, and environmental communications.

A guidance document, ISO 14004, accompanying ISO 14001, recommends methods of implementing the conformance standard. These guidance documents are not an auditable part of the registration process, but summarize recommendations based on the collective experience of participants in the drafting and review process.

Because of their common requirements, as well as the focus on documentation associated with ISO 14001, it is clear that a Quality-based Baldrige approach is an excellent preparation for organizations anticipating ISO 14000 implementation and/or registration. However, they will also need to identify and fill any environmental management system gaps.

"Quality control cannot be implemented by merely following national or international standards. . . .[B]eyond these standards, quality control must have the higher goals of meeting the requirements of consumers and creating quality which satisfies them." *Kaoru Ishikawa*

Should You Seek ISO 14000 Registration?

Not all companies will seek ISO 14000 registration. Cost is one barrier. The costs associated with initial registration under ISO 9000 are about 20 percent of the overall implementation costs. Registrar fees alone for a single, sizable facility range from $10,000 to $20,000. This does not include ongoing follow-up audits.

Some companies seeking registration will use third parties for both the audit function and registration. Others will prefer to perform their own internal audits, then seek registration through a less costly third-party verification process.

Yet others may simply elect to self-declare conformance, without verification, or to instead simply implement ISO 14000 requirements. If you elect to self-declare your conformance, be prepared to provide evidence when requested by customers or others. Philips Austria, a television manufacturer, used a third-party registrar to verify its conformance with a committee draft of ISO 14001 early in 1995.

"Customers have an interest in knowing how environmentally sound products are, so this step cannot be taken early enough. And by implementing ISO 14001 [now], we will also know much better where our environmental strengths and weaknesses are." *Philips Austria.*

The American National Standards Institute (ANSI), which is the U.S. member of ISO, will play a large role in determining how the accreditation and registration process unfolds in the United States, and how credible the process is. The consistency of auditors, and how they are certified, continues to be a concern with other ISO accreditation processes (e.g., 9000), and will need to be addressed. This is only one of many factors that companies will consider when deciding whether to register.

ADDITIONAL READINGS

Reimann, Curt W. and H. Hertz. 1993. "The Malcolm Baldrige National Quality Award and ISO 9000 Registration: Understanding Their Many Important Differences." *ASTM Standardization News* (November), pp. 42–51.

CHAPTER 3

LEADERSHIP

"As I grow older I pay less attention to what men say. I just watch what they do." *Andrew Carnegie.*

CHAPTER OBJECTIVES

Introduces the reader to the TQEM category of EHS Leadership*

Defines the critical elements of corporate EHS leadership

Provides examples of past and present-day corporate leaders—their commitments and actions

Outlines ways to overcome EHS leadership gaps

SENIOR LEADERSHIP MODELS

The Mark of a Leader

Companies become environmental leaders by choice, not happenstance. Some are led by ethical considerations, fostered by a strong top leader. A few

---

EHS Leadership Category: Looks at senior managers' personal leadership and involvement in creating the unit's EHS expectations, and a leadership system that promotes EHS excellence in the areas of public responsibilities and corporate stewardship of natural resources.

elect this path following a crisis. But many more at the forefront simply recognize the value of responsible stewardship, as well as the positive impacts on competitiveness of a well-integrated EHS program.

The leadership position brings with it both opportunities and challenges. Leaders in any sphere are visible, hence relentlessly scrutinized. When they fail, the descent is swift in an age where failed leadership is the norm. The most successful have learned through experience that public credibility depends not on rhetoric and footloose promises, but on actions and long-term commitment.

Few CEO's themselves have assumed the role of public spokesman on environmental or EHS issues. Each of the exceptions is unique, yet they have certain qualities in common. Max DePree, retired CEO of Herman Miller, and Sam Johnson, chairman of SC Johnson Wax, are venerable statesmen of the environment—their voices will be heard here and there in the pages of this book.

The Mark of a Leader

Leaders have the potential to mobilize thoughts and ideas, and energize people in new directions. . . .They are always out in front, but equally willing to stand behind you. . . .They have a vision of the future and a fine sense of how to get there. . . .They lend a unique style and culture to their organizations. . . .They are visible role models, who put resources where they say they will, so that visions and plans can be realized. . . .They know how and when to listen. . .and how to motivate and involve others in the process of change. . . .They create consistency through communication. . . .share ideas and information willingly. . . .and thereby win loyalty and support. . . .They create positive visibility for the organization by supporting initiatives that contribute to the public good. For this, they are valued and respected by the public and their colleagues alike.

An increasing number of CEO's preside over corporate councils with oversight over EHS management, participate in national and international forums, and approve policy statements in annual environmental reports. The day-to-day leadership falls to senior managers, most of whom were selected for their strong technical and/or policy backgrounds, as well as their ability as communicators. These individuals shape the ultimate culture, strategies, and level of success of their organization's environmental programs.

"We intend to make a contribution to society . . .through the products and services we offer, and through the manner in which we offer them . . . .We are committed to using responsibly our environment and our finite resources. We are devoted to outstanding performance through our stewardship of talent and resources. . . .All combine to provide a legitimate result in equity for employee owners, customers, investors, the public, and the communities in which we live and work." *Max Depree*

Leaders in the Largest U.S. Companies: A Context for Action

One of the real tests of environmental leadership during the 1980s was not an environmental disaster, but the creation of the Toxics Release Inventory (TRI). Mandated by the Superfund Act Reauthorization Amendment (SARA), Title III, Section 313, the TRI was a departure from traditional pollution control measures, requiring instead that companies track releases of specified chemicals, among other requirements, and make this information publicly available.

Corporate leaders had hard data before them for the first time. The magnitude of their waste streams presented a concern as well as an opportunity. Chemical manufacturers moved proactively to the forefront, rapidly drawing on process knowledge as well as safety management expertise to tighten down systems, reduce emissions, and eliminate accidental releases. Process redesign was the next focus, using a variety of pollution prevention approaches. At least some of the leaders of this period fit the white knight model, rescuing their companies in this case from sharp public pressures. Some also were even larger than life, setting high performance expectations that initially stretched credibility but eventually were realized. Reducing emissions reduced their public visibility, and the process changes made in many cases increased yields, thus contributing positively to the bottom line.

As a CEO, Caddbury's leadership was sometimes eclipsed by his sense of direction.

Industry sectors that were chemical *users* had different problems. Many of their processes were designed to emit solvents to the atmosphere to minimize safety and exposure risks to workers. Electronics manufacture, printing, spraying, coating and painting operations, for example, all depended on evaporative operations to remove volatile solvents, leaving behind high quality products. Process redesign for these sectors was often both extensive and expensive. Many companies were also driven by more than just the magnitude of their TRI data. The electronics sector, for example, discovered that the persistence of solvents used for circuit board cleaning threatened groundwater quality; some solvents were also associated with atmospheric damage. Proactive leaders at companies like AT&T, IBM, and Digital Equipment Corporation responded not only by substituting less hazardous materials and redesigning processes, but also by fundamentally altering the nature of the design tools themselves, to conform with a life-cycle based approach. All of these companies had one goal in common, however—the need to maintain product quality and competitiveness, whatever the process change.

Leaders within natural resource-based companies began to more proactively heed the public's urgency around endangered species and habitat issues associated with their landholdings and operations. Some of their issues and approaches are discussed in later chapters.

Industry leaders exerted their influence, not only at the company level but also through sector-level trade associations, where their participation was crucial in advancing programs such as CMA's Responsible Care Program, the American Forest Products Association's Sustainable Forestry Management Principles, and the Canadian Petroleum Producers Institute's programs to protect the marine environment.

Several corporate leaders instrumental in catalyzing change are briefly profiled in the sections below. Their selection was based on continuing prominence within their sector, and, in some cases, on their participation in initiatives with a national or international reach. Examples documenting their EHS strategies and performance can be found in later chapters as well.

SC Johnson Wax   Based in Racine, Wisconsin, this company employs about 14,000 employees worldwide at its 50 operations, and makes cleaning and maintenance products for the home and workplace. The company's third president, H. F. Johnson, established a tradition of incorporating personal ethics into business decisions. Johnson and a team of scientists went to Brazil in 1935 to determine the impact of harvesting palm trees used to supply the carnauba for the company's waxes (Smart, 1992). Johnson's memoirs, published in 1936, note that companies have an obligation to develop more sustainable ways to deal with natural resources. Following in the tradition of his great-grandfather, Sam Johnson, then chairman, announced in 1975 that the company would abandon the use of chlorofluorocarbons (CFCs) in the company's aerosol products worldwide, long before they were conclusively shown to be a problem for the upper atmosphere:

> When we set aside the obvious business benefits of being an environmentally responsible company, we are left with the simple human truth that we cannot lead lives of dignity and worth when the natural resources that sustain us are threatened or destroyed. We must act responsibly and we must act now.

During the 1990s, the company has continued its sustainable development leadership through continuous improvement of the eco-efficiency of its products and processes; that is, it "used less to do more, resulting in less waste and risk." Worldwide, the company's virgin packaging has been cut by nearly one fourth, and manufacturing waste has been slashed in half since 1990. The company also began a comprehensive global program with suppliers to focus these partnerships on helping the company achieve specific measurable eco-efficiency goals.

Today, Sam Johnson remains active as "corporate America's leading environmentalist" (Fortune, 1993) through his participation on the National Board of Governors of The Nature Conservancy, the President's Council on Sustainable Development, and the World Business Council for Sustainable Development.

> "Am I an environmentalist? Yes. Am I a businessman? Yes. But what I am more than anything else is a grandfather who wants his grandchildren to have the same kind of place to live and grow up in as I did." *Sam Johnson*, 1994, at presentation of Lindbergh Award

Georgia-Pacific Pete Correll, chairman and CEO of Georgia-Pacific, is a vocal supporter of continuous EHS progress. In the company's first environmental and safety report in 1994, Correll truly came to grips with the definition of environmental leadership:

> While profit leadership is easy to define, environmental leadership is not. At Georgia-Pacific we believe that environmental leadership means protecting the environment but at the same time being able to use our resources responsibly to make the paper and building products on which we all depend . . . .It means developing new and innovative approaches to addressing environmental problems. . .and it means involving all employees in carrying out our environmental commitments.

To do this, Correll increased the company's investment in employee training and development. He is also committed to the protection of tens of thousands of acres of ecologically and environmentally significant habitat. Visible nationally, Correll cochairs the Eco-Efficiency Task Force of the President's Council on Sustainable Development.

A Georgia-Pacific senior vice president, James E. Bostic, Jr., chairs a policy committee that oversees the company's environmental programs, and reports regularly to the board of directors on the committee's activities.

Dow Chemical Company Dow is a leader on virtually every front. Its best known environmental leaders are its CEO, Frank Popoff, and David Buzzelli, vice president, and director of environment, health and safety (Smart, 1992). Buzzelli cochairs the President's Council on Sustainable Development. He also serves on Dow's Board of Directors—a first for a high-ranking environmental officer in corporate America.

Dow's environmental stewardship programs trace their origins to 1966 when Carl Gerstacker, then chairman, introduced a progressive program that included source reduction, employee involvement, and the sharing of technical knowledge (Smart, 1992). Today, Dow's Board also has an outside advisory council comprised of academic, advocacy, academic, government, and other experts. Dow's leadership extends throughout the organization. Managers at all levels are educated and encouraged to speak out on EHS issues wherever the need arises.

Leaders in Small and Midsized Facilities

How do we place the efforts of smaller companies in context? Many of their issues are consumer-driven, and no less threatening to the bottom line than those of large companies. Their resources, however, are often severely constrained. Once compliance has been addressed, little is left for voluntary initiatives. Yet the track record of some companies proved that they can excel when strong leadership from the top is provided.

Below are several profiles of smaller companies that have taken an innovative approach to the management of environmental and social issues. Some of these are risk-takers and have great style in the way that they project their image. Their leaders also tend to be more accessible, both to insiders and outsiders, than their counterparts in larger companies.

Ben and Jerry's Homemade, Inc. If you are addicted to fine ice cream, you are probably a fan of Ben and Jerry's products (Scott and Rothman, 1994). This small-town company in Vermont, employing about 600, daily hosts thousands of visitors, who queue up to watch workers pack cartons, and also to sample the company's products. The unorthodox management style of its cofounders, Ben Cohen and Jerry Greenfield, permeates the place. Employees were encouraged to do the "10 steps of the Improvement Boogie," the company's version of TQM. In the past, the company regularly donated 7.5% of its pretax profits to organizations that address social and environmental concerns. The company also promotes recycling awareness, and recently installed an innovative solar system to purify dairy wastes from its operations. Ben and Jerry's also purchases rain forest products for its ice cream, to encourage preservation rather than destruction of these areas. A comment from its plant manager early in its history summed up the company's operating ethic:

Money's not always the issue. Sometimes in life you have to give something back.

At the end of 1994, the company unfortunately had significantly less to give back to society, losing $1.9 million on revenues of $148 million. New CEO, Robert Holland, brought in to sharpen the company's focus, intends to apply stricter financial and performance measures. His past management record suggests that he will probably follow the strong social consciousness model of his predecessors, but will have to take a strong hand in integrating the company's financial goals with environmental, social, and other objectives.

Herman Miller, Inc.   Another company with a "heart" is a manufacturer of fine office furniture in Zeeland, Michigan, that employs about 2800 people. Its former CEO, Max DePree, described the connection between leadership and stewardship as follows:

> The measure of leadership is not the quality of the head but the tone of the body... Leadership is a concept of owing certain things to the institution. It is a way of thinking about institutional heirs, a way of thinking about stewardship as contrasted with ownership.

The value system at Herman Miller is built on a strong social and environmental ethic that pervades the whole company (Murphy and Enderle, 1995). During the 1950s, its CEO established a policy that any new facilities constructed would retain 50 percent of their open areas as "green space." Natural lighting was favored to save energy. Today, that ethic has been translated into new standards for building construction that encompass everything from seasonal and weather design considerations to new materials, daylighting, fresh air, and landscaping. The company is a winner in many areas. Business Week bestowed 14 Industrial Design Excellence Awards on the company between 1980 and 1994. The company was also the first in the furniture manufacturing industry to require that any tropical woods used be obtained from "sustainable-yield" forests. Richard Ruch, CEO in 1990, describes the rationale behind that policy in business terms:

> The rain forests will survive only if we add value to them by encouraging their productive use rather than their destruction.

Brush Wellman, Inc.   This is a natural resource-based company headquartered in Cleveland, Ohio, that employs about 2000 people at its ten sites throughout the United States. Its Utah facility extracts beryllium from ores mined there. Elsewhere it is made into beryllium alloys and metal as well as beryllia ceramic. The company also makes precious metal products and specialty metal systems for worldwide markets. During the 1940s, the company's top management recognized the need for openness on the issue of potential health effects due to exposure to beryllium (a lung disease is associated with inhalation of beryllium in respirable form). It looked for advice on these policies and programs, including the appropriateness of warning labels on its products, from external health experts. The company president, Dr. C. Baldwin Sawyer, and the plant's manager wrote to employees on these issues, informing them of the company's policies and reminding them of the importance of their own role and responsibility in protecting fellow workers' health. Sawyer also implemented a policy of providing for medical care to any employees adversely affected by exposure. This early, proactive response, coupled with rigorous plant monitoring procedures and medical surveillance, contributed to the company's understanding of the types of work practices and equipment vital to protect employee health and the environment. It also undoubtedly protected the company from the type of disastrous lawsuits that plagued and in some cases bankrupted some segments of the asbestos industry. Today, the company's policy on this issue reads:

> The health and safety of our employees is of paramount importance. No operation or task will be conducted unless it can be performed in a safe manner. . . .We shall make every effort to minimize, to the lowest feasible level, occupational and environmental exposure to all potentially hazardous materials. We will go beyond regulatory compliance, striving for continuous improvement in all our environmental, health and safety control efforts.

The company continues to be the world's leading producer of beryllium and beryllium-containing products. Without its proactive stance on sound regulatory policy and its commitment to research, the industry itself might not exist today.

ENVIRONMENTAL LEADER-MANAGERS

The 1990s produced a more robust and proactive environmental leader, one who was not only a manager, but also recognized for leadership skills as a coach and mentor of people. These leader-managers were often senior or middle managers with strong technical backgrounds as well as operating and management capabilities. Their ability to network, lead teams, and provide top to bottom consistency and "constancy of purpose" is what distinguishes their companies from mediocre performers. Many have little formal environmental management education, but learned their skills and expertise on the job. The best of these are articulate high performers, respected by peers and subordinates alike. Their experience, career paths, and educational backgrounds tend to be diverse, thus making it easier to cross department or unit lines to get the job done. Some, despite intense internal responsibilities, were also drawn to address national and internationally significant issues. In many instances, a turning point during their career catalyzed a leap in both personal and job performance.

Role Model and Mentor

Kodak's Neil Connon personifies the leader/manager who is both role model and mentor. In the words of department staff:

> Neil's personal leadership got us moving and changed our culture. He recognized early on that waste minimization made good business sense and went personally to division managers to sell this concept. He also spends a lot of time on the plant floor talking to operators and chemists, and he encourages us to get out there as well.

Quality is an integral part of Connon's background from his production days, as well as his responsibilities as a senior manager in the site's large analytical chemistry laboratories. Quality was, in fact, the bridge between two career paths, production and environmental management. Like many of his counterparts in other companies, he brought extensive and varied management experience to his assignment as health, safety, and environmental manager in Kodak Park's synthetic chemicals manufacturing operation. Connon's credibility as a leader-manager is supported by his strong technical background (a Ph.D. in organic chemistry), as well as his operations experience as a development chemist and production manager.

Connon's division faced many hurdles in moving its improvement programs forward. His division makes specialty chemicals for Kodak's photographic manufacturing operations, and is, by far, the largest generator of hazardous waste at the site. Its other challenges include an aging physical facility, and high levels of waste designed into processes developed in earlier years. The need to make a strong business case for environmental improvements forced the division to be innovative. Connon points out that managers need to "get on the same page, and not set separate business goals and separate environmental goals." This year, the division received New York State Governor's Award for Pollution Prevention in 1995, demonstrating the success of its leadership team, the strong cooperation between operations and their EHS support staff, as well as what Connon terms the constancy of purpose of the division manager's support.

Public Policy Leadership

In Canada, it is not unusual for individuals to move from industry to government. This practice benefits both, and contributes to the more cooperative working relationship between the two sectors that is often envied in the United States. Wally Vrooman's career path is a good example of how this can work. He spent the first six years of his career as a chemical engineer in the Canadian paper industry. He joined the Ontario Ministry of Environment in 1968, at a time when the environmental movement of that decade was on the upswing. The last six years of this twenty-year hiatus in his industry career were spent as Regional Director for the Northwest Region.

Another turning point in Vrooman's career occurred in 1988 when he returned to industry and took on responsibility for all environmental issues in operations and woodlands in a forest products company, and two years later was named vice president of environment at Avenor. In this capacity, he drew on his chemical engineering background to catalyze the installation of environmentally beneficial production and treatment technologies in the company's pulp mills. Vrooman also drove the introduction of formal environmental management systems, participating at the same time in the development of ISO 14000 standards. Recognizing the need for greater environmental awareness and education for employees and stakeholders, he initiated the production of communications materials for the public, including videos for schools on recycling, forestry, and mill processes.

But Vrooman is probably best known throughout Canada for his effectiveness in high-level interactions with international, federal, and regional agencies to resolve policy debates critical to the forestry industry. He is also recognized nationally and internationally for his participation in business organizations such as the Conference Board of Canada, the Canadian Pulp and Paper Association, the Council of Great Lakes Industries, and the World Business Council for Sustainable Development.

Innovator

AT&T continues to produce truly talented leader-managers. Contemporary ones in the environmental arena include Braden Allenby, research vice president of technology and environment. Allenby contributed in a major way on the national and international scene to the development of tools for life-cycle assessment. His work with other AT&T colleagues in the area of industrial ecology recognizes the potential inherent in redirecting wastes to provide economic and environmental benefits.

Allenby's diverse educational background includes law, environmental science, and economics, and career experience with two regulatory bodies prior to joining AT&T in 1983 as an attorney. His unique perspective and capabilities led him eventually to the fields of energy policy, industrial ecology, and Design for Environment (DFE). Allenby's influence has also been felt at the National Academy of Engineering where he was a fellow, leading innovative efforts on industrial ecology.

Networking and Partnering

Tom Davis is another leader with national credentials who began his career at AT&T's Bell Labs. A turning point in his career came with the founding of the Global Environmental Management Initiative (GEMI), a business-based association. Davis and other colleagues recognized that although TQM was being applied by some companies to environmental management, there was a need to elevate attention on this nationally. They learned early in the life of GEMI the benefits of partnering both with business and with other stakeholder groups. Davis played a key role in founding two additional organizations that foster networking, the Corporate EHS Roundtable, comprised of senior environmental managers from individual companies, and the National Association of Environmental Managers.

Like many of his contemporaries, Davis' corporate background is diverse, including administration, public relations, training, government relations, and human resource development. His educational background, which includes degrees in journalism and communications theory, laid the foundation for his success. Today, as AT&T's director of environment and safety activities, he is the focal point for all external interactions with the regulatory community, trade associations, and the public. Davis is also recognized nationally and internationally in his role as senior director of the World Environment Center's International Environmental Forum, and as a member of the Board of the U.S. Environmental Training Institute.

World Business Leadership

Jane Hutterly's marketing and strategic business acquisitions background serves her well as worldwide vice president of environmental and safety actions for SC Johnson Wax. Hutterly views environmental management as essential to long-term competitiveness in the global marketplace, and has led company decision-makers to an understanding of the synergy between corporate financial and environmental goals:

> Responsible environmental management appeals to the heart and soul of a truly successful, competitive enterprise because it's essentially a dollars and cents proposition—today's investment equals tomorrow's cost savings.

Hutterly, who holds an undergraduate business degree from Centenary College of Louisiana and an MBA from Cornell, attributes the progress the company has made in environmental management to two key factors. The first is the "leave a light footprint" environmental philosophy and leadership of the Johnson family. The second is the success of both her team and the company's worldwide employees in turning that philosophy into realizable environmental policy, principles, and strategies in the 50 countries in which SC Johnson Wax operates. Hutterly argued for specificity and accountability in the company's first series of environmental and safety goals, gaining approval to publicly release both corporate goals and worldwide results—a first in the history of the 108-year-old privately held company.

> People tell me we're a leader in this area. Well, I believe leadership is two-pronged: action and communication. Our goals were designed to motivate action that could be measured, because what gets measured gets done. Communication is the logi-

cal extension. How can a company lead if no one knows where it's going and what it's doing to get there?

Hutterly's involvement in international environmental issues has grown steadily with the company's; her department was among the organization's first to effectively execute a global strategy. Within the company she is credited for her vision and strategic leadership in aligning environmental management and stakeholder interaction with the corporation's worldwide business focus. Today, on the national and international scene, she serves as a liaison to the Clinton administration's President's Council on Sustainable Development, and an Associate of the World Business Council for Sustainable Development.

Multitrack Careers as a Corporate Asset

A number of Fortune 500 companies have also attracted former government agency heads as senior managers or board advisors. Henry Habicht, former Deputy Administrator of EPA, now serves as vice president at Safety-Clean Corporation. R. Hays Bell, a former senior official in the Occupational Safety and Health Administration's (OSHA's) technical directorate, is Eastman Kodak Company's vice president of health, safety, and environment. Lee Thomas, former administrator of EPA, serves as senior vice president at Georgia-Pacific. William Ruckelshaus, now chairman and CEO of Browning-Ferris Industries, was also a former EPA administrator. Thomas Jorling left his position as New York State's Commissioner of the Department of Environmental Conservation to become vice president of environment at International Paper. William Reilly, former EPA administrator, serves on DuPont's board and chairs its Environmental Policy Committee. Such individuals bring leadership skills, a wealth of experience and knowledge, as well as credibility in policy and technical arenas.

These thumbnail sketches illustrate the caliber of leader that corporate America has been able to attract to the field of environmental management. Their leadership potential as well as their background experience led to their selection for assignments that are notoriously visible, frequently controversial, and always challenging.

CLOSING LEADERSHIP GAPS

Remember that your organization is unique with respect to its customers, its competitors, its capabilities, culture, and the personal qualities of its management and employees. The leadership model that it adopts needs to be carefully tailored to match those attributes. Does it, in fact, have an effective leadership model? *If not, why not?* Is top management unaware of environmental issues and their impact on the business of your organization? How can you raise that awareness? Perhaps your organization has already made a good start, but is stuck at a temporary but very real roadblock. How can its leadership improve, and be made more visible to others?

One of the most common barriers to success identified by environmental managers in companies of all sizes is the lack of support from above. Raising the visibility of "shopfloor" environmental issues to the level of a CEO in a large company can be daunting, due to the bureaucracy and competing priorities of big companies. If the chain of command drops the ball at any point, the wrong priorities and goals can be set. Failure to recognize such issues can be equally fatal to smaller organizations, since neither their operations, products, or ethics will satisfy customers, regulators, or the public. Without support from the top, companies will never be perceived as leaders among their peers.

Approaches You Can Take to Fill Gaps

Closing leadership gaps is a difficult task that requires persistence, sound information, and access. Below are a few approaches that might work for you.

1. *Capture attention with potential impacts of inaction.* Often, the greatest barrier to success is simply that issues and impacts have not been adequately evaluated or communicated. Top management, unaware of potential impacts, focuses on other priorities. Changing this mind-set may require a variety of tactics, including gathering more complete information on the potential impacts of inaction, such as accidents, injuries, violations, fines, and lawsuits, as well as information on the perceptions of the public of the company's values and ethics.

2. *Demonstrate impact on the bottom line.* Mismanagement of environmental issues can lead to impacts on both costs and revenues at virtually every point along the path of creating, distributing, and supporting a company's products processes, and services. By analyzing where additional costs are incurred, opportunities can be discovered to create additional value-added. (The value chain, a tool developed by Michael Porter and colleagues at Harvard in the mid 1980s, is discussed more fully in Chapter 6.) Another technique is to enlighten management on what the company's skunk works have accomplished through environmental improvement projects that create value. A third avenue is to provide intelligence on competitors' environmental strategies and successes, and the potential impacts on the organization's customer base and revenues of more competitive products or services.

3. *Find a champion.* If your problem is access, you may need to find a champion who can help you communicate with the company's leadership, using either the direct line or a more indirect route. Your champion should be someone who perceives value in your message, so your job becomes twofold, first finding, then educating your champion.

4. *Use environment as a rallying point.* Perhaps the morale within your company has been weakened due to restructuring or other changes. How do you

restore credibility when employees are preoccupied with saving their jobs, and short-term measures displace long-term thinking? In some respects, the area of environmental improvement is a "natural" as an element in such a restoration process. It provides an opportunity to demonstrate long-term corporate and personal commitment to broad problems both within and beyond the corporate fence, addressing global as well as community-oriented issues. The ethical attributes of these programs also inspire people to action. The visible presence and commitment of senior management lends credibility, and creates personal connections to people. Survival, in fact, depends on links between management and individuals, for it is people who bring such programs to life.

5. *Be prepared.* To say that an environmental manager needs to be a skilled salesman, fortune-teller, and magician in order to catalyze major cultural change is only a small exaggeration. However, you also need to do your homework. Don't proceed without sound data and a well-thought-out plan. Be prepared to demonstrate how your ideas can add value to the bottom line through more efficient and effective management approaches.

Questions to Answer on Leadership

■ Is your organization led by senior managers who display conviction and commitment to values and ethics? Are they personally involved and visible?

■ Is there a high level of commitment everywhere in the organization?

■ Do your organization's leaders effectively communicate, motivate, and enable others?

■ Do your leaders act as role models both within and outside the organization?

■ Do they provide resources to meet commitment in improvement plans, then reward efforts and excellence in performance?

■ Are they long-term or short-term oriented?

■ What barriers exist related to leadership? What can you do to inspire greater leadership by senior management, or by your organization in general? Do you need to become a better salesman, mentor, magician, or implementer?

ISO 14001 On Management Commitment

ISO 14001 is clear on the need for "commitment from all levels, especially from the top management" for success of the system. The Annex, which provides guidance, defines a specific role for management in defining and documenting the organization's environmental policy, including a commitment to compliance with applicable laws and regulations, as well as to continuous improvement. A guidance document, ISO 14004, lists key principles for managers, recommending that they:

- Recognize environmental management as "among the highest corporate priorities"
- Create a process to communicate with interested parties, both internal and external
- Determine applicable legal requirements as well as any environmental considerations relating to the organization's activities, products, and services
- Foster commitment on the part of both management and employees to protect the environment, and clearly assign both accountability and responsibility
- Encourage a life-cycle approach for environmental strategic planning
- Create management processes that ensure the unit will achieve its targeted performance levels
- Allocate resources, including training, so that performance levels can be achieved
- Compare performance against policies, objectives, and targets in order to make improvement as needed
- Regularly review and audit the unit's environmental management system and identify opportunities to improve both the system and performance
- Work with contractors and suppliers to establish an environmental management system (EMS)

ADDITIONAL READINGS

Ehrenfeld, J. R. and A. J. Hoffman. 1993. "Becoming a Green Company: The Importance of culture in the Greening process." *Greening of Industry Conference: Designing the Sustainable Enterprise.* Cambridge, MA: The Greening of Industry Network.

Hickman, Craig R. and M. A. Silva. 1984. *Creating Excellence: Managing Corporate Culture, Strategy and Change in the New Age.* New York: New American Library.

Hitt, William D. 1988. *The Leader-Manager: Guidelines for Action.* Columbus, OH: Battelle Press.

Weld, Royal F. 1993. "How CEO's See It," ECO *Magazine* 1:6–14.

CHAPTER 4

LINKING CORPORATE AND INDIVIDUAL VISION, VALUES, AND BEHAVIOR

"We commit voluntarily our energy and talent, as well as our financial resources, to those agencies and institutions whose purpose is the common good. We cannot live our lives isolated from the needs of society." *Max DePree*

CHAPTER OBJECTIVES

Describes how leaders, corporations, and individuals interact to make values and ethics come alive

Outlines approaches for deployment of EHS vision, principles, and values

LEADERS, VISION, AND VALUES

A vision defines where you are going. Values and ethics define how you behave in getting there, and help you frame principles and policies that govern decision-making.

What role do leaders play in this process, and how do individuals fit in? Leaders enable others to enter the leadership circle, articulate a consensus view of vision, values, and principles that govern behavior, and convey these to others in the organization. Without this structured approach, the organization would remain a chaotic collection of beliefs and behaviors. What sets some companies apart is a clear statement of ethics and values that comes from the top. Such a signal encourages employees with similar motivations and values to reflect back those corporate values through personal example, on or off the job, and to collaborate with like-minded counterparts in the organization. Some companies clearly excel at this.

". . .Understand that what we believe precedes policy and practice." *Max DePree*

"Doing the Right Thing"

"Doing the right thing" is a familiar term at Wegmans Food Markets, Inc., a family-run, regional business that originated in 1916 as a fruit and vegetable cart on Main Street in Rochester, New York (Bounds, 1994). Today this chain of 52 supermarkets and associated home and garden centers (known as Chase-Pitkin) employs 23,000 (two-thirds of whom are part-time). Wegmans has had its share of national fame through stories in the *Wall Street Journal* and *Fortune Magazine*, a feature story on CNN television, and a listing as one of *The 100 Best Companies to Work for in America* (Levering and Moskowitz, 1993).

What makes this company different? First and foremost, it is a company that is obsessed with satisfying its customers; a later section of this book talks more about this. But beyond its customer focus, the company also has a long tradition of "doing the right thing." Its scholarship program, for example, provides tuition awards to employees (the program won a Presidential "Point of Light" award). Its work-study program provides jobs for "at-risk" high school students. Its donations underwrite preschool programs for disadvantaged children.

With such a history, it is no surprise that Wegmans has also managed to combine both ethics and good business practices in solving what it identified as environmental challenges. Wegmans' management recognizes that its employees and its stakeholders are key to carrying out the company's commitment to its broad vision of a "better world for future generations." A simple statement summarizing its commitment appears in its 1994 Environmental Scrapbook, prepared for its employees and shared with the public:

> At Wegmans and Chase-Pitkin, we are aware that the ever-growing environmental concerns facing us today will have profound effects on the lives of our children and grandchildren. There are no simple solutions to the problems we encounter; no one person or group can ever hope to have all the answers. For this reason, we must work closely with our customers, employees, and suppliers to make the decisions which will lead us toward a brighter tomorrow. Only by working together and striving to continuously improve the way we work can we hope to provide a better world for future generations.

Leaders and Values

Articulating Values. Corporate values provide a governing framework for behavior, and a foundation for guiding principles, policies, and practices.

> "Clarifying the value system and breathing life into it are the greatest contributions a leader can make."   Tom Peters and Robert Waterman (1992)

Kodak's 1994 EHS report, for example, links its corporate values to EHS responsibility:

> The "rebuilding" of Kodak is based on five values: respect for the dignity of the individual, uncompromising integrity in everything we do, trust, credibility, and continuous improvement and personal renewal. Nowhere do those values have more significance than in the area of health, safety, and environmental responsiblity. *Chairman and CEO George Fisher, Vice President and Director of Health, Safety, and Environment, R. Hays Bell*

The role that corporate leaders have in articulating such values was eloquently summed up by Max DePree (1989):

> Leaders must take a role in developing, expressing, and defending civility and values....To be part of a throwaway mentality that discards goods and ideas, that discards principles and law, that discards persons and families, is to be at the dying edge.

The Chairman of the Stride Rite Foundation, Arnold S. Hiatt (1993) similarly recognized the need for ethical values that extend beyond corporate walls:

> With power and privilege comes responsibility, not only to stockholders, but also to other constituencies....the well-being of a company cannot be separated from the well-being of employees or the community.

Management as Mentor and Role Model   Hans Wolf (1993), former vice chair of Syntex (a leading pharmaceutical company) recognized the need for management example, and personally led seminars for his key managers on ethical behavior:

> ...Setting the right example is a top priority. To make sure subordinates act ethically, managers must be careful to act ethically themselves and to avoid the impression that they will condone unethical behavior to accomplish difficult tasks. In addition, they need to make it clear to their people that integrity and ethical conduct will be important factors in performance evaluation.

The Role of Individuals

Codes of Conduct for Individual Behaviors   A crisis situation at the NYNEX family of companies led that organization to recognize the links between individual behaviors, attitudes, and customer acceptance in the marketplace. Its management responded by redefining the organization's code of conduct. William C.

Ferguson (1993), NYNEX chairman and CEO, pointed out the role of account-ability in calling attention to expectations, noting that desired behaviors:

> [S]tart with integrity and leadership, emphasize communications...and end with a strong sense of accountability . . . . [T]here is a huge difference between compli-ance and commitment. If people are not seriously committed to ethics, expect to find them reading the ethics manual in order to find loopholes. If they are look-ing for loopholes, they are going to find them, no matter how good the code of conduct is.

Individual Choice The role of individual choice is recognized in the SC Johnson Wax 1994 environmental progress report in a message from its presi-dent and CEO, William George:

> Ultimately, every decision comes down to personal conviction. A deep down belief that it's the right thing to do. People making daily decisions, based on their own sense of responsibility to the world in which we live.

Dave Thomas (1994), the founder of Wendy's, a chain of fast-food restaurants, describes in a homely way the value-laden characteristics that lead to an indi-vidual's ultimate success in the business world:

- Inward ones that have to do with getting your own act together successfully.
- Outward ones that are all about treating people right.
- Upward ones—skills you need to know if you want to go beyond just doing an okay job and truly excel.
- Onward ones—attitudes you need to have when you put yourself second and other people first.

Ethics and EHS Professionals That many environmental or EHS professionals often encounter an atmosphere of distrust in working with regulators and the public points out the need for ethical values as the foundation for behavior:

> Ethics is the discipline concerned with concepts of right and wrong, with moral duty and obligation. It is an attempt to form boundaries on personal and profes-sional conduct to keep individuals from exceeding an acceptable range of behavior. . . . . [T]he responsibility of environmental professionals will be to provide the best information available to decision-makers about the environmental consequences or risk consequences of alternative paths of action. . . . As we insist upon the insertion of ethical considerations in these . . . decision-making processes, an amazing result will be achieved. Trust will begin to attach to these processes." *James B. Blackburn, (1994)*

Crises as a Proving Ground for Ethical Values

Crises are the ultimate proving ground for ethical values. Ashland Oil's response capabilities and its values were tested by a 4-million gallon diesel fuel spill from a new storage tank into the Monongahela River, which subsequently threatened water supplies downstream (Schrum, 1991). Ashland's response team was underway immediately and worked with local and other response agencies to contain, then mitigate, damage from the spill. The company hired contractors for cleanup, involved its own employees, alerted Coast Guard and other public response groups, and provided various equipment for spill cleanup. Temporary piping was installed to provide communities with clean drinking water.

During the first two days, the company's management uncovered a number of unexpected, and disconcerting, findings associated with construction materials, tank testing procedures, and the construction permit. Ashland's CEO, John Hall, decided to be candid with the public on these deficiencies, despite advice to the contrary, taking full responsibility for the spill, and admitting actions that had "clear legal implications."

His statement is telling: "I think you have to look at it in human terms. You have to try to do what's right and that's what we're trying to do."

While Ashland was subsequently held accountable for the disaster, the legal system was lenient. The presiding judge stated that the company had been straightforward in its conduct throughout the accident. Today, this event continues to be cited as an example of successful crisis management by the media, and was selected for case study use by students at the Harvard Business School (1990).

Ashland's response did not stop with a public admission of its accountability for the accident. The event precipitated the creation of new policies, plans, and procedures, as well as restructured departments. Recognizing the company as a leader, the following year, the EPA asked the company to direct a crisis management project for the agency.

MOVING FROM VISION AND VALUES TO ACTION

Frameworks for Deployment

Moving from values to substantive action requires more than an attitude adjustment. Most large companies take several years to create a complex framework of environmental values and policies, principles, standards, practices, as well as linkages to strategies, goals, and action plans (Figure 4-1). The process also requires significant effort to create consensus and consistency throughout the organization through communication, so that all elements of the framework can be effectively deployed. AT&T, for instance, deploys its environmental policy as part of its quality policy, and creates business plans that integrate both (Dambach and Allenby, 1995). Its corporate environmental policy was modified to reflect the desired change in direction toward Design for Environment (DFE), and action plans were developed to make this policy a reality:

> [We will] utilize design for environment principles to design, develop, manufacture and market products and services worldwide with environmentally preferable and

energy-efficient life cycle properties, and support our customers' and suppliers' efforts to do the same....[We will] promote achievement of environmental excellence by designing new generations of processes, products, and services to be environmentally preferable to the ones they replace.

Kodak's policies and guiding EHS principles are the basis for its EHS performance standards, which outline management intent and expectations for its units worldwide. The standards are also used in its assessment program to identify performance and management gaps.

Kodak's Health, Safety and Environment Performance Standards

Medical	**Environment**
Fitness to work	Waste minimization
Preventive medical services	Air emission control
Medical facilities and staff	Release reporting
Medical services liaison activities	Groundwater protection
Emergency medical care	Wastewater management
Medical surveillance program	Waste management
Medical records	

Safety	**Health**
Emergency preparedness and community involvement	Exposure assessment and hazard control
Facility safety	Product responsibility
Personal protective equipment	Occupational health record systems
Storage, handling and distribution of materials	Health, safety, and environmental education and training
Contractor safety	Company exposure limits
Fire protection	Chemical management control
Equipment safety	Ergonomics
Chemical and manufacturing processes and equipment	

If you find the use of such a management framework cumbersome or confusing, and wonder if you really need it, rest assured that you are not the first to ask. However, it is clear that at least some of its elements are essential to point your business, and its people, in the right direction. Specifically, you need to articulate what your core business is (mission), where you are going in the future (vision), what you stand for (values like integrity, trust, quality, environmental stewardship), and what principles govern your behavior.

THE HOUSE OF QUALITY

Standards & Practices	Plans & Resources	Continuous Improvement
Principles & Ethics	Goals & Targets	Measures & Review
Vision & Mission	Priorities & Options	Quality Tools, Processes, System
Values	Issues	Enabled Workforce

CULTURE   STRATEGY   DEPLOYMENT

■ **FIGURE 4-1.** Linking culture, strategy, and deployment.

Environmental Vision and Principles: Should You Write Your Own?

Getting Started   The answer to this is yes—and maybe. Yes, you should write your own vision statement. Only you know your business and where it should go. It is worthwhile comparing yours with statements written by other organizations. Ask your peers or look for examples in annual environmental reports published by a number of companies. The best of these are brief, clear, focused, emphasize end points rather than means, and are consistent with the organization's central mission.

Georgia-Pacific's Experience   Should you write your own environmental principles? Some companies and individual sites have done this. Georgia-Pacific's guiding principles on environment and safety, published in 1994, were developed by the company's Environmental Policy Committee, facilitated by Susan Vogt, director of corporate environmental policy, training, and regulatory affairs. The Committee looked at charters and principles developed by both corporations and environmental groups to find which points were common and essential. After six drafts over a twelve month period, consensus on a set of principles rel-

What we achieve reflects who we are, and, in turn, the breadth of our vision.

evant to Georgia-Pacific was reached. Six of these principles are management system-focused. Four more relate to the area of conservation and sustainable use of resources, including defining the company's commitment to sustainable development. The remaining eight address community awareness and protection of health and environment. Georgia-Pacific's principles are linked to specific goals and action plans, each of which has a senior management champion and an implementation team.

Herman Miller's Environmental Commitments In 1993, the Herman Miller company translated its corporate value of protecting the environment into a statement of its environmental commitments (or principles):

> Protecting the environment is one of the values of Herman Miller. As a corporate steward in our communities, through continuous improvement we will:
>
> > Minimize waste by following the priority order to reduce, reuse, recycle, compost, incinerate, landfill;
> >
> > Implement technologies to efficiently use energy resources;

Strive to surpass conformance to the law. Compliance will be the minimum standard by which we rate our performance;

Use company resources to promote environmental knowledge and awareness to those involved in our business, including our employees, customers, regulators, suppliers, neighbors, and competitors;

Review and improve the environmental impact of materials used in our products and processes.

Sustainable Development Principles The principles associated with International Chamber of Commerce's Business Charter for Sustainable Development (Appendix) were developed in preparation for the worldwide environmental summit in Rio in 1990. The principles are based on the concept of sustainable development and have received broad acceptance by the business community worldwide.

Responsible Care Principles The Responsible Care program was initiated by the Canadian Chemical Producers Association in 1984, and has now been adopted widely by chemical manufacturers associations in the United States and worldwide. Its principles (Appendix) include: a commitment to clean and safe operations; the protection of worker safety and health; safe products; supplier, customer, and community involvement; minimizing the use of natural resources; and responsible involvement in the public policy process. The forestry industry has recently issued principles for sustainable forestry practices.

The CERES Principles In the aftermath of the Exxon *Valdez* oil spill, the Coalition for Environmentally Responsible Economies (CERES) also published a set of environmental principles. Though initially controversial, a later version, revised with input from business, has gained somewhat greater acceptance. General Motors was the first major manufacturing company to endorse the CERES Principles, and also the first Fortune 50 company whose environmental principles were endorsed, in turn, by CERES.

Remember that you should be prepared to implement whatever you adopt, then to measure your progress. You may also find value in proactively providing the public with information on your programs and progress before they ask. Also remember that your principles and your action plans and goals should be consistent.

CHANGING PUBLIC PERCEPTIONS OF CORPORATE STEWARDSHIP

Some observers call "business ethics" an oxymoron, despite the strenuous efforts by business to better educate the public on stewardship programs and improved performance (Ferguson, 1993). Yet, surveys of corporate credibility continue to show that the public, as well as the media, remain unconvinced. Changing public perceptions is clearly a long-term objective, not one that can be accomplished overnight.

Perceptions also need to change from within before they can change externally in a meaningful way. This implies, in turn, that vision and values related to environmental responsibility go beyond written statements, that management "walks the talk," that ethical behaviors are valued and rewarded within the organization, and that individuals and corporate views on stewardship and ethics are consistent and reinforcing.

QUESTIONS TO ANSWER ON VISION, VALUES, ETHICS, AND PRINCIPLES

- Do you know where your organization is going? Is this documented in a vision statement and understood?
- Does your organization have a clear set of values? Do these include environmental responsibility?
- Do employees find the organization's values and ethics credible, or are they viewed as lip service? Does management walk the talk?
- Does your organization belong to an industry sector that has created a useful set of environmental principles that set a benchmark for the sector?
- Does your organization subscribe to those principles?
- Are your goals and objectives consistent with your principles?

ADDITIONAL READINGS

Cadbury, A. 1987. "Ethical Managers Make Their Own Rules." *Harvard Business Review* 68: 69–73.

Ciulla, Joanne B. 1995. "Leadership Ethics: Mapping the Territory." *Business Ethics Quarterly* 5: 5–28.

DePree, M. 1992. *Leadership Jazz*. New York: Currency Doubleday.

Howard, Robert. 1990. "Values Make the Company: An Interview with Robert Haas." *Harvard Business Review* 68: 132–144.

Minus, Paul M., Editor. 1993. *The Ethics of Business in a Global Economy*. Boston: Kluwer Academic Publishers.

PART II

STRATEGIC APPROACHES TO GREENING YOUR BUSINESS

CHAPTER 5

SOUND INFORMATION FOR SOUND DECISIONS

CHAPTER OBJECTIVES

Introduces the reader to the TQEM category of Information and Analysis*

Introduces the pivotal role of information in creating EHS strategies focused on competitive advantage

Describes how to strategically gather EHS information on customers, stakeholders, competitors, and organizational capabilities and needs.

GATHERING INFORMATION STRATEGICALLY

Building on Sound Information

Success in business starts long before planning. It begins with a clear idea of where an organization is going, its hopes, its vision. It builds on sound information about the entire scope of its customers' and stakeholders' needs, and other key issues. It scents out the past and likely future strengths of competitors as well as other threats to success. It takes an intent inward look at

---

Information and Analysis Category Looks at the effectiveness of management and use of EHS data and information to support customer/stakeholder-driven EHS performance excellence and marketplace success.

company competencies, including technical and management skills, culture, people, and investment base. Finally, it scrutinizes the company's products, operations, and services in terms of market needs, in order to discover opportunities to capitalize on a changing marketplace.

The Three C's   Much of the information needed to support your most critical business needs can be sorted into three major areas:

- Customers' and stakeholders' needs and expectations—current and unarticulated future needs
- Competitors
- Capabilities and competencies of your organization

These three areas, discussed in some detail in the sections below, are relevant whether you are working at the level of your overall business, or only focusing on environmental factors critical to success.

Gathering useful data and information, the subject of this chapter, is only the first step. In the next chapter, you will read about management, integration, and analysis of data and information supporting decision-making and planning at all organization levels.

Understanding Customers' and Stakeholders' Needs

Who Are Your Customers and Stakeholders?   Every business has a unique set of key customers and stakeholders or interested parties. Customers include both external and internal ones, anyone in fact who depends on you for a product, process, or service. Stakeholders (or interested parties) may not always be directly affected by your environmental standards and performance, but nevertheless may have interest, expectations, or concerns. Some like to list the environment itself as a stakeholder. However, there are many surrogates who speak vocally and effectively for the environment, such as regulators, citizens groups, and scientists and other experts within the research and development communities in academia, business, and government.

Think for a moment about your own customers and stakeholders—those who care about or are affected by the environmental aspects of your business. You can start with the following groups, then add any others relevant to your business:

- Customers, external and internal
- Internal clients
- Suppliers/contractors
- Employees
- Regulators, legislators, policy-makers, and others in government
- Community

- Shareholders, investors
- Lenders
- Insurers
- Board of Directors
- Research and development (R&D) community
- Advocacy groups and other nongovernmental organizations
- Media
- "General public"
- Peers

Prioritizing Needs Try to identify and prioritize the needs and expectations of the groups listed above, and add any other issues pertinent to your business that you may be aware of, such as:

- Compliance with laws, regulations, and other requirements
- Conformance with company policies, standards, codes of practice
- EHS risks associated with current operations, products, services
- EHS costs and benefits, looking both internally and externally
- Waste levels
- Efficiency of use of materials and energy
- Land use, habitat impacts
- Adverse impacts of products, processes, services on the environment and human health
- Attitudes and perceptions, both internal and external
- Environmental liabilities
- Incidents, fines, violations
- Community concerns
- Supply chain and contractor issues
- Effectiveness of communications

Table 5-1, showing a needs matrix of issues and stakeholder groups, is a composite developed from a series of TQEM workshops for businesses in the Great Lakes region. Use it as a model to list your own key customer/stakeholder groups and their most important needs, and to develop consensus around your organization's priorities.

Understanding the Strategies of Competitors and Peers

Where possible, benchmark your own environmental practices and strategies against competitors as well as against other sectors (Chapter 14). Identify your competitors' strengths and weaknesses, and the potential threats they pose to your business. For example, a number of companies have used "green marketing" strategies to attract buyers. Where this is valid, companies can

■ TABLE 5-1 Example of Completed Matrix for Customers' and Stakeholders' Issues and Concerns

	Issue/Concern [a]								
Customer/Stakeholder	Compliance	Safe Operations	Safe Products	Environmental Costs[b]	Life-cycle Approach	Incidents and Accidents	Fines and Violations	Emission Levels	Natural Resource Impacts
Customers	M	M	H	M	M	M	M	M	
Suppliers	M	M	M	M	M	M	M		
On-site contractors	M	H				H			
Employees	H	H	M	M	M	H	H	M	M
Regulators	H	H	H	M[b]	M	H	H	H	H
Community	H	H	M	M[b]		H	H	H	H
Shareholders	H	H	H	H	H	H	H	H	H
Lenders	H	H	H	M		H	H	M	H
Insurers	H	H	H	M[b]		H	H	M	H
Board of Directors	H	H	H	H		H	H	H	M
R&D community	M	M[b]	H	M	H	M		M	M
Advocacy groups	M	M	H	H[b]	H	H	H	H	H
Media	M	H	H			H	H	H	M

Source: Composite of input from TQEM workshops for business in Great Lakes region, G. Wever

[a]H = high concern; M = medium concern

[b]External costs (impacts to environment, human health)

achieve a first-mover advantage. This strategy, however, fails if customers discover that prices are set too high, or that claims are not valid. Companies with a long-term view will base their marketing strategies on sound business practices and ethics, rather than settling for short-term profits based on shortsighted strategies. Consider how you can use what you learned from benchmarking to add value to your business.

Knowing Your Organization's Capabilities

A sound environmental strategy will also be built on sound information about your organization's capabilities and weaknesses, its current position, and its vision of where it wants to be. This analysis should encompass your organization's:

- EHS vision, values, principles, and culture
- Training and education level
- Management system strengths and deficiencies
- Current products, processes, and services, including whether they are "environmentally sound"
- Current status of environmental performance in areas such as waste levels, compliance deficiencies, audit results, incidents, environmental costs, consent orders, permit requirements
- Technology, innovation, and other competencies
- Past and present performance (including trends) relative to objectives, targets, success measures
- Potential impacts on profitability when anticipated or unexpected change occurs (value chain impact)

Ways to Gather EHS Information

Consider putting your EHS needs for each of the three categories (customers and stakeholders, competitors, and capabilities) into a matrix format. This will help you identify information gaps, assign priorities to fill these gaps, and estimate resource needs. If you are unsure how to begin, look at Table 5-2, which summarizes some of the ways that companies typically gather such information.

DEFINING YOUR KEY INFORMATION AREAS

The following sections discuss some of the key information areas that environmental managers typically consider in planning and decision-making.

Regulatory Applicability and Compliance/Conformance

Compliance remains the number one priority of most managers, and often crowds out prevention-based programs. Even the process of determining applicable regulatory requirements is an onerous task. In the United States

■ TABLE 5-2 Opportunities to Gather Customer/Stakeholder Information

Group	Contact Point	Vehicle and/or Activityt
Customers	Marketing	Direct contact
	Sales	Sales data
	Environmental and other technical support staff	Hot lines: questions, complaints, assistance
Suppliers	Purchasing	Orders, contractual agreements
	Technical staff	Hot line: questions, concerns
	Operations	Use data
Employees	Management and supervision	One-on-ones, town meetings, performance reviews
	Human resources	Surveys, interviews
Regulators	Regulatory and other staff	Briefing sessions/workshops on proposed laws,regulations,voluntary initiatives
	Management	High-level dialogue with policy-makers
Community	Management/operations	Community advisory council, briefings
	Communications/technical staff	Hot lines: questions, concerns,
Shareholders	Board of Directors, chairman	Annual meetings
Directors	Management	Briefings on major issues, progress

Academics	Technical/scientific staff	Workshops, collaborative projects
Competitors	Business units, marketing Technical staff	Trade shows, new introductions Public records on regulatory submissions, analytical data on products Publications (e.g., media, books, patents, research, annual reports, technical reports) Benchmarking
Industry peers	Management/other employees	Benchmarking, conferences Trade associations, chambers of commerce Strategic alliances/projects Research
Advocacy groups	Management Regulatory, technical staff Employees	Roundtables, councils, partnerships Dialogue, workshops Membership in groups, participation in activities
Media	Communications/PR specialists Official spokesperson Technical staff	Meetings Interviews Technical interactions

alone, the number of pages of federal regulations has risen to about 80,000. In addition to regulations, many companies have adopted environmental principles and performance standards. To determine what regulations exist (let alone apply) with any degree of confidence to a given business or operation requires expert assistance from internal or external specialists. Determining how to comply is no easier. Small and midsized companies, although faced with fewer priorities, often face monumental resource limitations. Few have the luxury of highly trained and experienced staff in-house. Their compliance coordinator may also be the plant engineer responsible for manufacturing or maintenance operations. In the limit, the sole proprietor of a business may wear every hat imaginable: accountant, secretary, safety engineer, janitor, salesperson, clerk, and president.

Useful sources of information include national and state trade associations, local or state chambers of commerce, and some government agencies that provide information on new regulatory needs through newsletters and training programs. As a member of the supply chain, smaller companies may receive training and assistance from large customers.

Operational and Product Issues, Impacts, and Risks

Good data begins with the people closest to the action, who may already have a good idea of which issues are most important. For larger facilities, data should already be available on the volume and toxicity of wastes, requirements of operating permits, previous violations or fines, accident or incident records, and public concerns (e.g., complaints) expressed by the surrounding community. Customer support units in business units should have data on product returns, complaints, and questions.

Some facilities use customized screening tools to determine the applicability of process safety management, including identifying high risk processes and job hazards.

Some companies rely on external specialists to help them generate technical data on risks associated with products, operations, and management and operational practices (5-1). These specialists can help you identify and prioritize issues, impacts, and risks based on a wide variety of parameters, such as:

- Volume and characteristics of materials used/stored on site
- Waste stream volume and toxicity
- Chemical exposure data
- Accident or incident rates
- Groundwater and soil contamination
- Modeling data for air emissions, groundwater contamination
- Site data on proximity to fire/emergency equipment, residential communities, waterbodies, and so on
- Building construction; pipelines, sprinkler systems
- Public opinion

Such data may be drawn from sources such as emissions and exposure records, permits, process safety reviews, job hazard analysis, Material Safety Data Sheets (MSDSs) on chemicals, incident and accident records, external audits (e.g., insurance), inventory and waste records, and engineering and safety studies. You will need to determine the priorities of these risks and your ability to handle them, then determine what options you can take to minimize hazards and risks associated with operations. There are five stages in risk assessments associated with, for example, chemical exposures; these include: hazard identification; evaluation of the level of risk (e.g., dose of chemical present); determination of probability of undesirable impacts; determination of actual exposure; and lastly, characterization of the risk.

It is also important to determine the current and future liabilities associated with your business. This information will be used to create improvement programs (including risk management), and as input to business planning where future strategies and resource needs are addressed. Graedel and Allenby (1995) point out that "[R]isk. . . seems deceptively objective; risks are, in fact, intensely subjective. People worry about some risks all out of proportion to the actual potential for harm, and ignore others much more dangerous." This implies, then, that programs that deal with risk also need to include educating customers and others on real risks.

"Top management takes a major step when it realizes that the organization's information systems must support rather than dominate the discussions about core business issues. . . .Top management's principal challenge is not to design systems that will process data more efficiently but to create an environment in which people can exploit information more effectively." *Bartlett and Ghoshal (1995)*

While you are gathering data on your operations, remember to keep your eyes open for opportunities at all times. Look everywhere to try to link opportunities for reducing your risks, saving on costs, and improving your image and performance wherever possible. The earlier you embed these concepts in your thinking, the more "strategic" your approach will be. The best time to do this is at the product concept stage.

Environmental Costs

The EPA estimates that total annual pollution control costs in the United States increased from $27 billion in 1972 to more than $90 billion in 1990. Adding in control costs associated with health and safety regulations brings the total to about $200 billion annually (Hopkins, 1995; Economist, 1995, figure 5-1). These figures are, however, misleading, since they do not include other internal environmental costs, which bring this to about $500 billion per year. Dow Chemical Company estimates that for every new regulation, 80% of its costs go to documentation, and only 20% to other activities such as monitoring and equipment maintenance (Lash and Buzzelli, 1995).

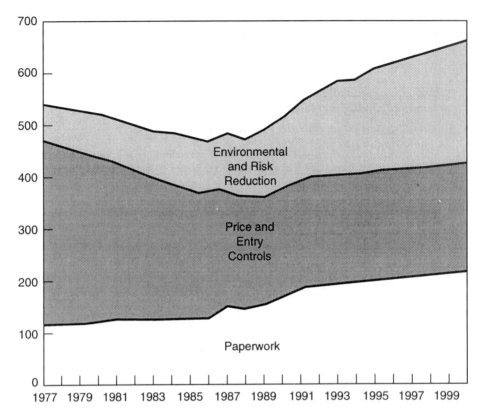

■ **FIGURE 5-1.** Annual pollution control costs (data from Hopkins, 1995).

While direct costs, such as capital expenditures, depreciation, and operating and maintenance expenses, are the easiest to track, "hidden" costs, such as waste treatment, compliance management, training, and legal support, are often included in overhead expense borne by all operations, rather than charged back to departments actually using the service. A few business organizations have become interested in "full cost accounting," an approach that considers not only direct and hidden costs, but also potential future costs such as remediation ("contingent liability costs"), public relations, and goodwill (GEMI, 1994) (2). Some companies have also begun to feel the effects of higher insurance and lending costs due to liabilities associated with their operations.

A number of advocacy groups have encouraged businesses to consider the costs associated with "externalities" such as depletion of the natural resource base or adverse effects on human health. Although research is continuing in this area, the data tends to be "soft" or inferential. For example, some methods estimate how much the public is willing to pay to gain an incremental small improvement in water or air quality. Others estimate the potential increase in revenues associated with such improvements (e.g., additional revenues from fishing license sales or increased tourism). Yet others compare the cost of controls versus prevention (GEMI, 1994)

Much has been written on the benefits of recognizing the full "cost of quality," or, as some would like to say, the "cost of *un*quality." The same kind of benefits apply to the recognition and application of knowledge about environmental quality costs. For one thing, recognizing these future costs may well set the stage for changing your approach to managing environmental issues, such as investing in cost-effective pollution prevention or Design for Environment (DFE) approaches to product design. Having sound data on EHS costs will also help you justify improvement programs with management, as well as estimate future costs of proposed regulatory measures and provide input to regulators. Analytical tools that will help you gather such data are discussed in the next chapter.

Audit and Assessment Data

Many companies use self-assessments to track and improve compliance with laws and regulations, as well as conformance with internal requirements. Although a few commercial software packages are available on regulatory compliance, these do not address site-specific requirements (e.g., specific permit conditions, consent orders), nor do they cover internal policies and practices. Some software packages are interactive; questions and reference materials can be added by either the software developer or the client. A few trade associations have developed self-assessment guides, such as the Chemical Manufacturers Association's annual assessment of members' conformance with its Responsible Care program. GEMI has a self-assessment guide (1992) for the International Chamber of Commerce's Sustainable Development Principles. Many companies rely on external auditors to supplement their in-house assessment programs, as well as to provide third party verification and potentially greater credibility (Chapter 9). Although a number of public and private organizations have attempted to develop compliance measures, it is becoming clear that a better method is to track repeat audit findings, rather than number and severity of findings.

Benchmarking Data

Companies with mature environmental management programs gather information about their competitors and peers through benchmarking exercises, and use this to selectively improve their performance (Chapter 14 covers benchmarking).

Performance Data

Many companies have recognized the value of tracking environmental performance, in areas such as waste stream volumes, savings from pollution prevention projects, spills, and safety accidents. This historical data, when compared with projected targets, is an important input to decision-making, performance-improvement programs, and strategic planning. It also provides positive feedback to departments engaged in improvement efforts (Chapter 11 discusses performance measures in some detail).

Gathering "Soft" Data

"Soft data" includes customer or stakeholder perceptions, employee attitudes, public opinion, and public policy trends. Understanding the expectations and needs of these groups can make the difference between survival or failure, short-term profits or long-term success. Another class of "soft" data is the determination of potential future risk or liability (lawsuits, fines, remediation costs) associated with existing or future operations, products, or services.

IMPROVING YOUR KNOWLEDGE BASE

The amount of environmental data needed to manage a business effectively is, at least initially, overwhelming. Don't try to address too many gaps at once.

Begin by prioritizing your information needs, decide what can be done in the short and long term. Then interject those resource needs into your action plans and get started. Some information needs can be addressed in fairly short order by simple procedural changes (e.g., creating a system to document customer concerns and complaints). Make a short-term plan, and assign responsibilities and timelines. Check to be sure you're going to meet your short-term objectives. Remember that for long-term improvements (e.g., computerizing information systems), you should prepare your case early enough to interject your resource needs into the annual plan for the following year.

Most companies begin with regulatory compliance, which has unfortunately always been a costly and moving target and a consumer of endless resources. Don't make the mistake, however, of shortchanging more proactive programs that avoid or minimize regulatory pressures, for these will almost certainly have a much higher payback for your organization in the long run.

ISO 14000 on Environmental Information

ISO 14001 requires organizations to identify the "environmental aspects" of their activities, products, and services, as well as legal and other requirements. "Environmental aspects" are defined as "elements of a company's activities, products and services which are likely to interact with the environment." The Annex is somewhat more specific on the types of data that might be useful (A.4.2.1 and A.4.2.2), such as:

■ Legislative and regulatory requirements
■ Management practices and procedures

- Feedback from investigations of incidents
- Industry codes of practices
- Agreements with public authorities
- Nonregulatory guidelines
- Environmental aspects of products, activities, services
- Emissions to air
- Releases to water
- Waste management
- Contamination of land
- Impact on communities
- Use of raw materials and natural resources
- Other local environmental issues

A guidance standard (ISO 14004) recommends that organizations do an initial review in a number of areas.

ADDITIONAL READINGS

Atkinson, John H., Jr., G. Hohner, B. Mundt, R. B. Troxel, and W. Winchell. 1991. *Current Trends in Cost of Quality: Linking the Cost of Quality and Continuous Improvement.* Montvale: N.J. National Association of Accountants and KPMG Peat Marwick.

Boden, Steven M. and G. Brayton. 1995. "Financial Issues in Environmental Liabilities and Decision-Making." *Environmental Strategies Handbook*, Rao V. Kolluru, Editor. New York: McGraw-Hill, pp. 261–288.

Russell, William G., S. L. Skalak, and Gail Miller. 1995. "Environmental Cost Accounting: The Bottom Line for Environmental Quality Management." *Auditing for Environmental Quality Leadership: Beyond Compliance to Environmental Excellence*, John T. Willig, Editor. New York: John Wiley & Sons, pp. 109–120.

Shank, John K. and V. Govindarajan. 1992. "Strategic Cost Analysis of Technological Investments." *Sloan Management Review* 34: 39–51.

CHAPTER

6

MAKING THE LEAP
FROM INFORMATION
TO INTELLIGENCE

"Technology provides the tool, information provides knowledge, and knowledge is power." *Lynn Johannson*

CHAPTER OBJECTIVES

Illustrates an array of information management tools that add value through analysis and integration

Explains and encourages the coupled use of life-cycle assessment and value chain analysis.

MANAGING INFORMATION STRATEGICALLY

EHS data is gathered for a purpose. Transformed into information, it is needed to demonstrate compliance and responsible stewardship to customers, share-holders, regulators, and the public, to support decision-making and planning, and ultimately to improve business performance. Systems that provide access to information should be designed to provide users at all organizational levels with timely, relevant, valid, comprehensible information that covers the scope of their needs.

Information technology has changed dramatically, particularly during the past decade. Most companies, faced with information overload, have chosen to computerize some of their EHS databases. Many of these systems are either personal computer (PC) based or local area networks (LANs), rather than centralized mainframe systems. Each of these approaches has limitations. While decentralized systems are initially less costly to develop and maintain, they also limit access. This may be expensive to correct when there is a need to link stand-alone systems that are noncompatible, in order to create unit-wide or corporate-level information for management decision-making and reporting.

Commercial software is available for a variety of applications such as tracking waste streams, auditing compliance with regulations, and documenting risk analyses. Some companies have tailored existing packages or instead developed their own approach to track pollution prevention projects, customer questions and follow-up, corrective action, and other EHS parameters important to operations and business units. Avenor, a Canadian forestry products company, is developing a computerized environmental database and network that will house daily performance information all of its facilities, link each of its operations, and provide a company-wide network for its environmental personnel. It is expected to serve as a communications and education base for environmental management.

In some cases, organizations have chosen to farm out certain data collection and management tasks to external sources such as analytical laboratories or engineering and consulting firms. Monitoring the quality of these external operations is essential to maintain credibility. It is also important to engineer carefully the link between systems designers and users in order to minimize misunderstandings due to jargon and other communications barriers, as well as to design systems that are truly user-friendly.

ADDING VALUE THROUGH INTEGRATION

Integrating EHS Information Systems

Geographic Information Systems (GIS) as a Value-Added Approach   Greater value can often be obtained by integrating EHS databases with spatial data (Douglas, 1995). Imagine, if you will, a system that can link many of your existing databases to an aerial map of your entire facility. The map can be viewed on a PC; then by pointing to a particular location, such as a building, it is possible to access databases showing types and quantities of chemicals used and emitted, MSDSs, emission sources and discharge points, location of control equipment, pipelines and sewers, safety and other incidents, three-dimensional images of soil stratigraphy, groundwater plumes, air dispersion patterns, and lists of contaminants. Such an approach enhances the ability of facility managers to access critical information pertinent to financial status, to risks and cost containment, and to environmental issues, in a format that contributes visually as well as conceptually to their understanding.

Use of GIS at Industrial and Other Facilities One Fortune 500 company uses this approach at its largest facility to display air dispersion modeling results, as well as to manage the data. GIS mapping is also used as a tool to manage its sewer and groundwater remediation applications, as well as for general construction projects. Such GIS applications can also increase a facility's effectiveness in dealing with external agencies and communities under routine as well as emergency conditions.

The Air Force is taking a somewhat bolder approach at its air bases, linking its site-specific environmental databases to provide base managers with a broader understanding of their major issues in order to support better decision-making in the areas of cleanup, compliance, conservation, and pollution prevention (Edwards et al., 1994; Haecker et al., 1995). The sources of data for these systems will include facility drawings (drawn from Computer Aided Design (CAD) layers from the base's archives), historical aerial photographs, land use classifications, sampling and test data, and past environmental reports. At one such installation, a GIS system models groundwater flow and contaminant transport to support health risk assessments at the site. To improve access, the base's systems are interactive and use a Windows-type operating environment, as well as off-the-shelf software.

A number of benefits are associated with this approach:

■ Integration of data in one place
■ Reduction in number and volume of reports
■ Better communication of information through combined graphics and photographic representations, including access to historical (or "change") data

Use of GIS for Natural Resource Management by Business GIS approaches are also being used for natural resource management. Avenor, a Canadian forestry and paper company, describes in its 1994 environmental report its use of information from third party audits of its operations for strategic planning at its British Columbia sites. GIS spatial modeling creates a computerized model of a forest area, incorporating factors such as the age and species of trees, types of soil, and habitats. This model can then be used to create a number of scenarios, allowing forest managers to select options for planning that minimize impacts of activities on the forest's ecosystem, thus ensuring the long-term health of the woodlands (6-1).

Limitations of GIS-Based Systems Although many facilities have been moving to GIS because of its advantages, there are still a number of shortcomings that you should be aware of with existing systems:

1. *For small facilities, cost and complexity are clearly limiting.* This is especially true where facility maps need to be converted to a format compatible with GIS applications.

2. *Many large facilities have now moved away from centralized mainframe applications to localized PC-based or LAN systems, and systems architectures may not be compatible when trying to link these distributed databases.* GIS is not compatible, in general, with a mainframe systems; transmission across the electronic backbone linking various areas of a facility may also be slow, depending on how advanced the technology of the backbone is.

3. *Software familiarization may also be a barrier, however "friendly" the design.* Occasional users may find that they need frequent assistance or refresher courses on its use.

INTEGRATING MANAGEMENT SYSTEMS AT A HIGHER LEVEL

Linking EHS and Other (Non-GIS) Databases

Value is also added by linking EHS with other facility databases, such as quality, operations, purchasing, financial, product, and human resources areas. While this is an ambitious and costly task, given that the data for many of these systems is distributed rather than centralized, linked management systems can minimize costs associated with auditing, planning, production, and other functions, and in time, could have a high payback. The linking also reduces the documentation burden by consolidating databases, rather than duplicating them.

Orlin and colleagues (1993, 1994) recommend a strategic approach to information management, applying the tools of information strategy planning. In this application, an information infrastructure is optimized to support the needs of the business, and aligned with strategic objectives. Enterprise-level information systems are used to recognize, describe, and characterize common inputs, processes, and outputs. When this is done both vertically (within the same function) and horizontally (across functional areas), then full alignment of organizational objectives, plans, and processes is possible. Given that the same resources are used across functions (people, time, equipment, material, energy, and money), it is possible to reduce the number of tracking systems, and simplify their use. Examples where such an approach can add value include the following:

- Linking personnel job files with medical and exposure records makes it easier to track chemical exposures over the lifetime of employees.
- Linking databases on waste, emission, and production makes it easier to create mass balance data, to meet reporting requirements associated with a number of waste reduction laws, and to track progress on pollution prevention and other projects.

- Linking purchasing data with departmental use of certain chemicals makes it possible to notify departments of new regulations, track chemical wastes, identify department-specific training needs, troubleshoot problems, and respond to emergencies.
- Linking databases needed for quality, planning, and EHS audits potentially provides auditors with easier access, and eliminates redundancies in database building and maintenance.

ADDING VALUE THROUGH ANALYTICAL TOOLS: LIFE-CYCLE ASSESSMENT AND THE VALUE CHAIN

Management often needs special-purpose analyses to evaluate the effectiveness of the organization's EHS management systems, as well as its plans and programs. Such analyses might include:

- The financial benefits associated with improved safety or waste reduction programs
- The effect of improved EHS training on performance (e.g., incident or accident rates)
- The impact of increased environmental support to customers on customer retention and revenues
- Customer acceptance of a recyclable versus a disposable product
- Comparisons of performance among business units with different levels of employee involvement in environmental improvement programs
- The effect of improved environmental performance on employee and public perception
- The effect of increased senior management visibility and support of environmental improvement programs on employee perceptions, involvement, and effectiveness

Two useful analytical tools are available that can help guide decision-making, improve environmental management, and add value to the bottom line. One focuses on environmental effects or impacts, and looks outwardly. The second focuses inwardly, examining costs associated with environmental factors. Both use similar frameworks. Value chain analysis is a tool that is already familiar to many in business. Life-cycle assessment (LCA) tools have been in use since the mid 1970s to support management decisions on product design, packaging, and other applications. Combining their use helps managers gain insight and refocus their efforts in a way that creates value.

Value Chain Analysis

The Value Chain Concept The concept of the value chain, developed by Michael Porter (1985) and colleagues at Harvard University during the mid 1980s (Figure 6-1), breaks down what a company does into discrete activities, deter-

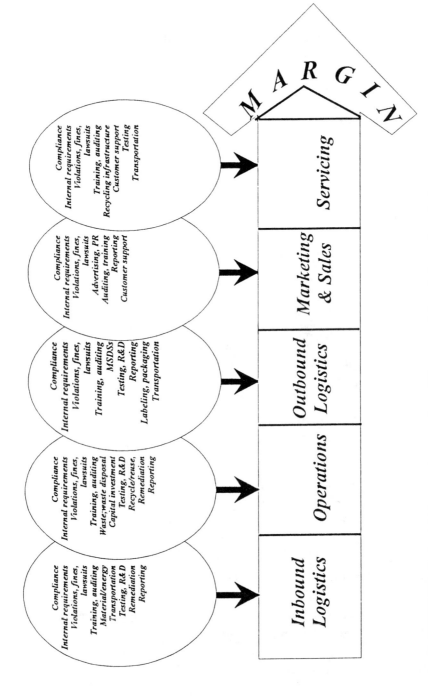

■ **FIGURE 6-1.** EHS costs incurred at different points of the value chain.

The image contains the following labeled value chain elements:

Inbound Logistics
Compliance
Internal requirements
Violations, fines, lawsuits
Training, auditing
Material/energy
Transportation
Testing, R&D
Remediation
Reporting

Operations
Compliance
Internal requirements
Violations, fines, lawsuits
Training, auditing
Waste/waste disposal
Capital investment
Testing, R&D
Recycle/reuse,
Remediation
Reporting

Outbound Logistics
Compliance
Internal requirements
Violations, fines, lawsuits
Training, auditing
MSDSs
Testing, R&D
Reporting
Labeling, packaging
Transportation

Marketing & Sales
Compliance
Internal requirements
Violations, fines, lawsuits
Advertising, PR
Auditing, training
Reporting
Customer support

Servicing
Compliance
Internal requirements
Violations, fines, lawsuits
Training, auditing
Recycling infrastructure
Customer support
Testing
Transportation

MARGIN

mines where costs and other factors relate to these activities, and provides a structured approach to creating competitive advantage. This tool examines sequential operations, starting with inputs such as raw materials and energy, then production, distribution, marketing and sales, and support beyond the point of sales. It also examines activities such as technology development and human resource management that are shared across the organization.

Value is added at each step along the chain. Total value equals what customers are willing to pay for the organization's products or services, its revenues, in other words. Obviously, costs are also incurred at each step. The difference between total revenues and total costs is profit or margin (although other financial adjustments can also affect the bottom line). Clearly, companies have an incentive to reduce costs, whatever the source, in order to maximize profits.

Impacts of EHS on the Value Chain Experienced managers recognize that EHS costs impact virtually every step in a typical manufacturing operation (Wever, 1991) (Figure 6-1). The cost of input materials is affected by EHS regulations applicable to production, transportation, and storage. At the production stage, added costs come from requirements relating to chemical emissions and exposure, chemical tracking, waste treatment, recycling, and compliance management. Permits, environmental impact studies, testing, fines, and lawsuits may also add costs to these stages. Research and development (R&D) may be needed to characterize toxicity effects or determine the fate of materials released to the environment. Distribution costs may be affected by regulations on transportation, packaging, labeling, and storage. Marketing and public relations costs related to EHS issues may be incurred. Once the product reaches the consumer, regulation-driven costs may be added to support customer needs, such as providing the infrastructure for product disposal, reuse, or recycling, as well as response to customer questions and concerns.

The magnitude of profits is obviously also affected by the company's total revenue stream. If competitors' products are more attractive due to their green attributes, revenues may shrink. Figure 6-2 illustrates how revenues and costs can be affected by EHS factors such as regulations, and how these interact to affect profitability. Organizations can improve their financial performance by changing course, improving their compliance performance and the way that they approach other EHS issues.

Using Life-Cycle Assessment Data to Improve Environmental Performance

The Product Life Cycle Five steps are recognized for the product life cycle (Figure 6-3):

■ Raw materials acquisition, or "premanufacturing," relating to supplier operations (input)

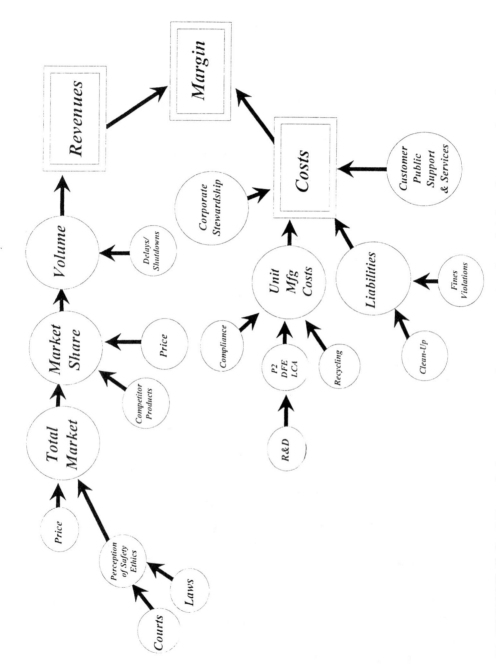

■ **FIGURE 6-2.** Life cycle impacts on environment, natural, societal, and economic systems.

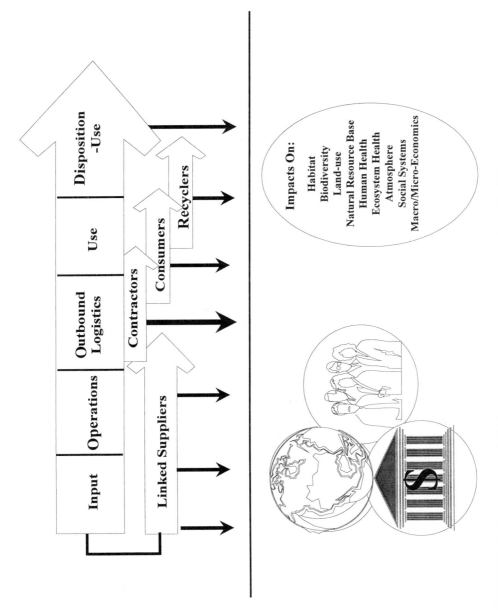

FIGURE 6-3. Impact of EHS issues on costs, revenues, and profitability.

Input | Operations | Outbound Logistics | Use | Disposition -Use

Linked Suppliers | Contractors | Consumers | Recyclers

Impacts On:
Habitat
Biodiversity
Land-use
Natural Resource Base
Human Health
Ecosystem Health
Atmosphere
Social Systems
Macro/Micro-Economics

- Manufacturing operations
- Distribution (outbound logistics)
- Customer use
- Product retirement or rebirth (e.g., disposal, reuse, recycling, recovery, remanufacturing)

Life-Cycle Assessment   Life-cycle assessment (LCA) is a tool designed to evaluate and, where possible, reduce the impact of products/services from "cradle to grave" on the environment. There are three stages in a typical LCA:

- An inventory process, which quantifies raw material, energy, and other inputs, as well as air emissions, water effluents, solid waste, and other outputs
- An assessment phase, which uses the LCA inventory to determine the potential impacts of inputs and outputs on human health, natural resources, and ecosystems
- An improvement phase, which uses information from the first two stages to reduce environmental impacts

LCA Approaches   A highly detailed LCA can take several years to complete. For this reason, many LCA practitioners prefer to use a shorter, less quantitative approach (e.g., the EPA and the Society of Environmental Toxicology and Chemistry (SETAC) methods). A life-cycle-based matrix approach developed by Braden Allenby and his colleagues at AT&T (Graedel et al., 1995) is useful to both perform and present a materials and process analysis for a particular design option. The matrix approach can also be used to examine, not only EHS factors, but other manufacturing considerations, as well as any social and political issues associated with the design option. These simplified methods are particularly applicable to sectors such as electronics, where the technology/product cycle is very rapid, and to sectors such as auto, where products are very complex (Gloria et al., 1995)(6-2).

While the methods used in the first step of an LCA are fairly well-defined and accepted, those for the second step, quantifying impacts, are only in their infancy. Some of the impacts (often called "externalities") that have been considered (e.g., Canadian Standards Association, 1994) include natural resource depletion, atmospheric effects (e.g., acid deposition, ozone depletion), human health and ecosystem effects, habitat loss, and even socioeconomic effects (e.g., cultural and population change, economic impacts). In many instances, these impacts are not easily quantified since commonly available methods produce only "soft" data on the costs or burden that is imposed on society and future generations.

The third phase of LCA asks decision-makers to use the data from stages one and two (inventories and impacts) to make environmental improvements.

This stage is the least developed of the three steps; it also depends on the development of better methods for stage two.

Use of LCA Approaches A number of companies have begun to use LCA approaches. A group at the Massachusetts Institute of Technology is working with industry partners such as Motorola, General Motors, and Hewlett Packard on applications of LCA tools. Bristol-Myers Squibb will complete LCAs of all its major product lines by the end of 1997. The need for a life-cycle approach is also recognized by sectors other than manufacturing. For example, Wegmans Food Markets in Rochester, New York, introduced the concept of an "eco-audit" of its in-house brands. Its suppliers are asked to provide environmental data in areas such as packaging (e.g., recycled content and packaging volume).

Use of Design for Environment Approaches A number of companies have begun to use Design for Environment (DFE) approaches for product design applications. Chrysler, Ford, and General Motors, for example, are using DFE to create vehicles that will be easier to disassemble and to recycle and reuse components. Increased recyclability of auto parts is an industry-wide goal. While 94 percent of U.S.-made cars and trucks are now returned to dismantling and shredding facilities, today only about 75 percent of the vehicle content, primarily metals, is recycled. Research is underway to increase the recycling of other materials, such as plastics, glass, sealers, fabrics, and so on, particularly where these are composite materials.

The Practicality of LCA Tools Will such tools ever become practical enough to use at the shopfloor level, or will they remain the more esoteric property of technical staff? In my experience, there is a ready audience for simplified tools for use by cross-discipline teams at all levels. Operators and other staff participating in pollution prevention and product redesign projects have asked: "What confidence do I have in making this process change? It might reduce the toxicity of my waste stream, but what about the effects upstream on my suppliers, and on the waste treatment plant downstream?" "Can consumers recycle this modified product, or will it have to be landfilled?" "What is the effect of changing this process so that it generates solid waste in place of wastewater?" The move toward simplified LCA methods is a positive step toward answering their questions, educating them to think more broadly about raw materials and eventual disposal or reuse.

The Value of Combining Life-Cycle Assessment and Value Chain Analysis

The frameworks for the two tools described above are nearly identical. The major difference is the way that the frameworks are used. The value chain focuses inwardly, quantifying internal impacts such as costs. LCAs look outward, evaluating external impacts, but generally excluding costs (6-3). What happens if you link the two frameworks? Figure 6-4 provides an illustration for a model company that manufactures a product whose constituents adversely affect groundwater quality when landfilled. Policy-makers and regulators respond with more restrictive laws and regulations; these in turn create additional costs for the company at a number of points in its value chain in order to manage the current manufacturing process as well as the disposal of the product.

Breaking this cycle requires a change in approach, beginning with a recognition of EHS costs associated with the current product and production process, EHS impacts on the environment, and an evaluation of design options. (This latter, in principle, is what the LCA "improvement phase" is all about.) The manufacturer elects to modify both the input materials and the manufacturing process, substituting a less toxic material and redesigning the product to be recyclable. These changes significantly reduce the company's EHS costs, and risks, as well as the product's and process' impact on the environment.

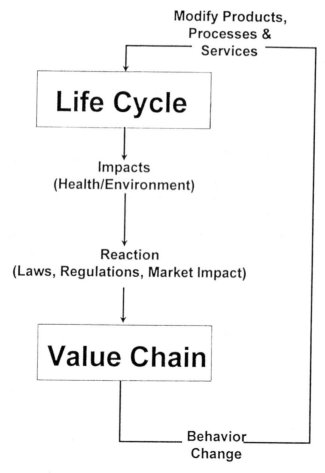

■ **FIGURE 6-4.** Linking the life cycle and the value chain.

Use of Full Cost Data for Decision-Making

Meeting Internal Financial Hurdles   Environmental projects are occasionally rejected because they do not meet internal financial hurdles, such as payback or return on investment. One reason is that cost engineers and decision-makers usually only have access to direct costs, and are unaware of, or do not know how to calculate, hidden, contingent liability, and "intangible" costs. If "full costs" are included in the financial measures typically used for decision-making, such as payback period, internal rate of return, net present value, and cost/benefit ratios (profitability index), the picture changes dramatically. The benefit of evaluating full costs is that you may be able to provide stronger justification for projects that appear marginal using standard financial measures. You may also be able to sell such projects based on risk considerations. This, then, means that environmental projects will become more competitive for funding, because you have done the extra homework that is needed to pull this information together. Better environmental cost data can also be used to provide more convincing information to policy-makers on the impacts of proposed regulations or initiatives. It can also be used to support strategic planning, since it deals with competitors' strategies and customer/stakeholder issues, as well as the organization's technical and other capabilities.

Use of Environmental Cost Accounting   Bristol-Myers Squibb is modifying its accounting systems to better capture EHS costs and benefits. Their approach includes methods for capital project evaluation and better linking of EHS costs to specific products, processes, and departments through activities-based accounting systems.

Procter & Gamble has applied "total cost assessment" (or TCA) to its pollution prevention projects worldwide at 150 sites in an effort to control its operating costs. Despite rapidly rising waste disposal costs, P&G was able to stabilize environmental costs as a result of the pollution prevention projects it justified using TCA as an analytical tool. P&G also found that strong top management support, as well as close working relations among financial and operations staff, were key to success.

A World Resources Institute's study (Ditz et al., 1995) looked at environmental costs and accounting practices at five global companies, Amoco, Ciba-Geigy, Dow, DuPont, and SC Johnson Wax, and at four smaller ones, Cascade Cabinet, Eldec Corporation, Heath Tecna, and Spectrum Glass (6-4). DuPont discovered through this process that nearly 20 percent of the total costs of manufacture for one of its pesticides were environmental in origin. Some study participants also found that most of their aggregated environmental costs were associated with a small number of products. Other environmental cost accounting case studies are underway, including EPA's studies of AT&T and Ontario Hydro's practices. The latter has begun to estimate external societal costs ("externalities") for its use of fossil and nuclear fuels.

Applying What You Learned

Try your hand at applying what you have learned about LCA and value chain analysis. Use the two frameworks described in this chapter to analyze the operations of a model company faced with growing environmental burdens and suggest possible solutions that add value to its current products, increase its revenues, and enhance its image.

Blackbourne Paint Systems, Inc., makes paint and other products for residential and commercial customers. Its SARA/TRI air emissions were the highest in the region from 1989 onward, prompting very negative coverage by the media and creating concern in its surrounding community. The company reacted by increasing its public relations and advertising budgets over the next two years to counteract public concern. The state environmental agency also reacted to its overall position on the national TRI emissions list by tightening its enforcement of air emission requirements and drafting more restrictive ones. The plant was forced to step up its plans to install pollution control equipment, and committed capital for the first such installation in one of seven major operations.

The plant's environmental manager was told that the state expects the remaining installations should be made over the next three years. New regulations affecting the company's paints and stripping formulations required the company to modify its product labels, cautioning consumers on toxic material present in its formulations and raising fears about effects on sales revenues. Blackbourne also had to fund costly toxicity testing on three new products, carried out by its parent company's laboratories. The company also knows that restrictive landfilling regulations will create disposal problems for its own operations as well as its commercial and residential customers.

As the plant's manager, what would you do? Illustrate the present situation using both the value chain to display costs, and the life cycle diagram to show impacts. Try your hand at indicating where external costs (externalities) might be incurred. Propose a course of action over the next one to five years that looks at a variety of options, and show how the company's bottom line, and the environment, might benefit.

QUESTIONS TO ANSWER ABOUT INFORMATION AND ANALYSIS

- How effectively does your organization identify its information needs?
- What major gaps exist in your information base? What resources will you need to fill them? Who has responsibility for this activity?
- Who are your major customers and stakeholders, and what are their needs and expectations? What are your key issues, short- and long-term? Your highest priorities? Your organization's strengths and weaknesses in meeting these needs?

- Do your information management systems meet your needs? Is the data you gather valid? Is it accessible to those who need it?
- Do you get the information you need for decision-making just in time, or too late to make a difference?
- Do you gather information "strategically," that is, does it support your strategic planning processes for both short- and long-term success?
- Do you integrate and analyze EHS and other information in a way that adds value to your organization?

ADDITIONAL READINGS

Johannsen, Lynn. 1995. "The Power of IT: How Can Information Technology Support TQEM." *Auditing for Environmental Quality Leadership: Beyond Compliance to Environmental Excellence*, John T. Willig, Editor. New York: John Wiley & Sons, pp. 275–280.

CHAPTER 7

PLANNING FOR SUCCESS

"Long-range planning should prevent managers from uncritically extending present trends into the future, from assuming that today's products, services, markets, and technologies will be [those] of tomorrow, and above all, from dedicating their resources and energies to the defense of yesterday." *Peter Drucker, 1985*

CHAPTER OBJECTIVES

Introduces the TQEM category of strategic EHS planning*

Describes the rationale for mainstreaming EHS issues into business plans

Outlines methods for effective EHS planning

Illustrates an array of corporate EHs strategies and examines their potential advantages

*Strategic EHS Planning Category Defines how the unit incorporates EHS needs and priorities into its strategic directions, and how it effectively implements plans that include EHS improvements.

LINKING PROCESS AND SUBSTANCE

Annual plans have become an institution in many companies. Some spend more time planning than doing. Success, however, is not a function of the mechanics of planning, but of the strategies adopted to reach the desired end points. Thus companies of any size can compete brilliantly if they avoid focusing on the structure and form of planning, and focus instead on substance.

Planning should begin and end with a vision of where you want to go. A straight line from the past to the future is often not the quickest path. More frequently, the path to the future actually *begins in the future*, recognizes its needs, then transforms the present to arrive there. The transformation process requires a framework that links vision with desired end points, creates success measures, and uses a systematic approach that includes objectives, targets, and action plans to make the vision a reality (7-1).

Hamel and Prahalad (1994) prefer the term *foresight* to *vision*, arguing that the latter suggests a dream or apparition, whereas foresight is based on "deep insights into the trends in technology, demographics, regulation, and lifestyles that can be harnessed to rewrite industry rules and create new competitive space." Their definition (whichever term you prefer) crystallizes the challenge that managers face in their struggle to create fully integrated EHS strategies within a broader corporate milieu.

"The best way to predict the future is to invent it." *Alan Kay*

Some companies, such as DuPont (Safety and Environment report, 1994) create corporate-wide strategic environmental plans, recognizing the extent to which such issues create costs and/or competitive advantage. Other companies prefer to create plans at the facility or business unit level, integrating EHS needs more locally with broader business, financial, and technology needs. Whatever the format, the process used should reinforce ownership and responsibility, and also allow such priorities to compete side-by-side with other legitimate business needs.

Setting Priorities

EHS Priority Considerations   The results of the priority setting process are only as good as the quality of the organization's input data. During the priority setting process, managers examine options, resource needs, risks, benefits, and payback associated with each. In the end, priorities should:

- Reflect the most critical customer and stakeholder needs
- Respond to new market opportunities and competitors' strategies
- Strengthen capabilities (e.g., core competencies in technology, management, and service)
- Provide for both long- and short-term needs
- Consider risk/benefit, and be cost-effective

"Management ... has to balance the immediate future against the long range. If it does not provide for the immediate future, there will be no long-range future. But if it sacrifices the long-range needs of "what our business will be" and "what our business should be" to immediate results, there will also be no business fairly soon. . . .Each business requires its own balance-and it may require a different balance at different times. Balancing is not a mechanical job. It is risk-taking decision." *Peter Drucker, 1985*

Selecting Options In some cases, options can be identified that are both environmentally sound and defensible from a payback standpoint. Some choices make obvious business sense. Gathering cost, risk, and benefit data on each alternative is needed before decision-making can proceed. These alternatives can then be fed into short- or longer term plans. Sometimes, intangible benefits override other considerations. A company that has repeated air emission violations, for instance, may identify various options, such as:

■ Installing new control or calibration equipment
■ Improving its existing procedures or documentation for calibration or maintenance
■ Substituting aqueous materials for volatile ones, thus reducing its emissions, its control and test equipment needs, and its material and operating costs

A company with a high accident or incident rate may evaluate its operations and management approach and identify options such as:

■ An increased corporate focus on EHS training and education
■ A revamping of the company's ergonomics program, including reevaluation of work areas and processes
■ Installation of modernized equipment

Companies that are wrestling with the issues of habitat loss and biodiversity may adopt conservation strategies that:

■ Minimize the effects of their operations on endangered and other species
■ Preserve or restore natural areas surrounding their facilities
■ Improve relations with community and advocacy groups through partnership projects that forge long-term relationships and that allow natural systems, jobs, and recreational uses to flourish side-by-side

Where problems and solutions are complex, selecting the best options often requires multidisciplinary input from environmental, financial, operations, and other specialists. But in the end, it is management's responsibility and choice as to where resources will be expended, what goals should be set, and what risks should be taken.

A Real-World Example of the Prioritization Process   At Kodak Park, a cross-discipline team from operations, together with EHS staff, prioritized the site's environmental projects, identifying and assigning weighting factors to a number of criteria, including:

- Risk reduction potential (the potential emission volume reduced)
- Toxicity
- Off-site exposure potential (exposure through air emissions, waste-water discharge or as hazardous waste)
- Opportunities for pollution prevention
- Regulatory drivers
- Project acceptability

Potential off-site impacts were evaluated by testing, flow/dispersion modeling, or other methods, then compared with existing regulatory standards or guidelines.

The pollution prevention criterion was rated using the waste management hierarchy (e.g., the highest weighting was given to projects where source reduction was achieved; the next to projects based on recovery/reclamation/reuse of a waste stream. the lowest to projects that were either R&D-focused or based on waste stream characterization). The "project acceptability" criterion was rated by the site's community advisory panel. Compliance requirements were also considered using a separate process that assigned a rating on a scale from 1 through 5. For example, a rating of 5 was assigned where there were clear regulatory requirements associated with a permit or license, or a standing regulation with a specific deliverable, and a rating of 1 where there was only a draft requirement with an expected time window of greater than two years. Table 7-1 illustrates some elements considered in the first stage of the prioritization process.

The site's environmental manager, Jeffrey Mathews, who drove the process, then used a second two-dimensional matrix (not shown) to group projects rated in this manner, and factor in compliance, then determined the final priority rating of each environmental project (high, medium, low priority). This information was then provided as input into the site's overall strategic planning process.

Mainstreaming Environmental Planning

Planning teams should focus on cost-effective, integrative solutions, rather than create isolated plans for environmental improvements. Integrating knowledge of environmental threats and opportunities and evaluating these within the context of other priorities will often make new opportunities obvious. The solutions developed should be more efficient in their consumption of resources and more effective in satisfying customer/stakeholder EHS needs than solutions developed addressing priorities in an isolated way.

■ TABLE 7-1 Illustration of First Phase of Prioritization Process for Environmental Projects*

Criterion	Rating Factor					Total
	10	20	30	40	50	
Release reduction potential (lb/year)	<100	<1,000	<10,000	<100,000	>100,000	—
Health/environmental toxicity	Low toxicity chemicals (lower group)	Low toxicity chemicals (upper group)	Moderate chemicals (lower group)	Moderate chemicals (upper group)	High toxicity chemicals	—
Potential for off-site impact	No standard or guideline, and innocuous	Below standard or guideline and only on-site receptor impact	Above standard or guideline and off-site receptor impact	Below standard or guideline and off-site receptor impact	Above standard or guideline and off-site receptor impact	—
Pollution prevention	Provides added process knowledge that may lead to pollution prevention	Appropriate media shift	Treatment utilized	Uses recycling, recovery, reclamation, reuse	Uses source reduction techniques	—
Project acceptance	Project benefits are not community-related	Perceived favorably	Perceived very favorably if adopted			—
Total Rating						

*Step two in process includes prioritization of compliance; this rating is then combined with the above rating to determine overall priority.

97

Ideally, cross-functional expertise should be used to identify issues and find solutions that realize both operational and environmental goals. Environmental managers should be an integral part of that process; in some companies, this type of access and involvement exists.

Creating Consistency Throughout the Organization

Consistency can only happen through effective communication channels created by people willing to share knowledge as well as progress toward goals. Consistency is needed at all levels:

- The organization's EHS vision and principles should be consistent with its goals and objectives.
- Action plans should be consistent at all levels, and, in the aggregate, achieve organizational goals.

Georgia-Pacific as a Model   A good illustration of consistency between principles, goals, and action plans is found in Georgia-Pacific's 1994 environmental and safety report. Sixteen goals and related actions were created to support the company's six principles related to management focus.

Selected Goals from Georgia-Pacific's Environment and Safety Program

- Establish a company recognition/awards program for operations and/or individuals that exemplify environmental stewardship, develop innovative pollution prevention practices, or provide outstanding service to the community in the environmental area. Present the first awards in 1995.
- Incorporate environmental performance into the performance review of appropriate salaried exempt employees in 1995.
- Develop an environmental plan for each business unit that will become an integral part of the business strategy in 1996.
- Communicate Georgia-Pacific principles to the company's customers and suppliers.
- Identify major areas of concern to customers and suppliers. Begin selected customer and supplier surveys in 1995. Use survey results to clarify and reconcile concerns and, where appropriate, develop a resolution.
- Analyze and classify each environmental professional's job in 1995 and set minimum environmental training/education requirements for each job classification.

SC Johnson Wax's Example   SC Johnson Wax also documented its environmental commitments as one of its overall corporate objectives in its 1993 environmental report:

To maintain our commitment to the preservation of our environment and be among the leaders in good environmental practice by incorporating consistently high standards in our formulation, packaging and processing.

Using this commitment statement, the company then identified in its worldwide corporate strategic plan six environmental goals, using 1990 as a benchmark.

SC Johnson Wax's Environmental Goals

To reduce pollution and waste by:

- Phasing out the use of some specific chemicals, and ceasing formulation of new or restaged products with these identified chemical ingredients worldwide
- Reducing our volatile organic compound ratio to total raw material by 25 percent by the end of 1995
- Reducing the amount of our virgin packaging as a ratio to formula weight by 20 percent by the end of 1995
- Reducing our air emissions, water effluents and solid waste disposal in our manufacturing operations by 50 percent as a ratio to total production by the end of 1995.
- Recycling 90 percent of wastepaper, cardboard, plastic, glass, and steel materials in our manufacturing and office facilities. This objective pertains primarily to North America and Europe, where recycling infrastructures are in place.

To support educational-based programs that promote meaningful environmental behavior by the individual.

Implementing Strategic Plans through Drivers and Action Plans

Once priorities, goals, and objectives are set, key business drivers can be defined that serve as the basis for action plans. Such drivers might include customer- and operationally driven EHS requirements such as partnerships, product and technology changes, and R&D. Action plans implementing these needs should define responsibilities, targets, and timelines. Long- and short-term measures should be selected. The organization should also decide how it will reinforce and communicate success.

"Momentum comes from a clear vision of what the corporation ought to be, from a well-thought-out strategy to achieve that vision, and from carefully conceived and communicated directions and plans that enable everyone to participate and be publicly accountable in achieving those plans" *Max DePree, 1989*

SUCCESSFUL STRATEGIES IN ACTION

Individual sectors and businesses have adopted a number of innovative strategies to respond to environmental pressures. "Business as usual" has been replaced by innovation in products, processes, and services, new ways of interacting with customers and stakeholder groups, alliances with competitors, advocacy groups, and government, and increased support for R&D and public education. Some companies have not followed a straight line from the past, but have used this opportunity to do a corporate "makeover" of their culture, the way they interact with their people, and their publics.

Compare the strategies profiled in the following sections (Table 7-2) with individual principles associated with the Responsible Care program, or those in the International Chamber of Commerce's (ICC's) Sustainable Development Charter (both can be found in the Appendix). You will find that many of these companies are indeed "walking the talk." The strategies we look at are:

- Pollution prevention
- Linking environmental improvements with capital projects
- Product stewardship
- Environmental research
- Innovative industry collaborations
- Capitalizing on environmental knowledge and technologies
- Supply chain partnerships
- Voluntary initiatives with government
- Community outreach and service
- Conservation and stewardship
- Public reporting on stewardship

In the remainder of this chapter, we explore how a number of companies have used each of these inward- and outward-directed strategies to address issues of key relevance to their customers and stakeholders, as well as to their business interests.

Pollution Prevention

Good business practices were the source of some of the earliest environmentally sound strategies of the 19th and 20th centuries, long before the concept of pollution prevention was developed. During the mid-1800s, for example, Coors Brewing Company found use for its waste hops in agricultural applications (Woods, 1994). Many manufacturers installed recovery and recycling equipment long before these business-wise decisions were recognized as beneficial to the environment. Today, virtually all major companies have formal programs in this area (Chapter 10).

■ TABLE 7-2 Examples of Strategies Applied by Individual Companies and Associations to EHS Management

Strategy	Examples of Strategy Application
Management Systems	Georgia-Pacific: Environment/safety principles; training; goals
	Air Force: Continuous improvement of environmental training; use of GIS for EHS management
	EG&G: Environmental Institute for managers provides combined environmental and financial training
	Dow, Amoco, Ciba-Geigy, Dupont, SC Johnson, A&T, Ontario Hydro, P&G: application of environmental cost-accounting
	Kodak: Weighting factors for prioritization of environmental plans; "Early Warning" system for chemicals
	Dofasco: Environmental management system as continuous improvement loop
	Sandoz: Risk portfolio approach
	Avenor: Third-party forest management audits; planning processes supported by computer simulation models and GIS
Employee recognition	Occidental, Xerox, Ashland, Dow: Internal environmental awards for employees
Pollution Prevention	Dow Canada: River Separation project
	Auto Industry Initiative in the Great Lakes region: Minimizing emissions of toxic chemicals
	Geon: Niagara Falls plant's emission reduction programs for vinyl chloride
	Upjohn: Process redesign to minimize emissions for its corticosteroid products manufacture
	Dofasco: Process redesign for blow-down systems to reach "no adverse impacts" from effluents
	Occidental Chemical: Replacement solvents for CFC's
	Canadian Petroleum Producers Institute: Oil response program
	Ford Motor Company: Process to turn paint sludge to activated carbon for use vehicle vapor-recovery systems
	Hoechst-Celanese: use of Molten Metals Technology process to convert hazardous waste to input materials for its production processes
	ITT Automotive's elimination of 1,1,1 TCE emissions from its air conditioning cleaning operations by material substitution

■ TABLE 7-2 (Continued)

Strategy	Examples of Strategy Application
Product Stewardship LCA/DFE	McDonald's Restaurants: Partnership with Environmental Defense Fund to evaluate life-cycle aspects of foam versus paper for the packaging of its take-out food
	Bristol-Myers Squibb: life cycle assessments of its major products
	Xerox: "Waste-Free Products," remanufacturing of office equipment/products
	Celestial Seasonings: Design out waste from packaging/product
	Browning-Ferris: Reuse/recycling of waste streams
	Wegmans Food Markets: Eco-audit of in-house brands
	Intel: Work with SEMI on EHS guidelines for manufacturing equipment performance
	AT&T: Pioneering efforts on industrial ecology/DFE
Linking - environmental improvements with capital investments	Forest/paper industry: Recycling goals, backed up by $10 billion in investments for plants and equipment allowing increasing use of recovered paper
	Intel, IBM: Installation of double containment underground storage for chemicals
	Herman Miller: Waste-to-Energy facility upgrade
Public reporting on stewardship	Responsible Care: annual progress report on member's conformance with principles and codes of practice
	PERI: consensus standards on environmental reporting
	Northern Telecom: Use of Internet for corporate environmental reporting
	Annual corporate environmental reports from many major companies
Supporting environmental research	IBM: Funding for computer system use for GIS-based studies of the natural environment
	Ford Motor Company: Funding for environmental research at Carnegie-Mellon, Munich, Southampton, Stuttgart, and other institutions

Industry cooperatives	USCAR (United States Council for Automotive Research): Research on materials, fuels and emissions, batteries, environmental science, recycling, and low emissions technologies
	Dow Canada, Dupont, Bayer Rubber: members of a unique industry environmental cooperative working with community, government, and academia in furthering environmental progress
Customer partnerships	New York Power Authority, Ontario Hydro: Energy efficiency audits for customers
	Ryder: Logistics management for customers
Voluntary initiatives with	Chrysler, Ford, General Motors: Participation in the Auto Industry Project addresses release reductions for a list of toxic government chemicals; also involves the supply chain
	Dow, Georgia-Pacific, General Motors, SC Johnson Wax, others: Participation in the President's Council for Sustainable Development
Community outreach and partnerships	Occidental Chemical: Niagara Falls plant's adopt-a-school program
	Dow, BASF, and Kodak: Community advisory councils
	CN North/Grand Trunk Western Railroad: training programs on safety/spill response
	Linde: "Rooting for America" tree-planting program
	Stora Forest Industries: community training on environmental awareness
	BASF: brownfield redevelopment of prime recreational site in Wyandotte, Michigan
Conservation/ preservation	Georgia-Pacific: Partnership with National Fish and Wildlife Service protecting the red-cockaded woodpecker
	New York Power and Ford Motor Company: Participation in the Wildlife Habitat Enhancement Council to protect habitat
Capitalizing on knowledge and technologies	Xerox: Innovative remediation technologies for the treatment of contaminated soil and groundwater.
	Dupont: Commercial safety services
	Dow Chemical Company: Commercial environmental consulting services
	Ontario Hydro: Commercialized environmental technologies initiative

For example, Dow Chemical Canada instituted a capital intensive, long-term "River Separation" project at its Sarnia facility to eliminate harmful discharges or spills to the St. Clair River. The project required a complete redesign and reengineering of water flow on the site over a 10 year period, beginning in 1989. Many individual companies, like Upjohn, Eli Lilly, and Bristol-Myers Squibb, have made major commitments to reducing solvent emissions through recycling, material substitution, and other process changes. Upjohn's goal, for example, is to reduce its volatile organic compound (VOC) emissions by more than 90 percent.

Linking Environmental Improvements with Capital Projects

A number of sectors and individual companies have been successful in linking key environmental objectives directly to capital improvements. Over the past decade, for example, the forestry and paper sector was hit simultaneously with a number of environmental issues:

- Regulations requiring a higher recycled content for its products
- Shrinking landfill space
- Consumer demands for "green" products
- Concerns about environmental effects of discharges from pulp mills
- Controversies around effects of forest management practices on endangered species.

The leadership of this industry, through the American Forest and Paper Association, committed to proactively addressing such issues through its planned capital investments as well as greater public awareness around recycling. In the area of recycling, the industry set an ambitious goal to recycle and reuse 40 percent of all the paper used in the United States by 1995. The industry actually met this goal two years early, then set a new goal of 50 percent by 2000. Future investments of $10 billion are planned to build new or update existing plants and equipment to allow increased use of recovered paper. However, physical improvements were not the only key to success. This strategy, to be successful, also required cooperation and support from local paper recovery programs, for example, companies, municipal governments, and other institutions, as well as a collection infrastructure. The strategy also required securing foreign markets for excess recycled materials.

Product Stewardship

The use of product stewardship, or life-cycle-based approaches, was briefly discussed in the previous chapter. Below are two additional illustrations that tie application to strategic needs.

McDonald's Although LCA tools have been in use since the 1970s, the public has only recently entered the debate at the point of sale. McDonald's Restaurants was caught up in such a controversy. Partnering with the Environmental Defense Fund, it began an intense evaluation of the life-cycle aspects of foam versus paper for the packaging of its take-out food. In the end, the company was able to identify a type of paper packaging that was both acceptable to the public as well as superior from an environmental standpoint (Environmental Defense Fund/McDonald's Corporation, 1991). Today, McDonald's continues to work with EDF on a far-reaching LCA project to determine the most preferable environmental characteristics of packaging, including its recycled paper content (7-2).

Browning-Ferris Industries Browning-Ferris Industries (BFI) owns a large piece of the life-cycle puzzle, as the United States' second-largest collectors and processors of commercial, industrial, and household wastes. It describes its business in its 1994 annual report as:

> [A] seamless system from collection, to processing, to ultimate disposition, be that disposal or back into commerce through recycling....As our industry has changed, we have evolved from simple collectors and disposers of waste, to sophisticated materials managers, extracting environmental and economic value from all components of the waste stream....

To accomplish this, BFI has had to emphasize efficiency in its operations, as well as increase the extent to which its inputs were recycled. Recognizing fully that it is "someone else's cost of doing business," BFI is responding to customers' desires for high quality service at a competitive price. Examining its waste stream, BFI found that 85 percent consisted of paper, half of which came from business. Today, BFI collects and bales these materials for sale directly to papermakers, thus minimizing landfilling as well as the use of third-party brokers for its downstream sales, and markedly improving its financial performance.

"We are beginning to view ourselves, particularly in our recycling business, as manufacturers of raw material "products" for end users." *William Ruckelshaus, CEO, Browning-Ferris Industries*

Environmental Research

Today, many companies leverage their own research by funding environmental programs at universities and colleges throughout the world. IBM, for example, provides funding for the use of its computer systems for GIS-based studies of the natural environment. Ford Motor Company's funding for environmental research is broadly based and includes universities such as Carnegie-Mellon, Munich, Southampton, and Stuttgart. At one of Avenor's forestry centers, researchers are using innovative methods, such as DNA fingerprinting, to understand and enhance forest health. Genetic research is underway to identify the strongest and healthiest trees and use genetic selection to improve them for replanting in harvested areas.

Innovative Industry Collaborations

The auto industry is collectively addressing a long list of environmental issues in areas such as emissions, toxic materials, recycling, and design for disassembly. The industry's U.S. Council for Automotive Research (or USCAR) recommends, monitors, and promotes precompetitive research among the Big Three automakers. Eight collective research and development consortia have been formed, covering areas such as materials, fuels and emissions, batteries, environmental science, recycling, and low emissions technologies. Projects underway include (1) benchmarking and improving dismantling technologies, (2) evaluation of materials identification and sorting technologies, (3) identification of higher value uses for recovered materials, and 4) demonstration projects for the most promising methods. The industry also is investing in research that will improve fuel efficiency and examine the use of alternative fuels, such as methanol/ethanol blends.

Capitalizing on Environmental Knowledge and Technologies

A number of companies that developed environmental technologies for in-house use are beginning to market these (7-3). DuPont and Dow Chemical, for example, market chemical safety and environmental expertise, respectively, through consulting arms of their companies. Xerox has commercialized an innovative two-phase extraction system for the remediation of contaminated soil and groundwater; in 1994, the EPA and Department of Defense rated the system the best among dozens tested at a demonstration project at McClennan Air Force Base in California. Ontario Hydro markets a variety of new environmental technologies through its subsidiary, Ontario Hydro Technologies.

Supply Chain Partnerships

Utilities are aggressively pursuing supply chain partnerships to cooperatively work toward reducing emissions. Between 1980 and 1990, New York State's electric utilities were successful in decreasing sulfur dioxide emissions by 15 percent. despite a 20 percent overall increase in energy use by their customers. Companies such as New York Power Authority and Ontario Hydro are also working with customers to reduce energy use through energy efficiency audits. Many manufacturers now provide processes and incentives for customers to return used components to the company for remanufacture or recycling. Kodak's "one-time-use" cameras, for example, are returned to the company by photofinishers, and have a very high return rate of about 60 percent.

Voluntary Initiatives with Government

The model of adversarial relationships in the United States with regulators and policy-makers is slowly dissolving through voluntary partnerships that maximize cooperative approaches to resolving environmental dilemmas. The publication of the TRI inventory data in the late 1980s put as much pressure on government as it did on business. The EPA's approach at that time was to initiate a voluntary emission reduction program. Though initially viewed as heavy-handed in its approach, the program in the long-run has been highly successful, involving over 1200 companies, and achieving its reduction targets at costs far below what would be expected from traditional regulatory approaches. Other initiatives have followed, again focused on emissions reductions, one housed in the auto industry, another in the printing industry.

Community Outreach and Service

Occidental Chemical's Niagara Falls plant participates in an "adopt-a-school" program aimed at stimulating partnerships between local schools and entities in the broader community. Activities include lecture series in areas like chemistry, protecting the environment, health/nutrition and life processes, technology classes, career education, tutoring, and plant tours. Programs like this give individuals such as Lana Dole, a young plant engineer, an opportunity to make a difference in the lives of young people, through personal contact and mentoring.

In 1990, Linde, a small Union Carbide subsidiary that supplies industrial gases, abandoned the company's traditionally low profile and announced that they would publicly celebrate the 20th anniversary of Earth Day. Employees, asked to define the nature of the celebration, decided to launch a tree-planting program, "Rooting for America," which involved employees with their surrounding communities (Secor, 1992). The program, in hindsight, is viewed by communities and employees alike as a great success.

Conservation and Stewardship

Many natural-resource-based companies have business strategies that recognize the need for conservation and preservation, in keeping with sound business goals. Through a 1993 partnership with the U.S. Fish and Wildlife Service, Georgia-Pacific launched a landmark endangered species agreement to protect the red-cockaded woodpecker on 4 million acres of company forest lands. The company also established goals associated with its forest management strategy that include regenerating every acre harvested on company-owned lands designated for ongoing forestry activities, and assisting private, nonindustrial landowners to manage their timberlands responsibly. Georgia-Pacific has goals to protect sites on company lands that have unique biological, physical or historical features, as well as integrate consideration of recreation into its forest management programs.

New York Power Authority and Ford Motor Company are members of the Wildlife Habitat Enhancement Council, which funds programs providing beneficial habitat for various wildlife species on the company's landholdings (Schmidheiny, 1992). Ford's Cuautitlan Assembly Plant twenty miles outside of Mexico City has a wetland enhancement project that provides reptiles and amphibians with habitat and cover. The project also maintains a garden for desert flora and a raptor management area for hawks, owls, and shrikes. Many utility companies also have aggressive conservation initiatives; for example, as an integral part of its "area for area" reforestation policy, Ontario Hydro planted 1.8 million trees.

Public Reporting on Stewardship

Recognizing the public's need for better understanding of corporate stewardship programs, a number of major companies collaborated to develop consensus standards for environmental reporting (known as the Public Environmental Reporting Initiative, or PERI). A growing number of firms now publish annual environmental reports, or integrate such information into their company annual reports.

Others have approached the issue of reporting in a structured way as well. Members of the Canadian Chemical Producers Association created the Responsible Care program during the 1980s, recognizing an industry-wide need for greater public credibility. Conformance with its principles and codes of practice is a requirement for membership in both Canadian and U.S.-based chemical manufacturers' associations. The program also commits U.S. members to a yearly assessment of EHS management issues, and reports publicly on industry-wide progress (7-4).

A number of companies, including Dow Canada, Bayer Rubber, and DuPont, participate in a unique local cooperative, the Lambton Industrial Society (LIS). Plant managers meet monthly to review environmental data collected by the cooperative, and make real-time data on air and water available to the public on a PC database housed in a walk-in office in the association's downtown office. The cooperative's long-term objectives include improving environmental management strategies of its member companies, as well as improving public understanding of their stewardship programs.

ISO 14001 on Planning

ISO 14001's Planning section includes both information gathering as well as the planning process (the previous chapter deals with the former topic). The standard recognizes the need to set objectives and targets, as well as to link objectives to key issues, such as legal requirements and environmental effects. The standard also notes that an integrated approach should be taken including factors such as "financial, operational and business requirements and the views of interested parties." The standard requires consistency between policy and objectives (including the organization's commitment to preventing pollution). It also requires that specific plans be developed that designate responsibilities, resources, and timelines.

An Annex to the standard provides guidance on objective setting. It also encourages businesses to consider best available technology "where economically viable, cost effective and judged appropriate by the organization." It specifically notes that organizations are not constrained to use environmental cost accounting methodologies (A.4.2.3). A guidance document (ISO 14004) also comments on planning, recognizing the need for long- and short-term plans that are either stand-alone or integrated into the organization's plans. It also recognizes the need for regular review and improvement. Finally, it notes the need to have highly specific action plans that deal with "individual processes, projects, products, services, sites or facilities within a site."

QUESTIONS TO ANSWER ON STRATEGIC PLANNING

- How can you create a strategy that best fits your capabilities, capitalizing on your existing mix of products and services as well as your knowledge base?
- Are you a company that not only has its "environmental act" in gear, but can profit by offering your expertise to others?
- Are your products marketable due to their "green" appeal, and is this appeal of enduring quality?
- Are you taking advantage of every option to make your operations more cost-effective, by incorporating "avoidance" strategies into future designs, by reducing waste levels and energy use, and by substituting less toxic materials where needed, thereby also meeting consumer needs?

ADDITIONAL READINGS

George, Stephen and Arnold Weimerskirch. 1994. *Total Quality Management: Strategies and Techniques Proven at Today's Most Successful Companies.* New York: John Wiley & Sons.

Kolluru, Rao V. 1995. *Environmental Strategies Handbook.* New York: McGraw-Hill.

Piasecki, Bruce W. 1995. *Corporate Environmental Strategy: The Avalanche of Change Since Bhopal.* New York: John Wiley & Sons.

CHAPTER

8

INVOLVING PEOPLE

"The purpose of an organization is to enable common men to do uncommon things." *Peter Drucker, 1985*

"Management based on humanity. . .lets the unlimited potential of human beings blossom." *Kaoru Ishikawa, 1985*

CHAPTER OBJECTIVES

Introduces the reader to the TQEM category of Human Resource Development*

Defines how organizations enable and motivate the workforce to contribute effectively to achieving EHS objectives

Describes the attributes of an effective organizational structure and model for EHS support

Outlines an approach to create effective EHS training and education for the workforce

Human Resource Development Category Defines how an organization's workforce is enabled to use its full potential in attaining the unit's EHS objectives. It also defines how an organization encourages EHS responsibility, and fosters individual and team behavior that lead to EHS and overall business improvements.

EFFECTIVE INVOLVEMENT OF PEOPLE

The business world has been literally transformed by rapidly advancing science, technology, and manufacturing practices. The revolution in information management technology alone has led many to the conclusion that today's capital is information. Yet human capital has always been the most important asset an organization can have. How can we manage, apply new science, develop new products, and converse with customers and the public without an enabled and motivated workforce? How can we realize our vision if it is not communicated, believed in, and internalized? How can we rationalize ethical and financial goals if our competencies do not include strategic thinking and planning?

While there have been many schools of thought on how to involve people in the life processes of an organization, from my perspective, three fundamental principles remain. Effective involvement depends on:

■ A robust organization that accommodates the basic needs of people to connect with each other and the operations they are associated with
■ The presence of a supportive culture, and a capability-building framework that enables employees to productively contribute to progress
■ A system that reinforces the right behaviors

If your organization cannot pass this three-point screening process, you have work to do.

The discussion that follows looks at each of these areas in turn, focusing on their relation to EHS management.

ORGANIZING TO MAXIMIZE INDIVIDUAL AND OVERALL EHS CONTRIBUTIONS

The ideal organization is responsive and enabling, robust but flexible. It purposefully provides its workforce with access, resources, and opportunities for continuous learning and growth.

Models for EHS Support

While there are no perfect models for EHS organization structure, experience over the last five to eight years allows us to make a number of useful observations. In many companies, reorganization is a regular event that sweeps up and re-sorts key functions in a constant drive for greater effectiveness and efficiency. EHS is no exception; when the dust settles, its centralized corporate-level functions are often linked with engineering, human resources, R&D, or legal departments. Although each of these areas has some functional commonality with EHS management, there seems to be no compelling reason to prefer one over another. The choice seems to be governed in some cases by whether the organization perceives EHS management as more technical in nature, or more policy-driven, where its major issues lie, and its relative strengths and interests.

The more important consideration is the degree of access the EHS organization has to top management through the line in which it is embedded, as well as the level of individual that leads the organization. Most large organizations have senior managers at the helm of their EHS programs. A 1994 Price Waterhouse study of 445 companies showed that over half of them have functional environmental managers that report to the CEO or other high-ranking corporate executives. More than 40 percent have elevated oversight of environmental management to the board level. Some facilitate this process through formal corporate-level EHS committees that include the CEO and other top managers, and that provide strategic direction to the overall program.

In some companies, EHS functions are managed by entirely different organizations, however there is a growing trend to consolidate these functions into a single department. This approach has merit because of the efficiencies that can be gained in the management systems area, and the commonalities of their customer and external stakeholder bases. Consolidation also offers opportunities for cross-training and, in turn, greater efficiencies in service.

As line operations' needs grow, the centralization versus decentralization debate is often resolved by a shift of technical resources toward line organization ownership. This is a healthy development, given the accountability of line management in areas such as compliance and waste reduction. Some organizations build flexibility into their EHS structure by contracting externally for services (e.g., analytical testing of air and water samples) and adjusting support level to need.

Within operations, larger departments also tend to have dedicated EHS managers or coordinators, some of whom supervise additional EHS staff. The competency level of line-level EHS staff varies greatly. Many have migrated in from operations; they have little formal EHS education, and obtain knowledge and training on the job. Some companies have created proficiency expectations for line staff. One useful approach is to rotate corporate or centralized EHS staff into line organizations on temporary assignment. Staff on such rotational assignments also benefit from their increased knowledge of operations issues, which then tends to increase the responsiveness and capabilities of the centralized unit when they return.

The lot of EHS managers on the front line of operations is also changing. Once they were unwelcome, viewed as bearers of "bad news" about more stringent requirements, increasing costs, and greener products from competitors. Today many are better integrated into the mainstream of operations and, in some cases, have considerable access to operations management. A number of departments have formed EHS teams that bring operations managers and EHS staff together to develop plans, follow up on corrective action, and provide review of progress.

The technical ceiling associated with EHS has also begun to crumble; some EHS managers have moved onward and upward into management-level positions in manufacturing, business units, and other areas.

A FRAMEWORK TO ENABLE AND MOTIVATE PEOPLE

The second principle listed at the beginning of this chapter is the need for a culture and a capability-building framework that enables employees to productively contribute to progress.

Enabling Employees

Enabled employees understand the full scope of their responsibilities. They have the authority needed to carry out their charge. Through training, education, and experience, they become knowledgeable, skilled, and competent. They are aware of the potential consequences of their actions, including their benefits and adverse impacts. They have the resources they need to get the job done. In a perfect world, they are also afforded the opportunity to add value by providing input to goals and targets, as well as to performance expectations. They contribute to success through innovation, supported by a safety net of trust that, in effect, protects risk-takers. They are reinforced for these and other, more mundane, accomplishments, but held accountable for shortcomings.

Organizations, then, need to create a working environment that fosters initiative, collaboration, and learning. Too many organizations fail by focusing on organizational structure and process, rather than on culture.

SC Johnson Wax's 1994 environmental progress report captures a number of these precepts:

> Our mission is organizational empowerment that enables people to take action that contributes to the competitiveness of the company and the protection of the environment. Better educated managers will make better choices. Better educated executives will foster the pursuit of technological advancements and initiatives that will ensure sustainability of our business in an increasingly competitive global marketplace.

Motivate People to Contribute

Management Messages   William Mulligan (1993), Chevron's manager of federal relations, talks freely about how his company motivated its people by changing its own focus. First, the company elevated environmental performance in the eyes of its employees by making it one of the company's six key strategy elements. It also framed several key messages to employees, including the fact that environmental image is an important factor in setting Chevron apart from its competitors, and that cost avoidance and competitive advantage can be gained through environmental efficiencies. Chevron also stressed that environmental excellence is essential if it is to continue to operate. Lastly, it developed an internal marketing strategy to sell these concepts to its employees, pointing out that "people, not programs, are responsible for environmental performance" (Smart, 1992).

Walking the Talk   Motivation is higher where management "walks the talks," responds to new ideas, and invests in EHS improvements. Custom Print, Inc., a 30-employee, unionized print shop in Arlington, Virginia, provides a good example of how this works. The company has been ahead of its time in environmental improvements; any major decision on equipment or process change has to pass hurdles in the areas of quality, environmental consciousness, and cost. Stuart McMichael, part-owner of the company, goes out of his way to credit employee contributions to leadership. For instance, in the area of waste minimization, employees suggested buying smaller quantities of inks, as well as custom-mixing ink colors for each job. Although this practice requires more expertise, it saves money and cuts back on waste ink. Employees also researched the use of silver recovery systems for the plant's three film processors. McMichael found a unique way to reward employees for their contributions; the silver flake obtained from the recovery system is sent off to a coin mint in Colorado each year and given to employees at Christmas. McMichael also recognizes and respects the need that employees have to say something about their jobs as well as how the business is run: "The more I listen and put into action what they suggest, the more they suggest. They know best what we need."

People Who Care   At Wegmans Food Markets, employees are involved and motivated through ideas like "imagineering," a process that combines the elements of imagination and engineering (used by Disney to create EPCOT, which revealed to tourists the wonders of the city of the future.) Wegmans first applied this concept in 1993 to evaluate the nature of their work and identify waste reduction opportunities. A combination of feedback from corporate headquarters paired with a friendly competitive spirit has had dramatic effects. Individual waste streams from all stores are tracked, reviewed at the corporate level, and monthly reports are sent to each supermarket location. At a Wegmans store in Canandaigua, New York, employees were perturbed that they had the lowest recycling rate of all 48 stores, and got together to find out why. The group charted possible reasons for the low rate, and discovered that employees needed more training on proper recycling procedures. Their enthusiasm was responsible for the store's improved recycling rate, which went from 22 percent to 51 percent in just one year.

Wegmans store teams also continue to work on materials for which recycling markets aren't yet in place. Today, plastic "peanuts" used to pack fragile goods now go to businesses that provide mailing and packaging services. Schools "adopted" by a local store receive donations of materials that were once landfilled, such as decorative streamers, egg cartons, and used computer paper for use in arts and crafts projects. Teamwork is also used to address safety incidents. Cross-functional members from operations, medical, risk management, and delicatessen departments meet to categorize incidents, identify root causes, and implement improvements in areas such as increasing employee awareness of safety hazards, providing more effective training, and identifying operations and procedural changes. Improvement programs are then implemented by each store's safety committee. Key to the success of all of these programs is strong and continued corporate support.

Total Employee Involvement Employees of Geon's Niagara Plant in Ontario, Canada, became committed to a goal of reducing the amount of vinyl chloride that escapes from resin operations. They used advanced technology to develop a thorough leak detection and elimination program. Employees also improved operating procedures and processes to minimize the occurrence of relief valve discharges. To reduce emissions in treated wastewater, employees improved the process used to strip vinyl chloride from product streams and wastewater. Laboratory operators took the initiative to reduce usage of solvents by eliminating unnecessary tests, and by returning unused resin samples to manufacturing. Their efforts have paid off dramatically, reducing vinyl chloride emissions from the plant to levels that are 99 percent lower than in 1980.

Improve Effectiveness Through EHS Training and Education

Motivating and mentoring the workforce is only the first step in effective involvement of people in EHS management. Providing them with the knowledge and skill base is also a prerequisite for effective performance, but is complicated by the fact that the EHS field is a relatively new discipline. As a result, many individuals are naive on the subject of EHS issues when they enter the general workforce. Few who migrate into EHS assignments from operations or support areas arrive with formal EHS training; thus there is a significant lag before they are proficient. This is even more of a problem in smaller companies, where a single individual may be responsible for EHS regulatory compliance across all operations.

To accelerate learning, some companies have developed broadly based EHS awareness programs to inform the entire workforce of the organization's EHS vision, principles, and policies and to create greater consistency. At the job level, training can be used to convey job-specific expectations and instill a prevention mind-set, thus avoiding future liabilities.

Here are some practical suggestions to help you improve your effectiveness through EHS training and education.

1. *Start by creating some overall objectives with input from operations, management, and support staff.* They will provide perspectives that you may not have considered. Stora Forest Industries, a pulp and paper company based in Nova Scotia, provides a good example of this (Johannsen, 1995). Stora not only created an environmental awareness program for all its employees, they asked employees to contribute to its development. The program was designed to spark innovation within the workforce, contribute to quality and competitiveness, better meet customer needs, and reduce any negative impacts of business practices. Its success led the company to offer it, at the request of employees, to family members and the community.

2. *Determine who needs EHS training.* Start with a plan that shows present and future needs, so that the entire package is clear to management. If your organization is typical, EHS compliance will have a high priority, so your training list will have a strong component of mandated training. It is important to get this in place first, since, in its absence, you may be subject to regulatory and other penalties. Other types of EHS training also need to be considered, such as job-specific requirements, new procedures, new regulatory or internal requirements, and general awareness of the organization's key environmental issues and goals.

   You can create a matrix that shows who needs training, training requirements, requirement sources (mandated, company policy, optional), frequency, and provider. Virtually everyone from managers, operations, and staff organizations needs to be aware of the organization's key issues, goals, and accomplishments; this type of training should be updated at least yearly. Employees or contractors whose assignments have a higher risk potential need job-specific training. In some cases, economies of scale are obtained by grouping employees with similar training needs.

3. *Develop a systematic way to document planned and completed training.* This provides the organization's management, as well as regulators and auditors, with evidence that training is being conducted and managed as required. Your system should also include information about frequency requirements. In some instances, frequency is mandated. In some instances, frequency is mandated. In other situations, you will have to determine needs yourself, based on accident or incident data, proficiency tests, and other such measures.

4. *Develop your own training where there are highly specific job-related procedures or tasks.* (You can also contract this out.) For regulations that have been in place for some time (e.g., hazardous waste, hazardous materials, hazard communication), prepackaged courses in both hard-copy and

electronic formats can be obtained from consultants or from trade associations. Training on new regulations can also be obtained from consultants, local chambers of commerce, and, in some instances, from regulators. You will need to decide whether to offer training on- or off-site, and also on-the-job, or off.

5. *Learn from other organizations that have made light-year improvements in their training programs.* Bristol-Meyers Squibb, for example, requires that facility environmental coordinators and other full-time EHS professional complete at least 40 hours of annual EHS training related to their job assignments. Procter & Gamble tracks certification of its Site Environmental Leaders regionally and worldwide at all its facilities. EG&G's Environmental Institute trains its managers not only on environmental management, but also on financial management. Georgia-Pacific's program is well worth studying. It trains employees on the environmental aspects of their jobs, but also addresses issues of environmental awareness, regulatory understanding, procedural requirements, and technical expertise. The program is backed up by goals and target dates for completion.

6. *Integrate EHS training and education into employee development plans.* These plans should be aligned with the organization's overall performance objectives, in order to capitalize on the strengths of the company's workforce. But challenge individuals to go beyond what they "must" know to what they should know in order to drive innovation and change.

7. *Demonstrate the value of EHS training and education to management.* EHS training and education programs should be viewed as investments that will save future costs, for they represent a net benefit to the value chain. You can convince management of this fact by gathering information on the potential liabilities associated with deficiencies in training (particularly for mandated training where penalties exist). You can remind management of incidents that occurred because employees were poorly trained initially or because employees were not regularly reinforced. You can describe success stories where knowledgeable employees suggested improvements that led to cost savings, such as pollution prevention or other waste/risk reduction projects. You can demonstrate how recognition and inclusion of EHS issues early in the development of core technologies and new products, processes, and services positioned the company more favorably along the learning curve than its competitors.

Georgia-Pacific's Commitments to Environmental Training

- Publish a corporate environmental training schedule annually beginning in 1994.
- Analyze and classify each environmental professional's job in 1995 and set

minimum environmental training/education requirements for each job classification.

■ Develop a generic orientation training module by Dec. 31, 1994 and specific environmental training modules for specific categories of facilities by Dec. 31, 1995.

■ Conduct at least 40 hours of environmental training/education for 100 percent of environmental coordinators in 1994.

■ Complete 16 hours of officer and key manager environmental training by Dec. 31, 1996. Set minimum annual environmental training requirements for these job categories.

■ Identify a communications contact and develop an environmental communications training program for all manufacturing facilities by Dec. 31, 1995. Provide basic environmental communications training for all designated contacts by Dec. 31, 1996.

■ Establish a tracking mechanism in 1994 to record completed training.

RECOGNIZING PERFORMANCE

Over the past few years, there has been much debate in management circles about the efficacy of reward systems and their effects on performance. Nevertheless, companies continue to provide pay for merit, as well as to publicly recognize individuals and teams that contribute to profitability, reduce waste, and engage in community service and other activities that signal responsible citizenship. These recognition practices probably will not change, whatever the management sages of the day tell us. (We know how we ourselves would like to be treated; fortunately, the golden rule still lives in some places.)

A 1994 survey of 445 companies by Price Waterhouse revealed that about 40 percent are factoring environmental performance into incentive compensation for executive and senior managers.

A number of companies have created internal environmental or EHS awards:

■ Occidental Chemical's awards program was broadened in 1994 to include three additional categories: awareness, improvement, and pollution prevention. Their selection process involves manufacturing directors as well as environmental staff. The company also gives special merit awards to facilities that have on-time completion of audit action plans, on-time submittal of goals and progress reports, and incident reduction plans.

■ A number of Xerox employees have been awarded the annual Xerox President's Award, the highest honor bestowed on the company's employees, for outstanding contributions to environmental protection.

- At Dow, company president and CEO Frank Popoff personally presents employees with environmental awards at annual employee meetings.
- Senior executives at Procter & Gamble, IBM, and 3M also present annual awards to individuals and teams involved in successful environmental improvement projects.
- Ashland's award program is unique in that it makes employees, retirees, and their families eligible for corporate awards in five categories: product stewardship/pollution prevention, educational outreach/public policy; conservation/habitat enhancement; safety, health, and wellness; and a general category. Awards also include a contribution to a conservation organization of the winner's choice.

OVERCOMING BARRIERS TO SUCCESS

Although most organizations recognize how important a well-motivated and informed workforce is to the success of their EHS programs, few have been able to realize its full potential. Some of the reasons for this are listed below; I also include a few practical suggestions to overcome these barriers (8-1).

1. *Human resource development, like Quality, EHS, finance, and other functions, has traditionally been sequestered in specialists' hands.* Rather than develop EHS training and other development programs in isolation, consider their development across functional lines, where they can foster a level of integration consistent with the organization's broad, long-term business goals.
2. *In many organizations, EHS is viewed as an additional and burdensome responsibility, rather than as a fundamental value and an individual responsibility.* The entire workforce needs to be made aware of the organization's EHS vision and principles, their impact on the organization's position in the marketplace, the organization's obligations as a member of the community and society, and their own role in carrying out the organization's goals.
3. *EHS roles, responsibilities, authorities, and job expectations are not well-documented or are not communicated effectively.* Area supervisors need to be sure that work procedures and documents describing job responsibilities spell out clearly what is expected of each employee. Understanding and competency need to be tested and demonstrated.
4. *Mobility and multiple assignments prevent full familiarization with needed EHS-related tasks.* This is particularly true for entry-level jobs where new employees may spend only a short time until reassignment. It is important to eliminate critical EHS tasks from such assignments. If this is not practical, then the organization needs to invest in more thorough training and provide effective feedback on performance.

5. *The potential consequences of departing from documented EHS procedures are not understood.* Supervisors as well as employees responsible for EHS tasks need to understand the risks and hazards associated with their assignments, including the potential for accidents, as well as any civil/criminal penalties or fines associated with deviations. They also need to be trained to respond effectively to an emergency and other nonroutine situations. Such information needs to be effectively incorporated into area training procedures.

6. *The potential benefits of EHS improvements have not been fully recognized.* Employees need to be encouraged to contribute ideas that could improve work procedures, reduce EHS hazards affecting themselves and others, and contribute to the organization's profitability and job security.

7. *Neither the culture nor effective vehicles and tools are in place to support implementation of EHS improvements.* Line management needs to be receptive to change, and willing to commit resources to implement beneficial EHS improvements. In some organizations, change needs to be precipitated from above to align the local culture with the organization's EHS values. Vehicles for employee contributions, such as suggestion systems, may need to be modified so they do not create an additional administrative burden for individuals, but instead funnel creative ideas directly into decision-making processes. The Body Shop, for example, expedites employees' innovative ideas through its newly christened Department of Damned Good Ideas.

8. *No effective reward or consequences system is in place.* Feedback is needed for responsible EHS performance so that employees know that supervisors and others in management care about performance. Creating and enforcing consequences for deviations from procedures, particularly where serious, similarly reinforces the organization's commitment to responsible EHS behaviors.

9. *The organization's structure fails to accommodate informal networks that are the vehicles for getting things done.* Organizations need to provide resources and legitimacy to the informal networks that get things done in most companies. (In one large company, e.g., a grassroots EHS team linking business units, R&D, and EHS sprang up to develop *ad hoc* ground rules for EHS decision-making for new and existing products. Legitimized after nearly five years, it continues to function and now facilitates top management decision-making.)

10. *EHS career paths are "terminal" assignments.* Organizations should consider using short-term assignments to enrich the background and experience of those destined for careers in business, operations, and/or management. They should also enlarge the skills of EHS staff through cross-functional training and rotational assignments in areas such as operations, finance, legal, public relations, and communications. EG&G's Envi-

ronmental Institute, for example, integrates both environmental and financial training for managers.

THE EHS SUPPORT MODEL OF THE FUTURE

The trend toward decentralized EHS support can be expected to increase, as line management assumes greater responsibilities in this area. However as competence increases, the overall size of corporate and line EHS support staff will probably stabilize and eventually, in some cases, even diminish slightly. Corporate programs will shift their activities toward tracking and review of operations programs, and provide a greater focus on value-added information in the areas of strategic planning and increasing internationalization of EHS management.

The selection criteria for corporate as well as operations-level EHS managers can be expected to become more stringent. Experience in operations, a technical background, and leadership skills will continue to be important. The information and skill base required for environmental leadership will increase in complexity and depth in areas such as science, technology, policy, and economics. EHS managers will be expected to have greater business and financial knowledge, as well as skill in dealing with grassroots and community groups.

Future managers can be expected to enter the field with more formal environmental training than in the past, as more universities consciously integrate such issues into business, technical, and other curricula, and establish executive-level training programs on environmental management and policy. Many entering this field in the next decade will also be highly computer-literate. A growing number will be hired for their capacity to manage the integration of information at higher levels, because of its strategic value.

No single individual will be competent in all of these areas. Most will depend on networking to tap the skills of internal staff and their peers in companies and trade associations. While EHS jargon will continue to provide a common language among managers, a common understanding of EHS management principles and values will also emerge to serve as the basis for dialogue with leaders in both the public and private sectors. In time, smaller companies will also have access to a larger pool of employees whose backgrounds include some formal environmental training, as the curriculum broadens. As these individuals move into management ranks, the commitment and performance of smaller companies will also improve in areas such as compliance, prevention, and quality management. While their risks and needs may be less extensive, poor EHS management can be just as fatal to the bottom line. As a result, the decision to hire a competent EHS coordinator or manager should be viewed as a wise investment. Such a candidate should be capable of meeting and communicating with all "interested parties," for the identities of leaders and companies tend to merge in the eyes of the public.

ISO 14000 on Human Resources

ISO 14001 primarily addresses human resources through the topic of environmental training, recognizing that effective environmental management depends on a workforce that understands its roles, responsibilities, and authorities. It also requires that management provide "human resources and specialised skills, technology and financial resources" in order to effectively implement the environmental management system.

The standard requires that top management assign a "specific management representative(s)" who is responsible for, and has authority for, ensuring that the organization meets all of the requirements of the system, as well as reporting on progress to top management so that improvements can be made to the system.

The standard addresses the key areas of training, awareness and competence, stipulating that the organization identify its training needs and provide appropriate training to all personnel "whose work may create a significant impact" on the environment. It also requires that the organization create procedures to make employees or members (not defined) aware of:

- How important it is to conform with policies and procedures as well as other requirements of the management system
- How their work activities might impact the environment, as well as the benefits of "improved personal performance"
- Their responsibilities with respect to compliance/conformance, including emergency preparedness and response requirements
- The potential consequences of departing from procedures

Finally, the standard requires that personnel who perform tasks that can cause significant environmental impacts "competent on the basis of appropriate education, training, and/or experience."

QUESTIONS TO ANSWER ABOUT HUMAN RESOURCE DEVELOPMENT

- How well does your organizational structure support responsible environmental or EHS management?
- How well motivated is your workforce?
- Is your workforce well-trained?
- Does it have the resources needed to accomplish objectives and targets within the needed timeframe?
- Do you effectively recognize the contributions of your workforce to excellence in EHS performance?

ADDITIONAL READINGS

Cahan, James D., J. Friss, M. Schweiger, and P. Nieroth. 1992. "Environmental Health and Safety Training and Education: TQEM Style." GEMI Conference proceedings, pp. 25–30.

Cramer, J. M. and B. Roes. 1994. "Total Employee Involvement: Measures for Success." *Total Quality Environmental Management* 3: 39–52.

Gantner, Bruce A. 1991. "Achieving Environmental Excellence at Browning-Ferris Landfills Through Quality Training Programs." GEMI Conference proceedings, pp. 99–106.

Wellins, Richard S., W. C. Byham, and J. M. Wilson. 1991. Empowered Teams. San Francisco: Jossey-Bass Publishers.

CHAPTER 9

QUALITY TOOLS THAT WORK

CHAPTER OBJECTIVES

Introduces the reader to the TQEM category of *Process Management**

Presents an array of quality tools and vehicles needed to effectively manage key processes affecting EHS performance

FINDING THE QUALITY CONNECTION

The mid-1980s were kind to corporate trainers, whose success was measured by how frequently they could replenish the training course hopper. The Quality wave was breaking over corporate America, and programs on statistical process control and other Quality tools began to surface on mid-managerial training matrices. As a relatively new laboratory director, I found myself in the nondescriptly titled "Deming 40-Hour Course." When the lights were dimmed for the overheads, the warm, dark rooms did little to foster alertness. The presentations and the material were only part of the problem. Not that most of us didn't appreciate our new Quality toys. We played with them regularly, even religiously, along with other sound practices in our Good Laboratory Practices (or GLP) manual. We also submitted to excruciatingly detailed audits. But we never

Process Management Category Defines key processes that ensure the unit's regulatory and customer/stakeholder-driven needs will be effectively met for the development and functioning of its operational processes, products, and services.

really understood the relevancy of our efforts. QA/QC was the goal, rather than the means.

This changed in the early 1990s. The customer connection was discovered, and we began to ask our customers what they really wanted. Quality moved from the purview of Quality specialists into the hands of operations. The connection between customers' needs and how goods were made and services delivered became clearer. Even our language began to reflect this change; the Baldrige category of "Quality Assurance" was retitled "Process Management," emphasizing the crucial link between customer-focus and the effectiveness of its key processes and systems, including those affecting its supply chain.

Some companies already far along the Quality path began to apply those principles and tools to EHS programs, beginning, in most cases, with the application of traditional approaches, such as documentation, measurement, audits, inspections, and corrective action, to operational areas in order to ensure their conformance with regulatory requirements.

But conformance and compliance soon became just a baseline for performance. Customers and stakeholders demanded as much of Best-in-Class companies in the area of stewardship as they did in the realm of product quality. To compete successfully for their attention, companies were forced to adopt effective, as well as responsible, strategies to manage the risks associated with their operations, products, and services. Senior management's role also became clear: it needed to put an organizational structure and resources in place, as well as to devise an effective and well-integrated system integrating business, financial, and EHS needs and solutions.

This chapter discusses a number of process management tools, beginning with those that ensure consistency in both management and performance. Chapter 10 illustrates how risk management, prevention, and continuous improvement can be used to elevate performance levels, as well as how the links between committed people, effective processes and systems, and satisfied customers and stakeholders are constructed and how they work.

PROCESS MANAGEMENT: GETTING IT RIGHT EVERY TIME

Documentation as a Key Process Management Function

Asked to identify their greatest weakness, environmental managers overwhelmingly replied "documentation" (Diamond, 1995). Yet, what is the first thing that auditors or regulatory agency inspectors request when they come to a facility? Examining the scope and quality of an organization's documentation is the most reliable way that outsiders can develop a sense of the degree of commitment of its management and employees to fulfilling its EHS principles and objectives. Documentation needs extend not only to operational activities such as procedures, record-keeping, monitoring, measurement, and process control systems, but also to organizational policy, goals, training, results, and review processes. In short, good documentation is a prerequisite for a well-managed EHS program, as well as a critical factor in minimizing risks and operational costs, and preventing surprises. Below, I list ten good reasons why you should pay close attention to the quality of your EHS documentation.

1. *EHS documentation is required by law, in a number of areas; its absence or falsification may be considered a civil and/or criminal offense in some cases.* EPA and other agencies have been directing more of their resources to uncovering violations of record-keeping. The severity of penalties has increased as well. Your management systems should be designed to help you comply with legal and regulatory requirements, following both the letter and spirit of the law. A well-managed program gives management and others a sense of security, knowing that the organization has done its best to anticipate potential civil and criminal liabilities. Learning about your obligations in this area and conveying this information to others in the organization requires training and education, as well as a close working relationship among operations, EHS, and legal staff.

Suddenly, Smedley realized that his 8:00AM was not an audition.

2. *Good documentation systems give an organization the opportunity to demonstrate to auditors (including those from regulatory agencies), the public, and others both its good intentions and its management capabilities.* Documentation of procedures provides objective evidence (in the words of ISO 9000, clause 5.2) that "a process has been defined; the procedures are approved, and the procedures are under change control." A well-documented EHS management system, and evidence that it is functioning, show both management's as well as operations' commitment to EHS. For example, the absence of repeat, as well as new, audit findings is evidence that the organization has an effective corrective and preventive action process in place.

3. *Through good documentation, employees know what is expected of them.* Well-written EHS manuals provide managers and other employees needed information on policies, responsibilities, and performance standards and job expectations. This starting material can be used to create area-specific manuals with specific procedures and work instructions that further define action. Fox Studios, for instance, documents in employees' job descriptions the requirement to reduce, reuse, and recycle.

4. *Good documentation and record-keeping practices instill workplace discipline, and reinforce the need for consistency in performance.* Following procedures ensures that the quality of a unit's product meets its customer/stakeholder requirements; it likewise ensures that the quality of its EHS performance will be as "designed." In both cases, waste and other adverse EHS impacts will be minimized by adhering to requirements.

5. *The act of generating and reviewing procedures gives employees the opportunity to think through processes, to identify potential weak points, and to work toward designing out factors that could contribute to accidents, injuries, and nonconformances.* Employees are often called upon to contribute to or to design workplace procedures, as well as to regularly review them, because of their intimate knowledge of the processes for which they are responsible. Knowing the results of current procedures enables them to determine the extent of improvements when changes are made, and to "institutionalize#4 improvement by documenting the new procedure. These activities lead to continuous improvement of both EHS management and performance. They also awaken and encourage a prevention mind-set within the workplace.

6. *Through good documentation and record-keeping, an organization gains the ability to track and trend the quality of its operations, and to make improvements where they are needed.* You can't get to sound operational control without effective documentation and record-keeping systems associated with the appropriate monitoring and measurement systems. For instance, equipment calibration and other process control data enable

operators to make needed process corrections so that air or wastewater emissions do not exceed permit limits. Well-designed and documented experiments provide credible, timely information for decision-making to those in operations, R&D, and management, and may support future product claims.

7. *Documentation of performance objectives, targets as well as results, provides management with a tool to track performance and reward those within the organization who contributed to meeting its goals.* Objectives and targets need to be written down, and results should be reviewed against agreed-upon targets. Managers who "walk the talk," in ISO 9000 parlance, also "say what they mean, put it in writing, and then do what they say." This, then, gives them great legitimacy in recognizing those who contribute to success.

8. *Availability of documentation at all levels provides the opportunity to collect, integrate, and manage it at a higher level, in order to gain insights and add value to the business.* This integration should occur not only within the EHS arena, but also at a broader level, so that cost savings result when management and operations systems are designed. Integration is particularly important when new regulatory developments emerge, so that those who track them and those subject to them can work together to put the right management strategies in place throughout the organization.

9. A *well-managed documentation and record-keeping system also saves money, by minimizing documentation duplication, consolidating testing and record-keeping requirements, and designing the system for easy access.* Organizations need to have a system to retrieve, work with, manage, and review EHS data. This is particularly important for nonroutine events, such as emergencies or unannounced visits from regulatory agency auditors.

10. *Submitting needed reports to the government also fulfills that sector's need to gather data and respond in a way that makes sense to its constituents.* For example, the good faith performance of many businesses, as demonstrated by their TRI emission reduction data, has encouraged government to continue its involvement in voluntary partnerships (e.g., the 33/50 program), and initiate a variety of other programs focusing on regulatory reform.

11. *An organization can improve its relationship with the surrounding community and other members of the public through certain aspects of its documentation.* For example, SARA Title III requires that a facility provide information to local planners on the volume of certain chemicals (over a threshold amount) that it stores on site, as well as on the characteristics of those chemicals. This provides the organization with an opportunity to work openly and creatively with the community to manage this

data as well as to plan for emergency response. An organization can also increase its credibility with the general public by documenting its EHS plans and accomplishments through publicly available reports (e.g., annual reports).

ISO 9000's Emphasis on Documentation How many organizations have a strong documentation ethic? Certainly those with ISO 9000 registration do. ISO 9001, for example, requires a Quality manual that documents the organization's Quality system, including its:

- Policies
- Procedures
- Plans (e.g., resource needs, action plans)
- Records
- Change procedures
- Organizational relationships, showing how people, organizational groups, and systems interrelate
- Documentation and data control requirements
- Approval processes
- Product design requirements *including applicable statutory and regulatory requirements*

The kinds of records required typically include inspections, testing, audits, training, and calibrations, as well as those associated with the Quality system itself (e.g., reviews that demonstrate conformance with objectives, audit and assessment results, and corrective action).

These four levels (manual, procedures, work instructions, and records) are the foundation for a sound documentation system (for a more complete understanding of these requirements, the reader may want to refer to ISO 9000 documents, as well as Robert Peach's 1994 book on ISO 9000). While these requirements place ISO 9000-certified organizations at an advantage with respect to certain aspects of EHS management, they do not guarantee that all of the requirements of ISO 14001 will be met. A cross-reference between ISO 9001, Baldrige, and ISO 14001 elements is provided in Table 2-2.

Moving from Documentation to Use An EHS manager at a large, diverse manufacturing site once commented: "There are two sides to documentation. First, you have to create it because it's required, and second, you have to use it. The second is, by far, the bigger challenge." People don't become motivated to use documentation until they have a valid reason to do so.

The ISO 14001 conformance standard requires that organizations inform their employees about the consequences of deviating from procedures as well as the benefits of conformance. Information about performance trends (e.g., spills, accidents, and repeat audit findings) can be incorporated into communication and training programs to reinforce the need for responsible behaviors.

Monitoring and Measurement in Process Management and Control

Using Data for Decision-Making   One of the most fundamental concepts of the Quality movement is data-driven decision-making. The process of measurement forces us to reflect on what is important, to determine where we have been and where we currently stand. It allows us to compare our performance against targets or limits. The techniques and tools used for this return us to the very roots of the Quality movement—to the early work at AT&T on statistical process control, and the subsequent contributions of other U.S. and Japanese experts to this field.

The need for sound data is common to shopfloor operators, laboratory technicians, sales personnel, R&D staff, in short, to all on whom product, process, and service quality depend. Sound data allows operators to confidently shut down production lines generating bad product, or to take equipment offline when it creates unsafe conditions. It permits lab technicians to stop generating test data until equipment malfunctions are repaired. It provides the driver for product recalls where safety or other concerns are discovered. It compels R&D staff to take pause and integrate new knowledge into the design cycle.

Quality-Based Tools   Many companies have incorporated Quality-based tools into their training programs, instructing employees on the use of graphs, histograms, Pareto diagrams, cause-and-effect diagrams (used for root-cause analysis), scatter diagrams, and flow, trend, and control charts (Ishikawa, 1985). Perhaps one of the best known of these tools is the Ishikawa diagram, more commonly called the fishbone, which shows the relationship between a given effect and its potential causes, and is usually developed through brainstorming exercises that identify, organize, and diagram potential causes of problems into categories (such as "materials, methods, machines, and manpower"). These diagrams also help to identify the types of data that should be collected to verify the actual cause/effect relationship for a given problem.

Using Tools Creatively for Problem-Solving   Data collected in such studies can be visualized in a number of ways. For example, Pareto charts can be used to identify the most common types of EHS problems, as well as to identify the most common causes of those problems. Many companies track EHS issues such as accidental releases, discharge levels, accident/injury rates, and compliance, and plot such data (e.g., on monthly charts using a moving average). Control charting allows "owners" and others interested in the process to determine whether it is stable and in control, and, equally importantly, whether it is capable of consistently meeting the requirements placed on it (i.e., does it fall within control limits?).

Before looking at how such tools are used in the EHS area, let's discuss another Quality tool, the corrective action process, which is a systematic process designed for problem-solving.

The Corrective Action Process

The first step in the corrective action process is to recognize that you have a problem that needs to be fixed. Before you begin any formal action, you have to assign responsibility for the corrective action process. You also have to evaluate the significance of the problem. The Deming cycle's Plan–Do–Check–Act–(P–D–C–A) loop describes the steps you can take.

1. *Figure out the underlying or root cause of a problem, then identify possible options to correct it, such as process controls, procedural changes, or employee training ("Plan").* Often, units choose to institute brainstorming to identify possible root causes. A cross-discipline team that includes operations, EHS staff, and others with process or product expertise may be needed to ferret out both the root cause and the solution. The corrective action selected should also include timelines for completion and responsible individuals assigned to the task (the "Plan" step). Both ISO 14000 and the 1995 version of ISO 9000 now require that such actions be preventive rather than just corrective. That is, the solution should be a "permanent" solution, rather than a short-term fix.

2. *Implement the corrective action plan ("Do").* Be sure you have management buy-in. Stay within the timelines and resource constraints identified. If you need to make midcourse corrections to the plan, be certain that these are acceptable to management.

3. *Verify that the problem has been fixed ("Check").* Use measures selected at the time the plan was created. Communicate results to those who need to know this.

4. *Take action, if the verification step indicates it is needed ("Act").* Repeat the cycle if the solution hasn't worked. If it has worked, institutionalize the solution by documenting procedural or process changes, modifying training, and taking other related actions. Look at the actual EHS impacts of the fix, and any effects on the organization's objectives and targets.

You may want to generate your own list of problems where corrective action should be applied, such as:

■ Audit/assessment findings
■ Process safety review findings
■ Accidents or injuries

- Accidental spills or releases to the environment
- Significant deviations from procedures or permit requirements
- Workplace inspections
- Situations posing significant risk or imminent danger
- Trends or patterns identified through systematic analyses, assessments, or other processes

APPLYING QUALITY TOOLS

A Case Study on the Use of Quality Tools

Let's look at an example of how operators used Quality tools to resolve a problem with irregular chemical discharges that led to wastewater discharge exceedences. Plotting these occurrences on trend and control charts, operators found that discharge levels often fell statistically outside the desired control limits set by the facility's permit. To use the jargon of Quality, the existing process was simply not "capable" of meeting the limit.

In order to improve the "process capability," operators initiated brainstorming to identify the factors that influenced the process, and identified the following candidates for the "root cause" of the problem: equipment failure, materials handling and storage, operator training, maintenance, and documentation. They organized these ideas using an Ishikawa fishbone diagram.

The team followed up on each of these potential causes, and eventually found multiple contributors to the problem. In one department, operators, unaware of the environmental consequences of their actions, would prop open valves and go on to other tasks, rather than wait until a filling operation was complete. Procedures did not specify that they remain with the equipment. If the operator did not return in time, this resulted in a spill, and on some occasions, the material released created a permit exceedance.

In developing a solution, the team considered productivity requirements, costs, as well as environmental risks and benefits, and came up with a solution that addressed each of these:

- New automatic shut-off valves were installed that allowed operators to initiate the filling event, then go on to other duties.
- Documented procedures were written describing how and when to check the integrity of the new shut-off valves, as well as how and when to maintain them.
- Responsibilities were conveyed to operators and maintenance personnel through training, as well as documented in the department's procedures.
- An awareness program was incorporated into training programs that informed operations and other staff of:

■ The need to conform with all verification and maintenance procedures

■ The consequences of not adhering to procedures, including potential adverse effects on the environment

■ The potential for permit exceedences and fines

■ The reflection of individual EHS behaviors in performance ratings

■ Control charting of all EHS incidents was instituted and reviewed at department team meetings by supervisory personnel.

EHS staff continued to track the performance of the process, and relayed to involved departments that the process was now "capable" of meeting the requirements imposed on it. Because permit exceedences remained a high priority with the facility's manager, the control charting process was continued and regularly reviewed by department and site management.

What factors contributed to the success of this solution? First, operators who were familiar with the process were involved in the solution. They identified potential root causes, and recommended likely solutions. Second, the process "owner" (in this case, the department manager) was willing to commit resources to achieve the solution; he also had the authority to make the needed change. Operators that have "line-stop" authority may well not have the authority or the access to resources. Thus management involvement, ownership, and oversight may be needed to effect a long-term change in behaviors. Third, the department was also willing to follow the process beyond the installation of new equipment and procedural changes, and to incorporate new knowledge into training and rating systems.

A Case Study of Problem-Solving Using Root-Cause Analysis

Here is another illustration that began with the same scenario but reached very different conclusions about both the root cause of the problem and the appropriate solution This story also involved a facility that had spasmodic discharges of a particulate material to the facility's wastewater, which then caused a permit exceedence. The team put together to solve the problem identified the following potential sources of the discharge.

■ Someone in operations occasionally opened the wrong valve and sent the material to the wastewater drain lines rather than to the recovery system (people/procedures-related).

■ The valves sometimes malfunctioned (equipment-related).

■ The lines were plumbed wrong in a particular department, and wastewater and recovery lines were switched (equipment-related).

■ Particulate material accumulated in the drain lines, and was periodically released to the wastewater treatment facility (process-related).

The group began its investigation by installing monitoring equipment on ͺom various buildings. After some time, they were able to pinpoint a par-ͺuilding as a source. They then began to investigate whether a procedur-ͺ▯ͺwas the cause of the discharge events, but were never able to link such ͺwith any recorded procedural deviations.

The team then decided to work on options associated with equipment. Maintenance and engineering staff began tracing the building wastewater and recovery system lines to determine whether they were correctly plumbed. They also examined the integrity of valving in the lines. No significant line or valve problems were found.

During this time period, a significant discharge event was again detected by the monitoring equipment, this time coinciding with the weekend production schedule. The team assembled to review the data, but once again, no connection with production events could be established. When the data was scrutinized further, however, a strong candidate for the root cause of the problem emerged. At the time of the event, a torrential rainfall began, inundating a team member who had been called in for trouble shooting that day, which fixed the time of the event in his mind. He and other team members suddenly realized that the torrent of rainwater ripping through the sewers must be dislodging deposits of the particular materials, thus creating the discharge event. (The team developed further support for this idea by checking the dates of past discharge events and comparing them against rainfall levels. For many events, there was a good correlation with weather.)

The team then developed a corrective action scenario. The lines were cleaned out, and all material removed from the lines was sent to recovery operations. Periodic inspections and cleaning were initiated. These steps eliminated future discharge events. The team also recommended investigating recovery of the particulate material from the wastewater stream before it entered the facility's external lines.

This story should tell you that root-cause analysis is not a simple, straightforward process. There will be wild goose chases, in some cases, and surprises in others. What solved this apparently intractable problem was a combination of persistence, process knowledge, and on-going engagement of team members. (And, in this case, doses of both serendipidity and luck.)

Use of EHS Audits as a Quality Tool

Why Audit?   The two most common EHS-related questions asked by managers I've known are: "What regulations apply to my area?" and "Am I in compliance?" The answer to the first question becomes the foundation for answering the second one: If you don't know what is applicable, you can't very well determine your level of compliance. In essence, audits (or assessments, if you prefer this term) can help determine whether an organization is adhering to regulations and policies, help management identify gaps, and confirm that effective EHS management systems are in place.

A 1995 Conference Board study found that more than 90 percent of companies using Quality-based management also engaged in environmental auditing. Most such audits focus on compliance, using a third party to verify compliance with both regulatory and company requirements. Some companies also used environmental audits of suppliers as a management tool.

A well-managed audit program provides a systematic approach to identify issues, risks, and problems, and then prioritize them for corrective action. It provides credible, documented information about deficiencies, based on regulatory citations or corporate standards. It offers the opportunity to correct recurring problems by identifying trends and root causes. It helps justify human and financial resource allocations to correct existing problems and prevent future liabilities. It often identifies potential cost savings and other benefits tied to improvements. It is an opportunity to recognize excellence and reinforce the need for continuous improvement of both management and performance.

Designing the Audit Process   Audits should be systematic. Their scope should reflect the unit's needs. They should cover not only laws and regulations, but also evaluate the extent to which a facility conforms with its external and internal requirements, as well as its internal commitments (for example, its EHS standards and other requirements of its EHS management system.)

Audits can, of course, be broader or more focused, extending to an evaluation of risks and hazards, as well as potential cost savings associated with improvements. Management system audits are essential leading indicators of performance (Wells, 1995). They help organizations anticipate problems in performance and make corrections before problems occur. Their frequency also needs to reflect the character of the organization. A large, complex manufacturing facility that is subject to a wide variety of EHS laws and regulations will need to be assessed more often than an installation that consists primarily of office areas.

Many companies conduct both internal and external third-party audits. The latter provide verification of compliance/conformance, as well as lend greater credibility than an internal program.

External, Third-Party EHS Audits   These audits usually entail a combination of activities, including personnel interviews, walk-around facility inspections, and documentation reviews. The first stage of this three-stage process is a preaudit phase, which establishes the scope of the assessment, specific preaudit documentation needs, and a detailed plan for the site visit.

At the second stage, the site visit, auditors become familiar with the unit's EHS management approach and various controls through interviews, inspections, and reviews of other on-site materials. They also gather specific evidence that verifies whether the unit is in conformance with regulatory, legal, and other requirements. Generally, the team reviews its findings, documented in an interim report, with the assessed unit's management before leaving the site, and any differences of opinion or interpretation are discussed.

At the third, or postaudit stage, a final report is submitted from the audit team to management that describes audit "findings," including a cross-reference to regulations and organization standards and other requirements. This report is (or should be) shared with others in the unit. Management in turn assigns responsibility for follow-up. The unit then prepares corrective action plans that include timelines for completion and specific responsibilities. The unit also reviews progress with management at suitable time points, and uses whatever leverage it can muster to drive corrective action to completion. In the best of all worlds, corrective and preventive action will eliminate repeat assessment findings on the next go-around.

It is important to set objectives and ground rules from the beginning. In some companies, departments are informed of an impending audit, and thus can be well-prepared when auditors arrive. Other companies favor unannounced audits to mimic regulator inspections. After the fact, findings should be treated as improvement opportunities. Too often, they can become a focus for fault-finding (and potentially scapegoating). Where positive comments are made by assessors, these should also be communicated. (Some auditors, however, like to point out that they are not there to record what is right, but what is wrong.)

Obviously, the quality and extent of the auditors' findings will depend on a number of factors, such the competence of the assessors, their familiarity with operations, the time allotted for the assessment, and the depth of the assessment. Not all assessors (or assessment events) are created equal. Recognizing this, most organizations elect to trend repeat findings and/or finding severity, rather than track the absolute number of findings.

Internal Audits   In some organizations, the audit function is simply a checklist combined with a walk-around inspection. For organizations with more complex regulatory requirements, a more detailed process is a must. Although some commercial software or on-line audit systems are available on regulatory compliance, these do not address site-specific requirements, such as permit conditions or consent orders, nor do they cover internal policies and practices. These systems are also country-specific, and many are further limited to only certain states.

Various storage media are available. Software packages can be ordered for PCs with hard disks; other programs are available on CD-ROM or are stored on remote computers and accessed through a modem and communications software running on a PC. Some software packages are interactive; questions and reference materials can be added by either the software developer or the client. Some companies, like Browning-Ferris Industries, develop their own programs or work with outside consultants to tailor existing packages to their needs, incorporating company-specific requirements (Johnson, 1995). While up-front costs for this may be significant, the company gains the capability to collect data for corporate-level reporting, thus eliminating a lot of manual work (Ruble, 1995).

A few trade associations have developed self-assessment guides for EHS principles. Examples include the Chemical Manufacturers Association's annual assessment of its Responsible Care program, and GEMI's self-assessment guide for the International Chamber of Commerce's Sustainable Development Principles.

Internal Versus External Assessments A few years ago, in a course on environmental auditing, I learned that the people who benefit the most from this process are the auditors themselves. So, logically, organizations benefit by having internal auditors who can preserve this knowledge base. However, there are also benefits associated with outside or third-party audits. They should be (and usually are) more objective than internal audits. The downside is that the auditors will not have the intimate knowledge of the unit's operations. While the best of all worlds, then, would be a combination of both, the ultimate check on both is an on-site inspection and audit by a regulatory agency. While facility managers can hope that their sites will never be subject to an in-depth audit by regulatory or enforcement agencies, these are becoming more common in an age of regulatory complexity.

Significant concerns still exist in the United States about the confidentiality of such audits. The EPA attempted to address these concerns through an interim policy released in 1995, which states that facilities that voluntarily disclose and address noncompliances satisfactorily will be subject to greatly reduced penalties and find "safe harbor" from criminal referrals. Nevertheless, the uncertainty associated with this policy should prompt companies to continue to emphasize management system improvements that minimize noncompliances.

ADDITIONAL READINGS

Greeno, J. Ladd, G. S. Hedstrom, and M. DiBerto. 1988. *The Environmental, Health, and Safety Auditor's Handbook.* Cambridge, MA: Arthur D. Little.

Ikenberry, Eric A. 1992. "Root Cause Analysis." GEMI Conference proceedings, pp. 109–114.

Roig, Randy A. and P. Schneider. 1995. *"Audits and Root Cause Analysis." Auditing for Environmental Quality Leadership: Beyond Compliance to Environmental Excellence,* John T. Willig, Editor. New York: John Wiley & Sons, pp. 176–184.

CHAPTER

10

DRIVING OUT SACRED COWS

"If it ain't broke, break it."   *Robert W. Peach (1994)*

CHAPTER OBJECTIVES

Demonstrates the value of continuous improvement in adapting to changing circumstances and customer/stakeholder EHS needs

Illustrates how companies use prevention-based approaches to proactively achieve superior EHS as well as financial performance

CONTINUOUS IMPROVEMENT

What are the dangers of over-institutionalizing the process of change? People get lost in the woods trying to understand the process. Continue to remind them of the big picture, the connection between customer/stakeholders needs and profitability. Then point out the connectors, which are people and effective ways of doing business. The tools are never the goal. We arrive at success by relentlessly adapting to change.

Effective process management means more than conforming with procedures and doing the same things in the same way. It also means adapting to changing customer/stakeholder requirements. It means scrutinizing the way we work and the nature of our products and services, and actively pursuing ways to improve all we do. Robert W. Peach said it well (1994):

> Corrective and preventive action are the two driving forces of continuous improvement. As far as the management system is concerned, one of the adages for any company seeking to constantly drive forward must be the cry—"if it ain't broke, break it." Only in this way can a constant process of improvement happen. The search for better ways of doing everything must be totally relentless—there can be no sacred cows when continuous improvement is the goal.

The level of debate on the topic of continuous improvement during the development of the ISO 14000 standards has been remarkable. One school of thought is that both management systems and performance should be subject to continuous improvement. The other contends that it should only be applied to the management system itself, fearing that organizations would be compelled to improve performance beyond the point where benefits to the environment could be demonstrated, thus shifting resources away from other, more critical, priorities, and weakening the business.

This argument can be defused if continuous improvement is understood as the process of modifying management systems and performance to meet changing customer and stakeholder expectations in a way that supports the long-term survival of the business.

This would allow the lens of continuous improvement to be focused on environmental performance, just as it is on all other parameters of keen interest to customers and stakeholders, *but only within the full context of the business setting in which the organization operates.*

Using this definition, the costs, benefits, and potential adverse outcomes of any alternative, including a proposed environmental improvement, would be weighed against other competing priorities. Under the best of circumstances, options will be found that integrate these priorities, thus benefiting both the business and the environment. In some cases, the most appropriate choice will be obvious. In other cases, decisions may be influenced by factors such as public opinion or employee morale (and sometimes compromised by personal biases). However, running a business mainly on "feel good" principles, absent good business practices, will support profitability (and morale) only as long as there is enough fat in the system.

Few small or midsized businesses have this luxury. Large organizations are also finding their excess resources slipping away, and their flexibility to do more than is absolutely required eroding. *Finding the fine balance between strict financial measures and other more personal ones, as well as a way to integrate both, is the real challenge of business leadership today.*

Continuous Improvement Vehicles and Their Application

What vehicles do organizations use to build in the process of continuous improvement?

The Baldrige Framework   At the organization level, the Baldrige framework itself provides both a context and vehicle for continuous improvement (you may want to look at Figure 2-1 again to verify this). Once the right processes and systems are in place, feedback from a variety of sources can be used to improve plans, objectives, and ultimately performance itself.

Deming's Continuous Improvement Cycle   Another framework, Deming's continuous improvement cycle (plan–do–check–act) can also be applied to any process at any level of the organization. Auditing, risk assessment/management processes, pollution prevention, and benchmarking are all continuous improvement vehicles, if they are regularly and consistently used for this purpose (see Figures 10-1, 10-2, 14-1). ISO 14001 itself is also based on this framework.

How Is Continuous Improvement Being Applied?   In its 1994 environmental report, Dofasco, a Canadian steel maker, delineates the elements of its corporate environmental management system as a continuous improvement loop. Dow Chemical Canada has adopted the ISO 14000 framework, which also incorporates a continuous improvement cycle, for environmental management at its sites.

The U.S. Air Combat Command uses the continuous improvement process in annual environmental training programs held for staff from its installations worldwide. Each training course is run three to five times during the week, depending on demand. Critiques gathered from participants at the close of each session are evaluated within 30 minutes, and an ongoing trend analysis is provided to the session's instructors. Often more than one instructor is involved in these multiple sessions, and each instructor's approach and expertise can be evaluated separately. Using the participants' feedback, each course is modified to better meet attendees' needs at the remaining sessions that week. The feedback obtained from students is also used to redesign the following year's offerings.

Using Process Mapping Before You Begin   Before you attempt to apply continuous improvement to any process, it is important to first characterize or "map" the process itself, following the points below and, only then, to apply a closed-loop corrective-action process (10-1). Process mapping includes determining:

- Who owns the process?
- Who is the customer for the output of the process?
- What are the process inputs and resources?
- What are the tasks or activities the process accomplishes?
- What are the desired goals and outputs?

DESIGNING TO MINIMIZE RISK

Facility Considerations

While well-designed systems and processes are no guarantee that things will go smoothly, they are our best line of defense. For this reason, many industry sectors have developed procedures to minimize risk by incorporating EHS considerations into the design and modification of new and existing operations, products, and services. From an operational standpoint, for example, the attention that a facility manager gives to process management should be strongly influenced by:

■ The intrinsic risks associated with the facility's operations (e.g., a large chemical manufacturing site and an office building may be at opposite ends of spectrum with respect to the risks it must manage)

■ The site's previous history and knowledge of peer or industry sector problems

■ The age and condition of the site's infrastructure and equipment

■ The knowledge and competency level of employees

■ The stage of development of the site's EHS management system (e.g., the formality of its documentation, policies, procedures)

■ The response capabilities of the site and local responders

Risk management will also be influenced by other considerations such as level of management commitment, availability of resources, competing priorities, and technical competencies.

Linking Risk Management and the Bottom Line

A Management Framework for Risk   Although every facility is different, the risks associated with the site, the area, and the individual job can be identified, quantified, and managed using the tools of risk assessment and management. The systematic tools of both provide a framework for identifying and prioritizing risks at the site and organization levels. (The framework is very compatible with the Deming P–D–C–A cycle, Figure 10-1.)

A Framework for Risk Assessment and Management

■ Define your business and EHS objectives.

■ Determine what resources are at risk and assess the level of risk.

■ Develop risk reduction options and prioritize these.

■ Implement risk reduction measures.

■ Review progress against targets.

■ Make course corrections.

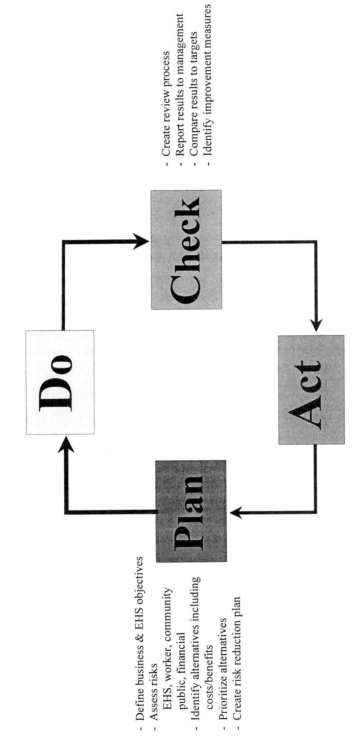

- Create project plans
- Allocate resources
- Set timelines, responsibilities and milestones
- Implement plant

- Create review process
- Report results to management
- Compare results to targets
- Identify improvement measures

Do

Check

Act

Plan

Act on improvement measures

- Define business & EHS objectives
- Assess risks
    EHS, worker, community
    public, financial
- Identify alternatives including
    costs/benefits
- Prioritize alternatives
- Create risk reduction plan

Data Uncertainty Data derived from this process is the key to improving performance at both the site and organization level, as well as to short- and long-term planning. One of the chief barriers to the use of such data is the inability of existing methodologies to fully quantify the more intangible elements of risk such as future liabilities, as well as the relative uncertainties that are associated with each category of risk. Management may be unconvinced when presented with worst case scenarios based on such data, as well as unimpressed with arguments to assign resources to the highest prioritized risks, given the genealogy of such data. Nevertheless, some companies are moving rapidly in this direction, supported by trade association efforts centered around quantifying risks associated with particular types of operations and circumstances. The American Institute of Chemical Engineers (AIChE), for example, provides data derived from plant experience and generic industry failures in its Safety and Reliability Analysis Center publications.

Some have attempted to estimate the benefits associated with averting mishaps (Kolluru, 1995a) For example, where a worker fatality is averted, the economic benefit derived might be equated with earnings capacity. Where a worker's disabling injury is averted, the cost of worker's compensation might be used to estimate the benefit derived. Where environmental resource damage is prevented, the cost of restoration might be used, or the estimated amount of a fine or lawsuit settlement. How these costs and benefits are used, and which are pertinent to the organization's bottom line and which to societal or individual benefits, still needs to be sorted out.

Use of Risk Assessment/Management Approaches

Despite the uncertainties bound up in such processes, some companies are developing an organization-wide understanding of the key EHS risks associated with their products, processes, and services.

Sandoz Sandoz, for example, described the utility of its risk portfolio approach as both a "measurement and an internal communications tool" (Ankers, 1992). Each of its sites identified its key risks, as well as their degree of control over these risks. Site managers also identified factors such as the potential of noncompliance, potential injury for a given hazard, as well as potential harm to the business or company's image. At the company level, this information was merged, taking care to note the relative contribution of each site to the overall risk portfolio. The result of this exercise provided management with insight into its key hazards, as seen through the eyes of its site managers. Other information that the company collected included the range of activities planned to address risks, particularly those of the most severe nature. Sandoz concluded that this approach helped them reduce risks over the two-year period reported in the study.

Bristol-Myers Squibb Bristol-Myers Squibb, for example, actively designs EHS awareness into its capital projects, and requires that all capital appropriations requests for new processes, products, and facilities be reviewed by a facility EHS coordinator. Such appropriation requests consider factors such as permitted environmental releases, waste generation and disposal, health and safety risks, energy consumption, and potential for accidents. In addition, capital projects involving new products or packaging also include an evaluation of total product life-cycle impact on the environment.

Kodak Kodak has an "early warning" program that links its EHS staff with R&D, operations, and business units to inform them of any potential concerns associated with the use of new chemicals before these are designed into new products, thus minimizing both EHS and business risks.

Conoco Conoco instituted a rigorous safety program to address risks in its operations in northern Russia, where there are no permanent roads and ice roads must be built during winter months. After its program for pipeline construction work went into effect, safety incidents dropped by 83 percent and the total recordable rate was cut from 1.79 to 0.41 injuries per 200,000 hours worked, thus demonstrating that high standards and a comprehensive safety program produce superior safety results globally.

Intel Intel minimizes risks associated with its operations by working with its chemical suppliers to keep its on-site inventories of chemicals at a minimum. Chemicals kept on site are stored in rooms designed to capture or treat any leak or release before it reaches the environment. These rooms also have state-of-the-art leak detection and monitoring systems that allow trained employees to respond quickly to potential problems before they escalate. Intel took a leadership role working with its industry sector trade association (Semiconductor Equipment and Materials International, or SEMI), to develop a common set of EHS guidelines for manufacturing equipment performance. The company has completed more than 150 EHS assessments of its fabrication, assembly, and test manufacturing equipment, following the same procedures used to qualify equipment used for quality and reliability testing, metrology, factory automation, and R&D purposes. According to Intel, equipment manufactured according to the new guidelines show fewer EHS problems.

Canadian Petroleum Products Institute Minimizing risks through prevention is a top priority of petroleum producers. Their programs engage not only their own facilties, but also receivers, government, and community in design and implementation, as well as in the response mode. During the late 1980s, the Canadian

Petroleum Products Institute (CPPI) conducted a voluntary audit, and publicly reported on its members' oil spill response capabilities. This study led to expanded industry-funded centers, with improved prevention and response capabilities, and created four new response corporations that provide equipment, skilled personnel, and training.

DESIGNING IN PREVENTION

The "Six Sigma" Approach to Prevention

Prevention means "never having to say you're sorry"—to borrow shamelessly from a contemporary cartoon series. Companies with a "six sigma" mentality rarely have to apologize for defects. There is evidence that the same philosophy is being applied to EHS management within the context of sound, cost-effective business practices. Although many may never reach such goals, their pursuit, where well-managed, leads to innovation, change, and ultimately both environmental and business gains.

At Herman Miller, Inc., for example, the "zero defects" theme translates to "zero waste to landfills in 1995." At Xerox, it becomes the "Waste-Free Factory." Dow Canada's interpretation is zero discharge of contaminated process and drainage water to the St. Clair River. DuPont's goal is "no chemical contact," no matter how small, at its Chambers Works plant in New Jersey. Duke Power Company's target is zero incidents by 1998. Dofasco envisions "no adverse impacts" from its effluents (R&D is underway on a system that will sequentially feed blow-down water from its steel making operations to its coke-making and iron-making works). To yet others, the stretch goal is zero accidents, injuries, or accidental releases to the environment, or zero repeat findings on compliance audits.

Designing Out Mistakes

Relentlessly pursuing and designing out waste is one way to *prevent* pollution. Designing and following procedures that minimize error helps to *prevent* spills, injuries, exposures, and nonconformances with regulations and internal standards. But prevention goes far beyond modifying procedures and practices. It also applies to areas such as product/process design, input materials and other life-cycle attributes.

Design Tools   Tools such as pollution prevention and Design for Environment (DFE) can be used to apply a life-cycle approach to product and process design, and to encourage the sustainable use of natural resources. Michael Porter and Claas van der Linde (1995) call attention to the greater "resource productivity" that is gained from pollution prevention–focused activities, which in turn makes companies more competitive at home and in world markets.

The Challenge of Product Versus Process Change Dambach and Allenby (1995) point out significant differences between products and processes, including their interactions with the environment. Process changes are more difficult to make once the technology has become embedded within a given industry, because of the investments involved. Product designers have somewhat more flexibility, in that they can choose from a spectrum of existing processes and materials. Ideally, both product and process are developed together, providing the opportunity to integrate EHS into the entire design scheme. But more often, in the real world, their design is distinct, involving different technical, operations, and business unit communities.

Pollution Prevention as a Tool for Continuous Improvement

Pollution prevention is the approach most commonly applied by facilities to improve the EHS impacts of their various operations (such as manufacturing, maintenance, R&D, and testing). The framework presented here is consistent with Deming's P–D–C–A continuous improvement cycle (Figure 10-2). Companies of all sizes have been successful in reducing emissions using this strategy.

Somehow, Barday's department never seems to have time for training.

A Management Framework for Pollution Prevention

- Gain management commitment.
- Mobilize and train the workforce to participate.
- Identify and characterize the facility's waste streams.
- Evaluate the environmental impacts of those waste streams.
- Identify the highest priority targets.
- Identify alternative technologies and other options.
- Estimate costs, risks, benefits associated with each alternative.
- Propose priorities to management and gain commitment.
- Create plans, including resources, targets, timelines, and responsibilities.
- Implement pollution prevention plans.
- Measure progress against targets.
- Communicate progress to management and others.
- Make course corrections, as needed.

A number of organizations have tools to manage the selection and tracking of such projects. McClellan Air Force Base, for example, has a comprehensive list of management tools for pollution prevention, including:

- Economic evaluation (e.g., payback, savings, internal rate of return, net present value)
- Reporting (e.g., life-cycle cost data, comparisons between present and proposed systems)
- Prioritization (six criteria are used in the selection process: achievement of Air Force goals, environmental benefits, compliance, economic feasibility, initial capital investment, and technical feasibility)
- Road maps (which provide a "big picture" approach to visualization of project goals and accomplishments)

Pollution Prevention Achievements

Ben and Jerry's Homemade: An Attention to Waste   Few of us think about waste (or waists) when we are busy devouring Ben and Jerry's products. The employees of this small company, however, have been active in devising ways to keep its own wastes to a minimum. Their ice cream bars are now packaged in flexible bags, eliminating the individual boxes they had been wrapped in, saving 8 to 11 million boxes annually. The company is also working with its suppliers to ship goods in larger, reusable totes. Dairy wastes are now composted, and the finished product is made available to the community for garden use. Measures are being developed for all the company's solid waste streams, as well as for

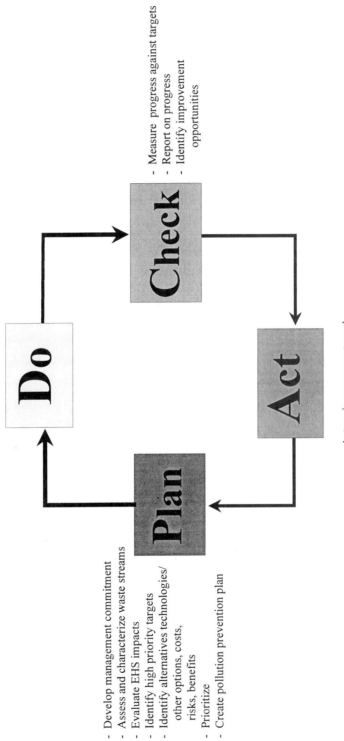

- Create project plans
- Allocate resources
- Set timelines, responsibilities, milestones
- Implement

Do

Check

- Measure progress against targets
- Report on progress
- Identify improvement opportunities

Act

Act on improvement needs

Plan

- Develop management commitment
- Assess and characterize waste streams
- Evaluate EHS impacts
- Identify high priority targets
- Identify alternatives technologies/ other options, costs, risks, benefits
- Prioritize
- Create pollution prevention plan

energy use, in an effort to focus attention on areas where the greatest improvements can be gained.

The Auto Industry   General Motors has a number of pollution prevention initiatives in place. It reduced the amount of organic solvents used per vehicle in painting operations by 70 percent over the past 15 years, and also met its TRI reduction goal of 50 percent for EPA's 33/50 chemicals. Its annual recycling volume for metals, paper, and other materials has reached 3 million tons. The company has also set a fee structure for on-site chemical services from its suppliers that encourages both to reduce the volume of chemicals in use on its sites. Facilities participating in this contract arrangement have realized an average 30 percent reduction in chemical use and annual savings of up to $750,000.

Ford Motor Company's highly successful Quality-based approach to product design has also been extended to environmental quality. Ford's scientists and engineers designed new models anticipating increasingly stringent emission standards, and met design objectives two years ahead of the compliance schedule. Its assembly plants have also been able to significantly reduce organic solvent emissions from paint areas.

In addition to these programs, the Big Three are working in partnership with their supply chain and with U.S. and Canadian regulatory agencies to reduce emissions of 65 persistent toxic chemicals.

ITT Automotive   ITT Automotive's facility in Rochester, New York, has been highly successful in eliminating emissions of a number of solvents. Ken Ladue, senior environmental engineer at the facility, describes their approach enthusiastically: "No chemical enters the facility without the buy-in of our environmental department. We are involved in purchasing decision, and at all stages of process/product design." Using this approach, the facility was able to totally eliminate its emissions of 1,1,1, trichloroethane (90 tons in 1991) by substituting the use of steam-cleaning for its air conditioner manufacture. It was also able to reduce its xylene emissions (529 tons in 1977) to zero by 1994, by switching from solvent-based painting of its compressors and blower motors to powder coating.

Other pollution prevention strategies were provided in Chapter 7.

Design for Environment

Design for Environment (DFE) is a prevention-based approach more commonly applied to product design; thus it often engages a different design community. It follows in the footsteps of other "Design for X" approaches (or DFX) to product design, where "X" refers to attributes such as assembly, safety and liability prevention, material logistics, serviceability, reliability, testability, or manufacturability. In the case of DFE, "X" relates to environmental factors, considered across the entire product life cycle (Dambach and Allenby, 1995).

DFE Practices in Use Within Industry

■ Substitute product/process constituents with ones exhibiting more favorable EHS profiles.

■ Design for disassembly and remanufacturability.

■ Design in recyclability.

■ Design to minimize impacts on the environment resulting from consumer use.

■ Minimize parts count.

■ Design for durability.

■ Minimize waste levels, discharges, and releases during manufacturing.

■ Reduce energy use, and design improved energy recovery systems.

■ Minimize environmental impacts associated with logistical aspects of the life cycle.

AT&T's Approach to DFE

The approach that AT&T took to implement DFE is worth exploring (Dambach and Allenby, 1995). The steps they used included:

1. *Find a home and a sponsor for the DFE approach.* AT&T concluded that DFE is so technology-intensive, its proper home is within the engineering and research communities, rather than with EHS functional areas. (Nevertheless, AT&T found a home for DFE initially within its own EHS organization.)

2. *Make whatever cultural changes are required.* This can include changing EHS vision, policy, and practices. AT&T updated its environmental policy to reflect its change in direction.

3. *Create a system of teams to address specific DFE programs.* A multidiscipline approach will be needed. AT&T created an umbrella coordinating team, under which fell subteams dealing with environmental cost accounting, technical methods, energy, product takeback, and so on.

4. *Formalize DFE training.* The target audience, while perhaps fully conversant with DFX principles, may not understand EHS issues, impacts, and management approaches. AT&T created two to four hour programs that covered DFE principles, the use of assessment matrices, and working sessions with designers. More intensified courses are planned for its technical designers, engineers, and managers.

5. *Choose targets of opportunity.* Select a few showcase projects as initial efforts, but be sure that they are not too complex.

6. *Deploy DFE as an integral module in existing DFX programs, where engineers and designers are already familiar with this approach.* This

approach will be easier than introducing EHS considerations after major design parameters have been established. The tools used, including software, checklists, Computer-Aided Design (CAD), and decision matrices, will need to be adapted to DFE use.

7. *Incorporate EHS needs in the product definition stage.* The earlier these concepts are introduced, the fewer changes will be incurred.

8. *Create a DFE outreach program.* network of external relationships is essential to stay current with the latest technical and management thinking, both domestically and abroad.

9. *Quantify cost savings and other benefits from your DFE and other prevention-based programs.* Xerox, for example, reported in 1994 that its estimated annual savings for its supplier partnership packaging program, implemented in 1990, were $20 million in resource conservation, disposal cost avoidance, and additional productivity.

DFE at Work

Xerox's goal is to minimize waste to landfills as well as releases to the environment throughout the product cycle, a strategy that calls for "waste-free" products and factories, realized through a DFE approach. (Barnes, 1993; Smart, 1992). The company's training for design engineers began in 1993. Initially, DFE principles were applied to copy cartridge designs, and are now also being applied to new copiers, printers, and multifunction products. Xerox engineers begin by limiting production materials to recyclable and recycled thermoplastics and metals. For instance, it uses recycled plastics in replaceable copy and print cartridges. Xerox also embosses plastic parts with recycling symbols to facilitate the recycling process at the end of their initial use cycle. In 1995, Xerox began marking its drawings with remanufacturing codes to expedite cleaning, testing, and reuse of parts. Snap-together designs that facilitate assembly and disassembly were incorporated. Replaceable copy cartridges are designed specifically for parts reuse, helping reduce waste at customer sites.

Chrysler has been able to minimize its emissions of persistent toxic chemicals, such as cadmium, lead, and hexavalent chromium, through new technologies and equipment in areas such as paint application, powder coatings, and battery manufacture. Using a DFE approach, the Chrysler Grand Cherokees made in its Jefferson North Assembly Plant now have:

■ Non-CFC air conditioning refrigerants
■ Asbestos-free brake linings
■ Noncadmium plastic fasteners
■ Plastic components identified to facilitate disassembly and recycling
■ New powder antichip coatings to eliminate VOC emissions

Transforming Waste Streams to Feedstocks

Proponents of "industrial ecology" like to point to the opportunities that exist to couple various industrial sectors through by-products and waste streams, yet, many segments of the chemical industry have been doing exactly this for decades. Canada's Chemical Valley in Sarnia, Ontario, for example, grew up precisely to capitalize on the availability of by-products that could serve as feedstocks for other chemical synthetic pathways.

Hoechst Celanese, will use innovative technology to convert the hazardous waste at a Texas Gulf Coast site to an organic chemical feedstock for its on-site production processes. Wastes are channeled into a molten metal bath where heat and catalysts convert complex molecules to elemental form. The system is the first of its kind installed by Molten Metal Technology of Waltham, Massachusetts, in production. The process has been designated a pollution prevention technology, rather than a waste treatment process.

Such coupling of by-product streams has also been successful between *different* industry sectors, such as utilities and cement manufacturers. Ontario Hydro has been selling fly ash (the properties of which are very similar to shale) from its coal-burning operations to the cement industry for nearly a decade. In 1992 its wet fly ash handling system was upgraded to a dry system, making it easier to market. The utility now has a ten-year contract with LaFarge Cement, which benefits both companies. LaFarge is able to reduce dust from its kiln operations, carbon dioxide emissions, and its nonrenewable resource use. Ontario Hydro avoids landfill disposal costs, as well as complies with provincial regulations on reducing landfill use.

Sand used at Ford Motor Company's casting plants, which make molds and cores for engine blocks and components in Cleveland, Ohio, and Windsor, Ontario, is now being recycled for use as paving and building materials. Spent sand was previously shipped to landfills for disposal. Today it is a useful commodity. Ford researchers are also working to turn paint sludge, a by-product from the automotive paint process, into a form of activated carbon. One potential use for this material is in vehicle vapor-recovery systems, where it absorbs undesirable gases and prevents them from entering the atmosphere during refueling operations.

Carbon dioxide, a by-product of certain manufacturing processes, is used in Xerox' office equipment refurbishment process. This new technology, borrowed from jet engine cleaning, removes grease, dirt, and oil by blasting used parts with carbon dioxide pellets. As the pellets hit the surface, they return to their gaseous state, lifting off any grime. The process has also completely eliminated the use of an ozone-depleter, 1,1,1 trichloroethane. It is also more economical, with annual costs savings for one facility estimated at $500,000.

ISO 14001 on Process Management

ISO 14001 groups the topics addressed in this chapter and the previous one under two major headings: Implementation and Operation, and Checking and Corrective Action.

Continuous Improvement The definition that ISO 14001 provides for continuous improvement is narrow:

> The process of enhancing the environmental management system to achieve improvements in overall environmental performance in line with the organization's policy.

All the same, the definition provided for an "environmental management system" is quite broad, including:

> [The] organizational structure, planning activities, responsibilities, practices, procedures, processes and resources for developing, implementing, achieving, reviewing and maintaining the environmental policy.

Prevention ISO 14001 incorporates the concept of "prevention" into the standard in two different contexts. In the Introduction section, "prevention of pollution" is described as the standard's overall aim, along with supporting environmental protection. Both, however, are viewed within the context of socio-economic needs.

Clause 4.1 of the standard requires top management to ensure that the organization's policy includes a commitment to both continuous improvement and preventing pollution. It also requires that its policy be consistent with the scale of its issues as well as its potential impacts.

Corrective and Preventive Action Prevention is also incorporated into ISO 14001 under the topic of preventive action (under the major heading of "Checking and Corrective Action"). The organization is required to create procedures, and to define both responsibilities and authority for action relevant to investigating any nonconformances, including any corrective and preventive actions. While ISO 14001 does not define nonconformance, this presumably includes regulatory and other legal requirements, internal procedures and commitments, and organization policy and principles.

Audits The topic of auditing is also included under the major heading of "Checking and Corrective Action" (clause 4.4.1). The standard, however, requires only that the environmental management system be audited to be certain that it "conforms to planned arrangements for environmental management including the requirements of this standard." (This statement is not clearly worded.) It also requires that any information derived from the audit be communicated to management.

Management Review The standard also requires that top management review, at appropriate intervals, the environmental management system in order to ensure that it remains suitable, adequate, as well as effective, from the perspective of its policy, objectives, and management system elements. It also requires that this review process take into account "changing circumstances and the commitment to continual improvement."

Documentation and Record-Keeping ISO 14001 requires that the organization document all requirements of its management system, including their interactions (the latter are not clearly defined). It also requires that the documentation clearly provide direction to any related documentation.

ISO 14001 provides somewhat greater detail on the topics of document control and record-keeping, requiring that the organization establish procedures to control all documents required by the standard to be sure that they can be readily located, that they are regularly reviewed and revised, and that current versions are accessible everywhere that accessibility is important to effective management. It also requires that any obsolete materials be removed so that no unintended use occurs, and that any materials retained for purposes other than use be suitably identified.

The standard also briefly states requirements for procedures to identify, maintain, and dispose of environmental records, such as training records and the results of audits and reviews. It requires that such records be legible, and that they can be readily identified. It also requires they be readily retrievable and adequately protected. Retention time requirements also must be established. Finally, the standard requires that records be maintained as appropriate to demonstrate conformance to the standard's requirements.

On the topic of operational control, the organization is required to identify operations and activities that may have a significant environmental impact, as well as to plan those activities so that they are well controlled. This is to be accomplished by creating documented procedures where they are needed to prevent unwanted impacts, and by stipulating appropriate operating criteria. The organization is also required to create procedures for any good and services its uses that might have significant environmental impacts, as well as to communicate to suppliers and contractors any relevant procedures and requirements.

Monitoring and Measurement The organization is required to establish procedures to both monitor and measure any parameters of its activities that can have a significant environmental impact; these procedures can include recording performance data, establishing appropriate operational controls, and assuring conformance with the organization's objectives and targets. The standard also requires that monitoring equipment be calibrated and maintained, and that records be retained according to documented procedures.

Emergency Preparedness and Response The standard includes the topic of emergency preparedness and response under clause 4.3.7 of "Implementation and Operation," and requires that the organization establish procedures to evaluate its ability to respond to emergency situations, and to deal with any environmental impacts associated with them. The organization is also required to review its procedures, particularly after accidents or emergency situations have occurred, as well as to test such procedures periodically, where practicable.

QUESTIONS TO ANSWER ABOUT PROCESS MANAGEMENT

- Is there a commitment to a prevention approach based on risk assessment/management?
- Is an effective pollution prevention program in place?
- Is an approach such as DFE used for product design?
- Are life-cycle considerations included in product and process design?
- Are cost savings from these approaches quantified?
- Has the use of a prevention-based and continuous improvement approach made a difference in any financial parameters that the organization tracks?

ADDITIONAL READINGS

Allenby, Braden. 1993. "Supporting Environmental Quality: Developing an Infrastructure for Design." *Total Quality Environmental Management* 2: 303–308.

Bringer, Robert M. and D. M. Benforado. 1995. "Pollution Prevention and TQEM." *Environmental Strategies Handbook*, Rao V. Kolluru, Editor. New York: McGraw-Hill, pp. 165–197.

Frosch, Robert A. and N. Gallopoulos. 1992. "Towards an Industrial Ecology." *The Treatment and Handling of Waste*, A. D. Bradshaw et al., Editors. London: Chapman and Hall.

Oakley, Brian. 1993. "Total Quality Product Design: How to Integrate Environmental Criteria into the Product Realization Process." *Total Quality Environmental Management* 2: 309–321.

Prince, Jackie and R. Denison. 1995. "Developing an Environmental Action Plan for Business," *Environmental Strategies Handbook*, Rao V. Kolluru, Editor. New York: McGraw-Hill, pp. 239–258.

CHAPTER 11

PERFORMANCE—
THE BOTTOM LINE

CHAPTER OBJECTIVES

Introduces the reader to the TQEM category of *EHS Results**

Provides guidelines for selecting and using EHS performance measures

Illustrates how companies use EHS performance measures to track progress against targets

Provides case studies of successful EHS performance in small and large companies

THE VALUE OF MEASURING PERFORMANCE

Quality-based management is, by design, results-oriented. But it is also fundamentally data-driven. Just as knowledge of the organization's needs shapes present-day strategies, so, too, does performance data inform future action. *The selection of performance indicators, and in particular, success measures, is a critical step, since its provides a link back to the organization's vision, strategic goals and objectives.*

*EHS Results Category Looks at the organization's EHS performance in key areas associated with its products, processes, services, and EHS management systems, as well as financial performance indicators linked to these areas.

We collect performance data for a number of reasons; for instance:

■ To compare where we are with where we want to be (our position vs. our vision)

■ To determine how well we have satisfied our customers and other interested parties

■ To evaluate where improvements are needed in the way we manage, operate, and design our products, processes, and services

■ To inform our decision-making and communications processes

We measure in each of these cases because the data adds value to our business. There are other equally valid purposes behind the measurement process. For example, the data serves as the basis for recognition and reinforcement of the right behaviors, for allocating resources, and for accountability.

Everyone is interested in the bottom line. Shareholders expect financial returns as well as responsible corporate behaviors. Customers demand high quality products and services. Regulators want compliance—and more. Employees look for meaningfulness in their contributions. And managers—accountable for all this—look to results as reinforcement that they are on the right track.

Types of Performance Measures

Relevance of Measures to Stage of Organizational Development   The mix of an organization's performance indicators tends to reflect the stage of maturity of its EHS program.

■ At the earliest stage, an organization tends to collect data on operational indicators such as waste levels, accident/injury rates, product safety concerns, and regulatory violations. These are also called "lagging" indicators since they are the end result of other activities (e.g., waste results from upstream management/operations-based activities).

■ At a somewhat later stage of development, an organization identifies underlying management system deficiencies, and begins to collect data on the quality of its training, audits, communications, documentation, and review processes. These "leading" indicators predict downstream operational effects.

■ At a more mature stage, an organization recognizes and begins to fill gaps in its internal competencies as well as its external relationships. It may collect data on the impacts of its products, operations, or services on public health and the environment and use this information to improve its performance. It creates measures in areas relating to its EHS R&D, information technology, capital investments and stakeholder and customer partnerships. It also strives to more directly link financial, human resource, operational, EHS, and other goals and measures, as well as to create predictive indicators signaling market and competitors' directions.

Not all indicators are directly linked to the organization's objectives. For example, many organizations gather trend data to determine their performance history in areas such as waste levels, packaging volumes, and costs. Only later, when data has been evaluated and integrated with other data, are objectives or targets set.

Because each organization is unique, its measures or indicators cannot reasonably be imposed from outside an organization, but should be selected based on an organization's issues, its facilities and products, its capabilities, its audiences for performance data, and, finally, the resources it can deploy to collect such information.

Measurement Categories   A number of schemes have been proposed to categorize indicators, such as the following (adapted from James, 1994):

- ■ Management system
- ■ Financial, technical, human, and other resources
- ■ Physical resource consumption (energy, water, materials, and other resources)
- ■ Emissions and wastes (mass/volume of discharges, releases, and other wastes)
- ■ Efficiency (ratio of useful output to input)
- ■ Risks (likelihood of harmful events; a proxy, for environmental impacts)
- ■ Impact (what happens to the environment as a result of business activities)
- ■ Customer-related (satisfaction)

Others advocate an even simpler approach (Wells et al., 1992):

- ■ Process measures ask if the organization is doing the right thing.
- ■ Results measures ask if the organization is getting the results it wants.
- ■ Customer/stakeholder satisfaction measures ask if their needs are being met.

Table 11-1 provides a number of examples of indicators. You may already be tracking performance in a number of these areas, such as waste levels, energy use, or training. Later in this chapter, we look at specific performance measures and goals for several representative companies (11-1). You may be interested in comparing them with measures you are currently using.

State of the Environment   Many organizations fund studies to determine whether their products, processes, or services have any adverse impacts on

■ TABLE 11-1 Examples of Indicator

Management System

Number and frequency of internal audits

Number of repeat audit findings

Timeliness of corrective actions

Number of products to which product stewardship was applied

Employee involvement in EHS activities

Percent of EHS staff "certified"

Number of hours of EHS training for employees with specific EHS
responsibilities

Percent capital project funding allocated to EHS projects

EHS costs per product line

Ratio of decentralized to centralized EHS support staff

Cost savings from pollution prevention program

Operational

Energy units/year

    Energy units/product

    Sources of energy, energy units of each source

    Energy units/ton of emission (avoided emission equivalence)

    Vehicle miles traveled

Waste generation

    Tons/year generated

    Toxicity of wastes

    Percent annual reduction

    Tons/year disposed of, recycled, reclaimed, sold

    Tons of virgin vs. recycled material

    Amount of recovered material as "takeback"

    Cost of waste disposal

Raw material

    Tons of material used per ton of product

    Tons of raw material reused in production process

    Percent recycled content in product

    Number of materials used

    Amount of nonrenewable material used

    Amount of renewable resources used/product

    Cost of raw material/product

public health and the environment, and use this information to improve both design and function. For instance, Avenor, a Canadian forest and paper company, conducts studies on the health and diversity of fish, plants, and aquatic life in receiving waters to determine whether its facility operations are adequately protecting the aquatic environment.

This activity, however, is quite different in its intent from evaluating the actual state of the environment (currently proposed as a category for inclusion in ISO 14031, a guidance standard on environmental performance evaluation). In most cases, it is virtually impossible for individual organizations or facilities to segregate out and measure (or approximate) their impacts from those imposed by other sources, whether resulting from human activities or from nature itself. Governments and others in the public sector (e.g., academics) can and should take the lead in monitoring, modeling, and researching "state of the environment" parameters, information from which helps to shape macro-level policy- and decision-making. Business entities also have a clear role as stakeholders and, on occasion, as contributors of scientific, technical, management, and policy expertise, where this is pertinent. However, business should not be the major player in generating such data (11-2).

GUIDELINES TO DEVELOP AND USE MEASURES

In selecting performance measures, it is important to take into account who needs such information, why they need it, and how they will use it. For example, performance measure data helps those responsible for day-to-day decisions make midcourse corrections. Management, too, needs performance data so it can reinforce compliance and stewardship efforts within the line, report to the board, shareholders, and other interested stakeholders, as well as continue to allocate resources in the right direction. Here are a few practical recommendations.

1. *Tie key measures to key improvement efforts.* Choose measures that are strategically linked to your EHS objectives. For example, if hazardous waste issues are your highest priority, you may want to track waste volumes and percent reductions, adjusted to production volume. If there are also financial costs and benefits associated with reducing these waste streams (e.g., pollution prevention projects, cost reductions due to avoided waste disposal, and documentation costs), you may want to measure these as well.

2. *Select only a few key measures to track at the corporate level.* While you may find you need many different measures at various levels of your organization, be selective in choosing your key measures. Top management, the board, and shareholders can focus best if they have a few measures that are long-term as well as reflective of major programs. This selection process may be difficult if you have many units or sites, each of which has quite different activities. ITT (until recently a conglomerate comprised of hotel, insurance, automotive manufacturing, and other units) chose to limit corporate-wide indicators to those common to all its units.

3. *Keep analyses associated with measures simple, where possible.* If you have to go through too many transformations of data to generate the out-

put data for your measures, the complexity of explaining these may confuse or lose credibility with your intended audience. If your measures are too obtuse, users may not be able to make a direct connection between actions and results.

4. *Tailor measures to your own organization's needs.* While you may find it useful to adopt measures identified within your own sector, recognize your organization's uniqueness and tailor those measures to best suit your needs. In some cases, you may find it useful to aggregate or normalize data so that it better supports decision-making. For example, waste volumes might be combined with production volumes to obtain a normalized measure. Weighting factors might be assigned to a set of measures and an aggregated value computed in order to compare performance among company facilities or products. Encourage all levels of the organization to use measures to track performance. Many of these may be tied to transitory activities, such as short-term improvement projects; nevertheless they are useful to drive progress.

5. *Create a process to update measures regularly* Review your measures at least annually, particularly key success measures associated with the organization's key objectives. Tie the review process to the strategic planning process, and as objectives change, adjust your measures. If you have selected them well, they should remain in place for several years, so that trend data can be developed to support planning and reporting.

6. *Use performance measure data to communicate progress to your key audiences.* Progress (even lack of progress) is news. Find the best vehicles to get information out to your key audiences. Use team meetings, town meetings, written reports, or electronic newsletters to reach your employees. Where relevant and appropriate, communicate successes to the public.

7. *Use performance measure data to justify additional resources where key targets are not being met.* Perhaps resources need to be reallocated at some point. Your programs should be flexible enough to move resources to where they are needed. Performance data helps you justify this change.

8. *Tie measures to accountability and recognition.* Create accountability around measurements and success, and document this. Recognize those charged with creating success. Don't wait until the entire program is completed. Many organizations now have small celebrations that recognize milestones along the way to success. Managers who are truly interested in people find personal ways to convey support on a day-to-day basis as well.

9. *Measure the quality of your management program.* Your measures should deal with your organization's performance, as well as its management system. Examine the effectiveness of your planning process, strategies, and level of management commitment. Use this information to determine gaps and correct them.

10. *Benchmark EHS progress against those you view as Best-in-Class.* Each company and each sector has its unique challenges. Some historically are farther ahead of others in setting goals as well as in measuring and reporting progress, for a variety of reasons. Compare your progress with those that are Best-in-Class and use this information to improve your performance. (See Chapter 14 for more information on this topic.)

MATCHING PERFORMANCE TO GOALS

The examples below, drawn from annual environmental reports and other sources, illustrate how companies track performance against key goals and measures in both management systems and operational areas. Not all companies set numerical goals at the corporate level, but allow individual units the flexibility to set local targets, or express the corporate goal as "continuous improvement."

SC Johnson Wax

SC Johnson Wax set an ambitious goal of improving the "eco-efficiency" of its products and processes ("making more with less"), reducing waste and risk at the same time. Sam Johnson talks about this in what he calls "common sense" terms (Weld, 1993):

> Common sense says that if you reduce what you use, you reduce your cost of production and waste disposal. Companies who make the most progress toward eco-efficiency are positioning themselves to prevent waste from becoming an uncontrollable cost of doing business in the future. Customers want reassurance that the products they buy cause minimal environmental harm. So, by improving our eco-efficiency we stand to gain both competitive advantage and the customer trust.

Performance data quantified and reported in its annual environmental report for 1993 focus on operational (lagging) indicators. However, SC Johnson Wax's strategic objectives and success measures go beyond waste reduction goals, extending to areas such as supplier and customer partnerships, educating youth, and community outreach.

SC Johnson Wax 1994 EHS Performance Measures		
EHS Performance Measure	**Goal**	**Performance**
Virgin packaging volume	20% reduction by 1995	14% by 1994
Total solid, air, water waste	50% reduction by 1995	Surpassed goal
Waste recycling	90% recycling by 1995	On target
VOC emissions	25% reduction by 2000	17% reduction

"World-class results is the performance standard we set for ourselves at SC Johnson Wax. From product development to manufacturing to marketing to customer service, we aim to be the best. Today, as a result, our business is stronger than ever, with sales and profits at all-time highs."

DuPont

DuPont is the tenth largest corporation in the United States, with 175 chemicals and specialties plants, 6 refineries, and 32 natural gas processing plants. Its safety record is better than the industry average by an order of magnitude. DuPont has a goal of zero waste and emissions. Its 1994 report describes seven safety and environmental goals:

- Highest standards of performance and business excellence
- Goal of zero injuries, illnesses, and incidents
- Zero waste and emissions
- Conservation of energy and natural resources and habitat enhancement
- Open and public discussion, and influence on public policy
- Management and employee commitment and accountability.

Performance goals and measures in its 1994 report include both operational and management systems areas. Quantitative data is provided on a site-

---

DuPont's 1994 Performance

EHS Performance Measure	Goal	Performance
TRI air emission reductions	80% by 2000	Down 65% since 1987
TRI waste reduction	Continuous	Down 24% since 1991
33/50 chemicals reduction	Exceed 50% by 95	Down 43% since 1988
Deepwell disposal	Eliminate	Down 5% since 1987
Packaging waste to landfills	50% by 2000	Down 24% since 1991
Greenhouse gases	40% by 2000	Down 4% since 1991
Airborne carcinogens	90% by 2000	Down 70% since 1987
CFC sales	Phaseout by 1995	Down 75%
Use of double-hulled tankers	100% by 2000	57% of fleet
Double-containment fuel systems	All outlets	135 installed
Energy use reduction	Continuous	37% less per pound of product since 1973
Total recordable illnesses/ injuries	—	10X better than industry average
Environmental incidents	—	Significant decline since 1995
Wildlife habitat enhancement	—	21 facilities with enhancement programs
Responsible Care: five Codes	75% in place	Completed by year end 1994

by-site basis for its performance on the Responsible Care management practices. Anecdotal information is also provided on projects and performance associated with each of the individual codes. DuPont also tracks indicators such as environmental investments and costs, fines, and customer conversion to other products. DuPont's data on more than 3000 projects and programs showed that:

> [V]oluntary environmental initiatives costs less than 20% of those driven by regulation to achieve the same results. When we are able to fully integrate business and environmental strategies, we not only save energy and raw materials, but we more quickly develop new products and services that result in a cleaner environment and improved business performance.

Intel

Intel has been one of the most rapidly growing semiconductor manufacturers in the world; between 1987 and 1994, its revenues increased sixfold to nearly $12 billion. Like others in its sector, Intel was faced with a variety of chemicals management issues, and responded aggressively, removing ozone-depleting chemicals and PCBs from its systems. Although its production doubled between 1990 and 1994, its VOC emissions have increased only 18 percent.

Intel reported progress on a number of operational goals, but it also is tracking desired management system improvements. Goals and targets were set for compliance, risk management, conservation of natural resources, safety and health, product stewardship, and reduction of environmental releases. Intel also tracks its fines, violations, corrective action, awards, and other accomplishments. In the area of product stewardship, Intel's goals included the design of energy efficient computers, fax modems, and video cards, by including a "sleep" mode feature that reduces energy consumption while the computer is idle. It is also working to redesign components to facilitate reuse and recycling. An interesting innovation is its plan to deliver at least 70 percent of all product manuals and documents to customers via electronic media.

Intel's 1994 EHS Performance

EHS Performance

Measure	Goal	Performance
Solid waste recycling	50% recycling	Exceeded 1994 goal
VOC emissions	50% reduced in next generation despite production volume doubling	Reduced per unit volume
Injuries/illnesses (lost day case rate)	20% reduced in 1995	Reduced below industry sector level
Plastic tray recycling	50% recycled by 1995	18% in 1994
Plastic packaging		67% reduction since 1992
Natural gas use reduction	20% in newest factories	

Avenor

Avenor is one of the world's leading forest products companies, producing newsprint, pulp and white paper, and lumber, as well as one of Canada's leading exporters of market pulp. Despite major restructuring pressures, the Canadian pulp and paper industries have committed over $30 billion to environmental improvements focusing on the industry's key issues. Avenor's own investments in new technologies and procedures make its mills the largest producer in North America of post-consumer recycled-content newsprint. It has also adapted its bleaching process to use chlorine dioxide in order to reduce the levels of chlorinated organic substances released to the environment. Its objectives and performance measures for 1994 included operational ones such as optimizing the performance of existing pollution control systems and continuing its program for full effluent treatment at all facilities, as well as management system goals and measures such as eliminating exceedences of regulations from operations.

After years of company research and development, Avenor has developed a state-of-the-art treatment system at its Thunder Bay newsprint mill that will allow the mill to operate totally effluent free (TEF). A physical/chemical treatment process added to its primary clarifier, followed by secondary treatment, will allow recycling the resulting effluent back into the newsprint and kraft pulp production processes. This will reduce total discharge from the complex by 50%.

Avenor's 1994 EHS Performance

EHS Performance Measure	Performance
Volume of effluent flow from pulp mills	Reduced annually in each facility since 1992
Reduction of BOD and TSS in effluents*	Both below regulatory limit in all facilities
Levels of chlorinated organics in effluent	Well below regulatory limit
Air emission levels of particulates	Below limits in some plants; over in others
Emissions of total reduced sulfur	Above limit in some plants
Solid waste to landfills	Decreased overall since 1992
Exceedences and legal proceedings	Full list provided

*BOD (biological oxygen demand) and TSS (total suspended solids).

Georgia-Pacific

Georgia-Pacific is one of the world's leading manufacturers and distributors of pulp and paper and building materials. Its 400 facilities employ about 50,000 people. The company manages more than six million acres of timberland in the United States and Canada. Georgia-Pacific's broadly based performance measures are based on objectives associated with operational, management systems, and conservation-related improvements, each of which is tied to a specific corporate goal and action plan. In the United States the company has virtually eliminated dioxin in the mill effluents.

Georgia-Pacific's 1994 EHS Performance

EHS Performance Measure	Performance
Pulp and paper mill water use	Decreased more than 70% since 1972
Recovered paper usage (millions of tons)	Increasing steadily
"33/50" program emissions	Meeting its 1992 and 1995 commitments
Discharges at pulp and paper mills	TSS and BOD down about 90% since 1972
Safety performance vs. industry group	Outperformed average in every category
Notices of violations resulting in fines	82 notices resulting in fines over four years
Environmental capital spending	Doubled between 1993 and 1994
Number of closed-loop chemical facilities	13 out of 20 facilities are now closed loop
Compliance with Forestry Best Management Practices	97 % acceptable level for compliance
In-service equipment with PCBs	50% of equipment with PCBs removed at pulp and paper mills

---

Duke Power Company

Duke Power Company is the sixth largest electric utility in the United States. The company adopted Total Quality Management (TQM) in 1990, the same year that it initiated environmental performance measurements. Its environmental objectives include reduction of waste at the source, increased utilization of ash, prevention of environmental incidents, and improvement of its performance on corporate and facility assessments.

Some of its selection criteria for measures included simplicity, importance to the business (e.g., long-term and results-oriented), broad appeal to employees, alignment with TQM (e.g., driving prevention, continuous improvement, and customer focus), and "stretch" goals (Davidson, 1994).

Duke Power Company 1994 Performance

Measure	Goal	1994 Performance
Ash utilization	Reuse 75% by 1998	55% reuse
Source reduction	Reduce all solid/hazardous	~25% reduction
Incidents	Zero by 1998	Reduced ~70% since 1992
Corporate assessments (based on Baldrige)	90% score by 1996	612 out of 1000 points
Facility assessments (compliance/management systems)	90% score by 1996	~83% in 1994

ISO 14000 on Environmental Performance

Although the evaluation of environmental performance through the appropriate selection of metrics is an integral part of an environmental management system, a separate guidance standard (ISO 14031) is being developed on this topic. At the time of publication of this book, the language of the standard was still in draft. The draft makes clear that performance evaluation should be linked to the organization's objectives and targets, and that performance evaluation is primarily considered a measurement tool. Data from such evaluations can, of course, be used at the discretion of the organization for a variety of other purposes, such as reporting and communication, but this is not the purpose of the standard.

Three categories of indicators currently proposed include management system, operational or process-related parameters (related to physical facilities, equipment, their design and operation, and the material and energy flows associated with products/processes and services), and "the state of the environment." Each was discussed earlier in this chapter.

QUESTIONS TO ANSWER ABOUT EHS PERFORMANCE

- What kinds of performance measures do you have in place?
- Are measures in place for each of your environmental objectives and targets?
- How do you use performance data?
- Do you use it to determine improvement opportunities?
- Do you use it to recognize excellence in workforce contributions to progress?
- What do you do when your performance lags?
- Does your environmental performance position your organization as a leader?
- How does it position you with respect to your competitors?
- Is there any correlation between your environmental performance and your financial results?

ADDITIONAL READINGS

Fitzgerald, Chris. 1992. "Selecting Measures for Corporate Environmental Quality: Examples from TQEM Companies." *Auditing for Quality Environmental Leadership: Beyond Compliance to Environmental Excellence*, John T. Willig, Editor. New York: John Wiley & Sons, pp. 137–146.

Wever, Grace. 1994. "The Need for Ecosystem-Based Performance Indicators to Drive Responsible Policy and Management Strategies." *Indicators of Environmental Performance and Ecosystem Condition*. National Academy of Engineering Conference, Woods Hole, MA.

CHAPTER 12

THE ART OF ACTIVE LISTENING

CHAPTER OBJECTIVES

Introduces the reader to the TQEM category of *Customer/Stakeholder Focus and Satisfaction**

Describes effective processes to determine and proactively anticipate the EHS needs of customers and other interested parties

Outlines methods to measure customer/stakeholder satisfaction with EHS performance, and use satisfaction data for improvement

LISTEN, LEARN, AND CHANGE

"The business of business is to stay in business." *Peter Drucker*

The customer's opinion of our products and services determines whether we can sell them. The public's perceptions of our integrity determine whether we can operate. Our ability to listen, learn—and act on that learning—determines whether we will stay in business.

Customer/Stakeholder Focus and Satisfaction Category Defines the unit's systems for customer focus, learning, and relationship-building. It also looks at key measures such as customer/stakeholder satisfaction with the unit's EHS performance, and competitors' performance in this area, as well as impact of EHS considerations on the unit's market share.

From an EHS perspective, organizations have many practical ways of learning what their customers and stakeholders want. Acting on what you learn is the ticket to staying in business.

Customers expect to receive, for example, product information that is mandated by law, such as Material Safety Data Sheets (MSDSs). Packaging laws in many states require that data on recycling content or the presence of heavy metals be printed on the package. Customers also want reliable information that helps them fulfill their own regulatory requirements in areas like recycling or disposal. *Regulators and the public* expect compliance with Right-to-Know laws, which require timely submission of data on chemical use and waste levels, as well as inventory levels of selected chemicals stored on-site at company facilities. The *public* wants assurance that products are safe, for them as well as for the environment.

Practical Ways to Listen and Learn

Advocacy and legal staffs can:
- Monitor policy and regulatory trends
- Meet regularly with regulators and policy-makers

Customer relations, technical, and sales staff can:
- Use hot lines to receive input from customers and the public
- Meet directly with customers
- Learn from customer response to their own and competitors' EHS marketing strategies

Senior managers can:
- Hold town meetings to receive employee input
- Hold high-level discussions with public officials and decision-makers
- Interact with civic leaders and the community prior to initiating projects with community impact, and throughout the project life
- Seek input from subordinates and peers

Communicators and public relations staff can:
- Use response cards in newsletters or annual reports to seek public comment on EHS performance
- Track media coverage of EHS issues related to their organization
- Use surveys to gather input from employees, customers, the community, and other public groups

Supervisors at all levels can gather feedback during:
- Team meetings
- One-on-one meetings
- Performance reviews

Many organizations complement their compliance programs by setting up systems to respond swiftly to customer and stakeholder calls, questions, and concerns. Many provide a toll-free number and maintain an elaborate log categorizing such calls. A complex internal network may be needed to move questions efficiently to the right place for response, and targets set for response turnaround time. Continuous improvement may be applied to remove bottlenecks. These arrangements are particularly critical where regulatory requirements are involved, or where emergency situations exist.

EHS Hot Line Areas Commonly Tracked

- Question or concern
- Product or service affected
- Customer data
- Customer type
- Geographic region
- Action taken
- Turnaround time for response
- Repeat calls from same customer

As companies move to more proactive modes of interacting with customers and stakeholders, they also use information derived from these activities to improve EHS strategies and planning. Marketing and sale teams gather information in order to improve products or services.

The Herman Miller Company proactively addressed the need for customer and public information by installing an information database with up-to-date information on its environmental programs. The system includes data on recycling, rain forest management, "minimal packaging," and its Energy Center (waste to energy facility at Zeeland). The database answers actual client questions and is accessible through its sales offices. The company is also working with its suppliers to gather information on their environmental practices, such as recycling efforts, environmental policies, and accomplishments.

Some companies integrate safety and environmental issues with other product concerns in the design of their customer support programs. Occidental Chemical's technical experts work with customers, offering assistance with equipment and process evaluations, information on handling and storage and regulations, safety seminars, laboratory testing, and formulation recommendations.

Geon's Product Quality Team determines the root cause of customer concerns about products. The team uses a multifunctional approach to solving problems, and includes cross-functional representation from manufacturing, business management, sales, R&D, customer service, purchasing, technical service, and production planning. Analysis of customer concerns led the team to conclude that about half of all complaints were traceable to product design and usage issues, rather than to manufacturing problems. Over a year, the rate of customer complaints dropped by 60 percent.

BEFORE THEY ASK

How successfully do you anticipate public interest about your EHS performance? You would be well-advised not to wait until issues surface. Instead consider what other companies are doing, and adapt those strategies that best fit your business needs. Here are some recommendations you can explore:

1. *Create a summary of your EHS plans and accomplishments to share with the public.* Recognizing increasing pressure for public disclosure, and the need for consistency, a business cooperative, the Public Environmental Reporting Initiative (PERI), published a set of reporting guidelines for such information. The core components they recommended include:

   - An organizational profile
   - Policy
   - Environmental management
   - Releases
   - Resource conservation
   - Risk management
   - Compliance
   - Product stewardship
   - Employee recognition and stakeholder involvement

   By 1994, over 150 companies worldwide had issued annual environmental or EHS reports. While many organizations are still in the early stages of such a reporting program, others have a longer history, such as Dow Canada and Ontario Hydro. Most reports of this nature emphasize goals, performance, and voluntary initiatives, but a few are also open on fines, violations, and other EHS liabilities. A few trade associations also regularly publish annual reports focusing on sectoral environmental accomplishments, such as the Canadian Pulp and Paper Association, the Canadian Petroleum Products Institute, and the U.S. Chemical Manufacturers Association (CMA). The latter organization includes progress on its members conformance with its Responsible Care program, identifying areas where strengths and improvement opportunities exist.

2. *Keep employees and the community up-to-date on newsworthy EHS issues and events.* Occidental Chemical's newsletter, *EnviroNews*, is highly inclusive, covering environmental awards, progress on projects, training opportu-

nities, employee profiles, environmental information system updates, regulatory requirement changes, and incident statistics.

3. *Increase the knowledge base of your neighbors about your operations.* On Intel's tours for interested local citizens and government officials, technical staff explain the workings of their chemical storage and emergency response systems. The company also provides special training classes and donates equipment to local responders.

4. *Lend a hand to communities on emergency and other planning.* Intel works with local officials and agencies in creating local plans for chemical management, waste reduction, and emergency response. Occidental Chemical, along with other chemical firms in West Virginia's Kanawha Valley, joined with a local planning committee to communicate worst case release scenarios to the local community. Thousands of local residents visited booths set up in a local shopping mall, where employees and corporate environmental staff were on hand to answer questions posed by visitors.

5. *Seek public input through public advisory councils.* Dow Chemical Company's high-level advisory council reports to its Board of Directors, and includes perspectives from government, public, business, and advocacy group leaders. Community advisory councils at Kodak Park and BASF interact with site management on local issues, and provide input on management approaches to environmental issues, new project proposals, and future directions. A 1994 study found that over 200 such councils were in place within the chemical industry alone (Lynn, 1994).

MEASURING SATISFACTION

Selecting Satisfaction Measures

One of the most telling measures of customer satisfaction happens at the point of sale. If your revenues and market share are falling, and those of your competitors are growing, you have somehow lost that magical connection with the customer. Satisfaction measures won't bring your customer back, but they may put you on the right track for recreating that connection. Such measures should include both leading and lagging indicators, and should track customer action as well as opinion. Leading indicators get at the heart of the problem most quickly, and lead you to needed management system changes that will deliver customer value, before you have permanently lost your business base.

How do companies determine what EHS attributes and behavior customers and stakeholders value? How do you, then, measure their satisfaction with your actual performance? Here are a few guidelines, based on the experience of others in business.

1. *Determine whether you are effectively meeting their needs for regulatory information.* Customers can be surveyed through a variety of avenues to

determine whether the regulatory information you provide with your products meets their needs for relevance, scope, clarity, and other important characteristics.

2. *Quantify their satisfaction with the organization's response time and nature of response to their questions or concerns* Analysis of this information can then be used to create more effective response systems.

3. *Measure market impacts when product changes are made in response to customer or other stakeholder EHS needs.* Look at revenues and market share changes when you introduce products that are safer, have higher recycled content in product or packaging materials, or increased product recyclability. If no market impact occurs, then consider modifying your communications strategy to inform the public about changes that are beneficial to the environment, or to the health and safety of product users.

4. *Use opinion polls to determine the public's views on industry sector or individual company's environmental record and stewardship practices.* The chemical industry was one of the first to recognize and respond to the need for better information. Its programs inform the public about the nature of the industry itself, its products, and the safety of its facilities. Many other sectors have also recognized the need for better public information, including increased advertising emphasizing a commitment to product design from a cradle-to-grave, or cradle-to-cradle perspective.

5. *Ask the community whether you are a good neighbor.* You may be surprised with the response. Companies like Bayer Rubber and Dow Chemical Canada are members of an industry cooperative that surveys the community regularly to determine its views. Many other companies also conduct third-party surveys to ensure credibility.

6. *Ask your employees to rate the EHS leadership and performance of the organization.* Consider including such questions in broader surveys already in place, to minimize costs of collecting and processing such data.

Use of Satisfaction Measure Data to Improve Public Understanding

SC Johnson Wax's Study. Business has a stake in an informed public. Sound information is important to support decision-making (including purchasing) as well as to recognize economic and social impacts when dealing with environmental issues. Recognizing this, SC Johnson Wax commissioned four research studies of public attitudes, beginning in 1990. The study was carried out in consultation with the EPA. The company also partnered with three environmental groups on public outreach, and provided results to policy-makers, academics, environmental leaders, and media. The studies documented a disturbingly low rate of environmental literacy among the public. They also documented links among environmental knowledge, concern, and activism. The company went beyond the study and initiated programs to educate schoolchildren and teachers, as well as creating a youth forum.

Company-Sponsored Environmental Education Projects   A number of companies have extended their traditional approach to training and education far beyond corporate walls. Kodak's $2.5 million grant to the World Wildlife Fund (WWF) is also designed to further environmental literacy. This grant supports WWF's program "Windows on the Wild," which is designed for use in U.S. middle schools and which uses biodiversity as its organizing theme. Dow Chemical Company provided substantial support to the construction of a "tall ship" fitted out to train schoolchildren on water quality. Both Upjohn and General Motors fund educational programs for young people, and provide practical field experience in the area of water quality sampling, testing, and improvement.

The Occidental Chemical Corporation's Niagara Falls plant's Adopt-A-School program provides funds and personnel to develop training modules on safety, technology, chemistry, and the environment. Students also tour the facility in a program that includes hands-on interaction.

The Adopt-a-School Program

The Niagara Falls plant of Occidental Chemical Corporation is involved in an effective Adopt-A-School program with the LaSalle Middle School. Activities are coordinated, and collaboration fostered through four individuals volunteering for the program:

- Lana Dole, a senior environmental engineer
- Gerald Nardelli, the plant's technical manager
- Thomas Franklin, school principal
- Lynn Tompkins, science teacher

The program is designed to benefit students through personal contact, mentoring, and workplace knowledge provided by volunteers from all levels of local industry and business. Its activities include Earth Day observances, recycling, selection and donation of science kits, model bridge building and testing, annual career day, and sponsorship of teachers to special workshops.

VISIBLE PUBLIC RECOGNITION

One clear sign of stakeholder satisfaction is the public recognition and awards that many companies have received from government, advocacy groups, and trade and professional societies (12-1). For example, both Johnson & Johnson and Herman Miller were awarded *Business Ethics* magazine's 1989 award for excellence in ethics (File, 1989).

Awards such as these were designed by groups within government, advocacy groups, trade and professional societies, and the media to reinforce as well as recognize responsible stewardship. The evidence that companies or facilities do not give up or rest on their laurels is that many have received multiple awards over a number of years, indicating their ongoing commitment to environmental improvement.

A Sampling of the EHS Award Spectrum

■ Geon's Terre Haute, IN, vinyl manufacturing plant, for instance, received the US Senate Productivity Award, recognizing among other things its environmental performance and safety awareness.

■ Xerox has received numerous environmental awards, including the prestigious World Environment Center Gold Medal Award in 1993.

■ Georgia-Pacific was awarded the first Sustainable Development Award from the Earth Pledge Foundation for its efforts in protecting the environment and promoting economic growth through sustainable development through its plan to protect the red-cockaded woodpecker. Marshall Hahn, chairman of Georgia-Pacific, was honored with the 1993 Vision for America Award by Keep America Beautiful.

■ Dow Canada was honored with a 1991 Wildlife Greenbelt Award from the Fish and Game Association, and the Emerald Award from the Alberta Foundation for Environmental Excellence for environmental leadership through Dow's WRAP (Waste Reduction Always Pays) program.

■ IBM Japan received the Grand Prize for the Global Environment, an award sponsored by World Wildlife Fund, Keidanren, and MITI (Ministry of International Trade and Industry), for its aggressive environmental management programs.

■ 3M has been widely recognized by organizations such as the National Wildlife Federation's Corporate Conservation Council and the World Environmental Center.

■ Herman Miller was the recipient of the National Wildlife Federation's 1993 Environmental Achievement Award in recognition of its "exemplary private sector achievements." Some of its other awards include the President's Environmental and Conservation Challenge Award Citation, and America's Corporate Conscience Award for Environmental Responsibility, from the Council on Economic Priorities.

■ SC Johnson Wax was awarded the Gold Medal by the World Environment Center in 1993.

■ Occidental Chemical's Niagara plant won one of seven Energy Efficiency Awards presented as part of CMA's Energy Efficiency Continuous Improvement Program.

■ Wegmans Food Markets won the Best of the Best award for supply chain management for its programs in working with suppliers on packaging and other issues.

ADDITIONAL READINGS

Bole, Leslie and S. J. Nelson. 1992. "Environmental Community Relations: A Vital Component in TQEM." *Total Quality Environmental Management* 1: 363-367.

Sands, Tom. 1991. "Developing Customer and Supplier Relationships at Dow." GEMI Conference proceedings, pp. 59–68.

Stewart, Scott. 1992. "Consumer Feedback and Communications: Procter & Gamble's 800-Line to Customers." GEMI Conference proceedings, pp. 39–42.

Wright, Patricia D. 1992. "Community Relations in the Face of Uncertainty." GEMI Conference proceedings, pp. 239–245.

CHAPTER 13

ENGAGING YOUR NETWORKS

CHAPTER OBJECTIVES

Continues the discussion of the TQEM category of *Customer/Stakeholder Focus and Satisfaction*

Illustrates how companies join hands productively with customers and stakeholders to address EHS issues of mutual concern

Provides guidelines for value-added partnering

DESIGNING IN SATISFACTION THROUGH SUPPLY CHAIN PARTNERSHIPS

The productivity of business travelers is often suspended by circumstances. Stranded on runways by inclement weather or faulty equipment, business passengers swap small talk about home base and job interests. On one such trip, I learned my seatmate was with Ryder: "The company with the yellow rental trucks you see everywhere. Consumer rentals are only about 5% of our business," he added. "I'm really in the logistics end of the business. We work with Saturn, Xerox, Chrysler, and a lot of other large manufacturers" (Fortune, 1994). I began to listen more closely. Transportation is an enormous consumer of time, energy, and materials. And while sound business performance and productivity tools like Just-in-Time (JIT) are the primary drivers to meet the demands of a highly volatile marketplace, doing all this *in the right way* also benefits environmental quality. And this was at the bottom of my interest in Robert Dawson's story.

Dawson explained that the transportation sector was once viewed from a job-shop perspective as a simple vehicle to move goods between suppliers and customers. Today, the lines between customer, supplier, and service providers have blurred as partnerships have developed. Relationships, in some cases, are even dominated by service providers with far greater expertise. While industrial ecologists were just beginning to apply life-cycle analysis tools to the product cycle, market forces and the need for logistical systems that would meet real-world needs propelled technology and supplier partnerships forward. Customer requirements (including EHS needs) were designed into the service and supply chain through such alliances, and customer satisfaction was secured.

Today, through these transformed relationships, Ryder has grown to be the largest logistics management company in the United States. While much of their early learning came from the Japanese (Ryder has worked closely with Toyota), their challenge in the States was to bridge distances orders of magnitude greater than in Japan, while meeting customer needs for JIT delivery schedules. The payback from streamlining redundant supply chain activities was enormous, in terms of time, inventory, energy, materials, and human resource savings.

The redesign process didn't stop, however, with the distribution and warehousing systems themselves, but included handling and distribution equipment and packaging. Customized equipment, trailers, and packaging were designed. Returnable packaging, often made of materials such as steel, aluminum, and plastic, has been used in the automotive industry for decades to protect the quality of supplies, and is back-hauled to suppliers for reuse. But the packaging and trailers themselves are now designed to become an integral part of the production process itself, in many instances moving right to the production line where parts are removed directly into the assembly process.

Customer contract requirements in many cases encourage both good business practices and conservation practices, such as supporting programs for recyclable packaging. The customer may also specify that it will pay for fuel based on a specific miles per gallon target. This drives transportation companies toward greater efficiencies, both in vehicle road miles and in design. To accomplish the latter, Ryder works with its own supply chain to drive the development of vehicles that are aerodynamically configured, as well as of engines that are more fuel efficient, including exploring the use of alternative fuels. By meeting the need of logistics firms like Ryder for more efficient vehicles, the automakers are in fact helping themselves by driving down the costs required to move their own vehicles, parts, and other components to assembly plants and to market.

Ryder's honeymoon with the automotive industry is only beginning. Invited in at the start of planning for the new Saturn assembly plant in Spring Hill, Tennessee, Ryder had the opportunity to partner with Saturn and its suppliers in designing a supply chain that extended from supplier to factory to showroom floor. Over $100 million was invested in equipment alone. Performance metrics were set at the beginning, including for example, the percentage of suppliers that use returnable packaging. Other environmental metrics were used. Now qualified as a sole supplier after its initial contract, Ryder will become an "evergreen" supplier if it continues to measure up and satisfy this major customer. One indicator is the fact that over a four year period, the production line was only stopped once—for 18 minutes—due to a delivery glitch.

Reflecting on Robert Dawson's story reminded me of other customer/supplier success stories that also bear on environmental gains. The rail industry has also worked productively with manufacturers. After long negotiations, an agreement was recently concluded among the Big Three and major rail companies to use common railcar tie-downs for auto and truck shipments, thus reducing overall shipping distances, energy use, and increasing productivity.

Supermarkets have similarly begun to find value in more efficient movement of materials using the same kinds of strategies for inventory management, warehousing, packaging, and routing. In fact, they have been rapidly playing catch-up with mass merchandisers such as Wal-Mart, who play the logistics game brilliantly. Although the environmental benefits of their strategies have not been quantified using a life-cycle approach, Mike Lloyd of Wegmans Food Markets in Rochester, New York, was quick to list a large number of areas where energy and materials are saved by minimizing:

- Movement of materials into and within warehouses (e.g., decreased use of electric automated equipment)
- The number of warehouses constructed (decreased materials consumption, energy use)
- The number of warehouse installations in operation (decreased energy consumption for heating, lighting, other operations)
- The number of transportation links and miles driven (decreased numbers of vehicles built, used, repaired, maintained; decreased fuel consumption)
- Road wear, and impact on congestion (less fuel wasted in traffic jams/slowdowns)
- Overall inventory requirements (decreased material, energy use)
- Packaging materials (decreased materials, energy use)

From both the retailer's and the logistics firm's perspectives, there was consensus on two points:

- Business efficiencies often translate directly into environmental benefits (recall the early introduction of recovery and reuse strategies by many manufacturers early in the twentieth century, long before environment was an issue).
- Partnerships among manufacturers, retailers, and transportation businesses are the only effective way to guarantee that satisfaction extends fully throughout the customer/supplier chain.

Building on this knowledge, further environmental gains could be made by applying LCA tools to this complex chain to determine how to optimize business and environmental benefits, by mobilizing the entire supply chain and its powerful partnerships. In my view, Wegmans commitment statement on customer/stakeholder involvement and partnership sums this up neatly:

> There are no simple solutions to the problems we encounter; no one person or group can ever hope to have all the answers. For this reason, we must work closely with our customers, employees, and suppliers to make the decisions which will lead us toward a brighter tomorrow. Only by working together and striving to continuously improve the way we work can we hope to provide a better world for future generations. *Wegmans Environmental Scrapbook, 1994*

The environmental aspects of logistics are taken into account by the U.S. Department of Energy's (DOE's) programs, which coordinate packaging, packing development, training, regulatory compliance and assessment, as well as tracking systems. DOE also uses communications equipment and an upgraded satellite positioning and reporting system to track its shipments. The scale of Department of Defense logistics systems dwarfs any other such application. Their "Integrated Logistics Support" system was developed in partnership with their contractors for use at very large facilities. Nevertheless it can be adapted to large industrial applications, such as, for example, the design of multisectoral industrial complexes where the coordinated movement of inputs, outputs, by-products, waste recycling, and treatment will lead to economically and environmentally sound operations (13-1, 13-2).

PUBLIC AND PRIVATE PARTNERSHIPS

Part of the charm of many European cities is the way that waterways are beautified and made accessible to visitors. Parks, gardens, restaurants, and boathouses welcome both tourists and residents. Public and business coffers alike benefit from this dual recreational and commercial use. Prime waterfront space in many U.S. cities, in contrast, often consists of long-forgotten industrial complexes, left behind as suburban sprawl drew investments away from city centers to new "greenfield" sites. The costs to society are enormous; consider the expense of constructing new infrastructure to service outlying areas, and of moving people over ever longer distances to reach new workplaces. Consider increased energy outlays for transportation alone; think of lost jobs and a declining urban tax base.

The revitalization of cities is tightly interwoven with the coupled issue of "brownfield" development. How will we restore these vacated industrial properties with varying degrees of contamination to productive public use? The barriers to redevelopment are many: (1) financing the costs of demolition and new construction; (2) complex regulations imposed by agencies whose jurisdictions overlap; (3) conflicting regulatory requirements; (4) lack of clarity around cleanup standards; (5) costs of remediating soil and groundwater to pristine conditions; (6) unrealistic public expectations and fears; (7) and a lack of sound regional planning.

BASF's South Works property, an 84-acre site located downriver from the City of Detroit, was a case in point. Built in 1895, the site was ready for retirement after nearly a century of steel making, ship building, and a variety of chemical operations. Its phaseout began in 1980. Site investigations during demolition revealed the presence of subsurface contamination, and BASF began groundwater extraction activities as a part of the facility's decommissioning. Recognizing the site's prime waterfront location, the City of Wyandotte expressed interest in its reuse as a part of its revitalization program. This then set the stage for a remarkable stakeholder partnership beginning in 1988, that was to productively link business, municipal, regulatory, and public interests even beyond its completion in early 1996.

Before the project began, BASF recognized the potential liability associated with ground contaminants and initiated a comprehensive risk assessment study to ensure appropriate land use at the site, funding over 90,000 analyses of soil and groundwater. The study incorporated population and exposure assumptions drawn from the city's zoning classes, and was also based on procedures and guidelines specified by the state agency and the EPA. With this information, the City of Wyandotte and BASF began work together on a site redevelopment plan, concentrating on recreational uses. Areas with the highest levels of contamination were to be further isolated by paving or placement of additional soil.

A broad-based task force, representing local residents, local and state government, and BASF, was formed to develop recommendations for redevelopment. The outcome was a plan that included a rowing club facility, amphitheater, riverfront walkway, hiking trails, "green space," and a nine-hole golf course. To implement the plan, BASF and the City of Wyandotte signed a lease agreement that preserves BASF ownership of the property and ultimate responsibility for the development activities (in order to ensure its compliance with regulatory and risk assessment study requirements). The company also donated $2 million for park development, and the State itself awarded $1.5 million in grants to the City. The site was formally dedicated in 1995 by Governor John Engler. BASF summed up the secret to the project's success:

> This project illustrates that brownfield redevelopment for the benefit of the community can be accomplished when a diverse set of stakeholders form partnerships and share a common goal of property use enhancement. . . .[T]o overcome some of the challenges to brownfield redevelopment projects. . .bring all the stakeholders together early in the project, foster partnerships, and keep the lines of communication open throughout the process.

The project also identified a number of areas for future cooperation between regulators and business. These include the development of cleanup criteria that take into account future land use; the concept of voluntary cleanup initiated by business, where regulatory oversight is minimal; the use of financial incentives or equalizers for individuals or corporations that purchase and develop brownfield sites so that their redevelopment is more competitive with greenfield sites, and finally, the elimination of multiple sets of cleanup standards arising from state and federal agency jurisdictions.

Ciba Geigy has also learned from its experience in managing over 100 cleanup sites at its facilities throughout the United States (Wise, 1995). Four regional teams were created to interact with the regulatory community and public in a more structured way than in the past. The teams identified and eventually overcame a number of traditional mind-sets that were barriers to effective communication, learning that:

- Regulatory agencies are not always adversarial.
- The public is not uninformed on "good science."
- Technically trained staff are not the only ones qualified to make intelligent decisions.
- Top management does not always have all the strategic knowledge.
- The value of an individual's ideas is often independent of his/her title and position.

The company also learned that a mixture of skills were needed to bring projects to completion, including technical, customer and public relations, and general business skills. As a result of the teams' highly structured approach, as well as their willingness to work with regulators and the public, many sites have moved forward into the design and construction phase, while others have moved successfully into the settlement mode.

ACADEMIC/BUSINESS PARTNERSHIPS ON MANAGEMENT EDUCATION

Prior to 1987, courses on environmental management were virtually nonexistent in U.S. business schools. By 1993, about 50 schools had remedied this gap, propelled forward by both the business community and government. The first serious move in this direction was taken by a joint business/advocacy group in the late 1980s, the National Wildlife Federation/Corporate Conservation Council, which included a number of prominent business leaders from companies such as AT&T, Dow Chemical, DuPont, Johnson & Johnson, Monsanto, USX, and Waste Management.

The Council's outreach activities were initiated in 1988 to develop pilot courses in environmental management for graduate and undergraduate business school students. Participating schools (Brown University, Loyola of New Orleans, and the University of Minnesota) have since offered these courses to several hundred business school students, and have also shared resource materials with faculty from a number of other countries.

Founded in 1990 with joint support from government and business (EPA, Department of Energy, AT&T, and the Rockefeller Brothers Fund), the Management Institute for Environment and Business (MEB) provides infrastructure support for university-based environmental education. Today, MEB partners with a number of leading business schools on environmental education, including Carnegie-Mellon, Duke, Indiana, Michigan, Monterrey Tech (Mexico), Northwestern, Stanford, Texas, Virginia, and Yale. Case studies and other resource materials developed through these arrangements are being integrated into basic business courses at these and other schools (Chapter 16 describes MEB and Carnegie-Mellon's case study focused on use of TQEM.)

Tufts University's Greening of Industry program links together a large international academic network that recently has begun to expand its interactions with the business community. One of the objectives of its ambitious ten-year cycle of conferences and workshops is to foster the integration of issues such as "clean technology," environmental cost accounting, and sustainability into the academic research agenda.

In 1995, MEB itself published a collection of case studies documenting partnerships on environmental and natural resource issues as diverse as ozone layer protection, waterfowl management, urban growth management, wastewater treatment, pollution prevention, and demand side management (Long and Arnold, 1995).

GUIDELINES FOR VALUE-ADDED PARTNERING

Perhaps your organization has been involved in partnership arrangements such as collaborations with local civic organizations or joint R&D initiatives. It is important to review their relevance during strategic planning to determine the extent to which they add value to the organization. The steps involved in this process should include the following (the framework presented below is consistent with the now-familiar Deming P–D–C–A cycle):

1. *Identify all your existing partnership activities and initiatives.* Characterize them, including participating organizations, objectives, status, and accomplishments relative to targets. These can include, for example, local

community-based projects; R&D jointly sponsored by academics, government, and/or business; joint projects or initiatives with environmental advocacy or public interest groups; or joint business ventures.

2. *Evaluate them to determine how well they support your current strategic direction.* Compare their objectives with those in your organization's strategic plan, including how well they are aligned, the extent to which they address your organization's key risks, and how well they match your organization's key priorities. (If they do not, determine also how midcourse corrections might be made.)

3. *Compare the resources required to support these initiatives with those assigned to the organization's other key priorities.* Include human, financial, and technical resource commitments.

4. *Estimate the added value their success would represent in terms of risks reduced, and benefits gained for the organization, as well as benefits to the environment.* Estimate also their likelihood of success.

5. *Take stock of your progress* Identify what is working as well as what you wouldn't do again the same way. What should you stop doing?

6. *Examine your existing EHS strategies and determine where else a partnership approach might propel you more rapidly forward.* Obviously, some up-front exploratory work must be done well before you get to the point of a full-blown plan. Often, someone will approach you with an idea that can be interjected as a potential solution to one of your key issues. Evaluate various alternative approaches, and identify those with the most favorable cost/risk/benefit profiles. Talk to insiders who have participated in similar initiatives and find out the pitfalls encountered, how they were resolved, and the benefits derived. A partnership may not always be the best way to address your particular issue.

7. *Integrate these needs into your short- and long-term strategic plans.* Allocate resources, and develop objectives and targets.

8. *Implement your partnership plan.* Create well-aligned action plans for implementation including timelines, responsibilities, and success measures. Communicate these commitments throughout the organization.

9. *Review and measure progress.* Communicate results to management and to other levels of the organization. Develop an external communications strategy. Determine benefits to the organization as well as to the environment.

10. *Determine where the program is falling short.* Gain commitment to make needed course corrections.

11. *Incorporate your learnings from this process into the next round of strategic planning.* Make improvements in your plan as needed.

Obviously, partnering is not a stand-alone activity. It is one of a number of potential strategic vehicles that organizations can use to address issues of key concern to their own and their external constituencies.

ISO 14001 on Stakeholders and Interested Parties

The international community engaged in the ISO 14000 process elected to use the term "interested parties" rather than "stakeholders." The definition given in ISO 14001 is "individuals or groups concerned with or affected by the environmental performance of an organization."

The Introduction to this document acknowledges that "interested parties" continue to be concerned about environmental issues, including the topic of sustainable development, and that their concerns can be addressed by business in a systematic way, through a management system that considers their needs as well as those of society. The Introduction also points out that organizations themselves can benefit from this systematic approach, by demonstrating that they have successfully implemented ISO 14001. Part of that systematic approach includes considering "the views of interested parties" when setting and reviewing objectives. It also includes setting up procedures to receive, document, and respond to "relevant communication from external interested parties." The Annex to the standard elaborates on how this might be done, including creating a dialogue with interested parties and responding to them as appropriate, noting that this is particularly critical in the case of emergency planning.

The Annex to the standard also cautions organizations to make their environmental policy clear enough so that it can be readily understood by internal as well as external interested parties. On the topic of management review, the Annex instructs organizations to include in these reviews "concerns amongst relevant interested parties."

QUESTIONS TO ANSWER ABOUT CUSTOMER/STAKEHOLDER SATISFACTION

- What processes are in place that enable you to listen to what your customers and other interested parties have to say about EHS issues/concerns?
- How well do you anticipate their needs?
- What measures do you have in place to determine their satisfaction with your performance?
- Are you recognized externally by the public for your EHS performance?
- How well do you network and partner with external organizations?
- Do these partnerships support your strategic EHS objectives?

ADDITIONAL READINGS

O'Dea, Katherine and Gregg Freeman. 1995. "Environmental Logistics Engineering: A New Approach to Industrial Ecology." *Total Quality Environmental Management* 4: 73–85.

CHAPTER 14

USING BENCHMARKING TO IMPROVE YOUR PERFORMANCE

CHAPTER OBJECTIVES

Introduces the benchmarking process

Provides guidelines for benchmarking

THE BENCHMARKING PROCESS

Once you have successfully implemented your TQEM program, and have evidence that your program is in the maturing phase (Matrix cells 7–10), you may be ready for the challenge of benchmarking. Let's first define this activity, then describe some of its key characteristics.

> Benchmarking is the search for best practices that will lead to superior performance. *Camp, (1989)*

The term originated from a land surveyors' practice of establishing a reference point for subsequent measurements, and is used today to describe the rigorous process described below. Many use the term to describe a variety of intelligence-gathering activities about peer and competitor practices and trends. Here are a few general statements and guidelines that may help you decide if you are ready to devote your energy and resources to the more formalized process to improve your environmental performance. (Additional references are found at the end of this book.)

1. *Benchmarking is a labor intensive process.* Don't begin unless management is solidly behind you, and is willing to commit the needed resources to the process both before and after the fact.

2. *Benchmarking should be used at a mature rather than early stage in a Quality-based program.* At this point, it is easier to target areas where improvements will add the highest value.

3. *Benchmarking is not a shot in the dark.* Instead it is a carefully aimed study. You should design a narrowly focused exercise designed to uncover best-in-class practices of leaders.

4. *Benchmarking is not an end in itself.* It is one of many tools that allow you to continuously improve your operations and remain competitive. It is also not a one-time commitment but an ongoing requirement, since a benchmark, or best-in-class practice, does not remain fixed, but changes with time.

5. *Benchmarking can be used to create incremental improvements.* This includes improvements in your products, processes, or services. But benchmarking can also be the start of a major transformation in the way that you do business when you uncover major differences between your own practices and those that are best-in-class—those that require you to leapfrog your competitors.

6. *Benchmarking is useful for both internal and external partners.* Begin with internal partners to get experience, then branch out to competitors and others inside and outside your sector.

7. *Benchmark findings often have to be creatively adapted before they can be most effectively used.* In some cases, their very discovery will be both a combination of luck and insight.

8. *Benchmarking should not be an isolated process.* It is only one of many tools used to gather key environmental data for decision-making. Whatever data is gathered should be shared and integrated, both into the day-to-day improvement process and into strategic planning.

9. *The benchmarking process itself continues to improve.* This occurs as more companies explore its use. So be prepared to adapt the process to your own design.

Getting Started on Benchmarking

This book groups the formal stages in benchmarking into the following areas: commitment, planning, collection and analysis of data, implementation of change, and review of effectiveness. The steps you will take include, for example:

- Gaining commitment to benchmarking as a legitimate and desirable tool for improvement
- Selecting a team
- Defining a project plan and objectives

- Identifying what needs to be benchmarked
- Selecting the right partners and defining how to collect data
- Collecting and analyzing data
- Determining your performance gaps
- Creating objectives to improve your practices
- Applying (implementing) what was learned
- Assessing progress
- Reinitiating the benchmarking cycle

Let's look at some of these steps with particular emphasis on a few case studies drawn from the environmental area.

Identifying Benchmarking Areas

Benchmarking should be focused, not general in nature. Some have described it at as a rifle shot, rather than a fishing expedition where everyone "flounders" around. To determine where to begin, you might start at a generalized level, then become increasingly more specific, considering such elements as:

- Your mission (i.e., identify its deliverables, including products)
- Factors responsible for customer/stakeholder satisfaction
- Key issues or problems associated with a particular operation or product
- Areas or operations with the greatest costs, or where regulations are the most demanding
- Areas where competitive pressures are the greatest
- Existing performance metrics

You might also take a strategic approach, focusing on the three C's introduced in earlier sections of this book (Customers/Stakeholders, Competitors, Capabilities).

You should be aware that some areas are easier to benchmark than others (e.g., areas that are not particularly sensitive or confidential).

Digital Equipment Corporation's list of factors it considers important in selecting areas to be benchmarked includes (Kristof, 1992):

- Group problem areas
- Cost and productivity goals
- Improvements in products or functions
- Improvements in industry "standards"
- Requirements of new external standards
- Highest impact areas
- Factors critical to the success of the business

Environmental benchmarking has been applied in a number of areas, for example:

- Digital's Corporate Strategic Waste Management department determined that it needed an environmentally sound method to dispose of thousands of used CRT's that were being warehoused by the company, and benchmarked with other companies to determine best-in-class practices.
- Independent benchmarking studies were initiated by Weyerhaeuser and Browning-Ferris to identify best-in-class environmental management practices.
- Intel and AT&T selected the area of pollution prevention for benchmarking (Klafter, 1992, Klafter et al., 1993).
- Intel's facility in Oregon was one of six manufacturing sites selected nationwide as Best-in-Class in a pollution prevention benchmarking exercise.
- Texas Instruments and Martin Marietta benchmarked their approach to ethics programs (Skooglund, 1993).

Identifying Benchmark Partners

How do you begin to create such as list? Clearly, your benchmarking partners should include those identified as being Best-in-Class practices in a given area. Those experienced in benchmarking will tell you the best starting point is through networking with peers, customers, suppliers, and process experts. Information can also be gleaned from trade association and other publications, reference materials, library literature searches, conference proceedings, annual reports, environmental reports, and lists of environmental award winners. Other objective data should also be considered, such as emissions reductions, recycling programs, resources invested in environmental improvement projects, and so on.

Certain consulting companies have databases of companies and best practices, such as Arthur Andersen. A Canadian consulting firm's 1993 report lists companies that excel in the following areas:

Pollution prevention alliances	McDonald's Restaurants and EDF, packaging materials Loblaw's and Pollution Probe, "green" products
Compliance and emergency response procedures,	Chemical companies along St. Clair River, Sarnia, Ontario (members of Lambton Industrial Society cooperative)
Emission reduction	Dow Canada/Sarnia facility, River Separation Project
Waste reduction targets	Quaker Oats, food processing waste minimization Bell Canada, office recycling programs

Procurement policies	B&Q (do-it-yourself retailer), environmental practices questionnaire for suppliers Home Depot, documentation by suppliers of green product claims
Tracking and reporting	Noranda Minerals, annual environmental report

An AT&T and Intel study of pollution prevention practices based partner selection on the track record, reputation, and participants' own evaluation of the maturity of their programs in this area (Klafter, 1992, Klafter et al., 1993). The partners in this study included Dow Chemical, DuPont, Xerox, 3M, and H.B. Fuller.

In some cases, selection criteria will be more specific, for example, size, geographic location, customer base, types of equipment used, or regulatory overlap. A benchmarking study on waste minimization of photographic waste streams initiated by the Department of Energy drew in as partners both NASA and Kodak, each with its own expertise and needs (Levin, 1994). The DOE selection process was quite specific in its requirements, looking at size of staff associated with operations, diversity of operations, waste minimization efforts in place, best management practices, and willingness to share data.

Benchmarking partners can be selected internally, as well as externally. In some cases, you will want to move beyond your own industry sector when you benchmark functions that are common to all. This would apply to many aspects of environmental management practices, such as corporate environmental policy, environmental information management systems, and customer/stakeholder interactions.

Collecting Data

Although your first inclination may be to schedule site visits, this should be postponed until sufficient data has been gathered from other published sources, as described above. Then prepare your team for a site visit by drawing up an inclusive and highly organized list of questions and discussion topics. If possible, have benchmarking partners complete the material ahead of time, then review the results on site. Stay alert for areas or items you may have missed, or for observations that may apply in totally different areas (serendipity applies, as usual). Reinforce your impressions by recapping highlights at the end of each session, and have the team meet in the evenings as well as immediately on return to your facility to be certain of data accuracy.

Analysis

During the analysis phase, the team will review the benchmarking data; they may also reorganize it to make interpretation easier. It is important to complete this analysis soon after the visit to keep memories sharp as to both recorded data and the team's impressions, which may lead to more refined follow-up with benchmark partners. In the case of the AT&T and Intel benchmarking study, the team actually made several passes at organizing the data for subsequent use, and this contributed to the way in which the data was profitably used for subsequent improvements. In general, the results of the exercise will reinforce that Best-in-Class partners as well as practices were identified through preliminary work. The exercise should reveal to participants the most innovative, cost-effective, and strategic approaches in use. Some elements identified by the study may be irrelevant or of low priority. In other cases, there will be surprises. For example, when Digital examined the current practices of industry leaders in the area of CRT disposal, no Best-in-Class process was found.

Determining Performance Gaps

Once the benchmarking team has finished gathering and analyzing benchmark data, it is time for participants to critically examine their own performance. In some cases, "gap analysis" will reveal that a company is already Best-in-Class with respect to its practices in a particular area. Such a company should not rest on its laurels but recognize that competitors committed to continuous improvement (and greater market share) will not remain static.

Companies that have identified performance gaps should carefully consider the need to improve their position either by matching or "leapfrogging" competitors. Each case must be considered on its own merits, considering the resources required to close gaps, and the strategic value to the organization.

USING BENCHMARK RESULTS TO IMPROVE MANAGEMENT AND PERFORMANCE

Benchmarking is not an end in itself, but only one of many inputs to planning. The results of a benchmarking study should therefore be considered along with other competing short- and long-term priorities, and fully mainstreamed into activities such as R&D and strategic planning. This should prevent creating a bureaucracy to deal with benchmarking issues, including separate plans and resource commitments. If benchmarking is designed to create value, the priorities it generates should be able to compete with other priorities.

Similarly, a review of the effectiveness of benchmarking should not be conducted in isolation, but integrated and evaluated along with other corporate or site performance measures.

Passing on Your Knowledge about the Benchmarking Process

The skills that the benchmarking team has learned are important to the organization. Thus it is important to document how the process was organized

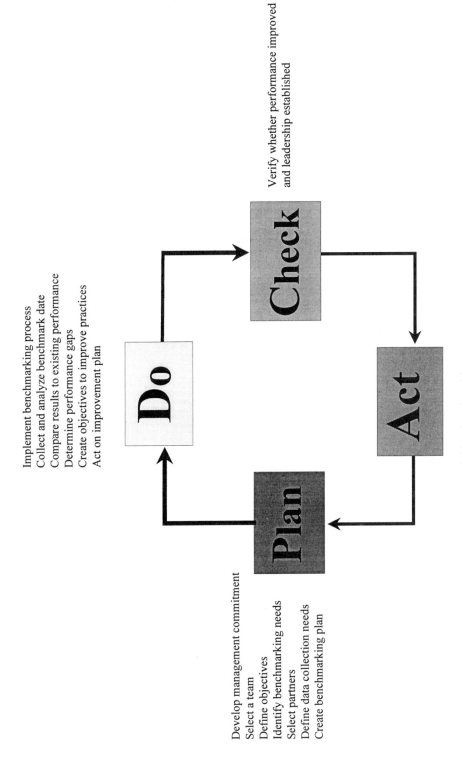

Verify whether performance improved
and leadership established

Check

Do

Implement benchmarking process
Collect and analyze benchmark date
Compare results to existing performance
Determine performance gaps
Create objectives to improve practices
Act on improvement plan

Act

Reinitiate benchmarking process

Plan

Develop management commitment
Select a team
Define objectives
Identify benchmarking needs
Select partners
Define data collection needs
Create benchmarking plan

195

and implemented, and how it can be improved. Institutional memory depends on people as well as documentation; however the former seem to be far more portable. If you have learned some important lessons with respect to efficiency and effectiveness, write them down. Also, you should be prepared to train others who want to repeat the process in areas that are ripe for improvement. Mixing experienced and inexperienced individuals on the next team is also a useful way to pass on this knowledge.

ADDITIONAL READINGS

King, Peter J. and Gordon West. 1994. "Environmental Benchmarking." Environmental Management Roundtable, Government Institutes conference, Hilton Head, SC.

Watson, Gregory H. 1993. *Strategic Benchmarking.* New York: John Wiley and Sons.

CHAPTER 15

CASE VIGNETTES: TQEM SUCCESS STORIES

Previous chapters in this book introduced you in a fragmented way to the concepts of TQEM, including the seven major elements of the Baldrige management framework. The case "vignettes" presented in this chapter bring all of this together, and illustrate how a Quality-based approach works. Through these real-world examples, you should come to realize that responsible stewardship is never an accident, but the end result of systematic planning and execution, from beginning to new beginnings. Each example in this chapter should illustrate most, if not all, of the following key management elements:

- A visible commitment from management
- The integration of the organization's most critical EHS issues into the organization's strategies and improvement programs
- Effective involvement of the workforce
- A prevention focus in strategy and practice
- A focus on measurement to support decision-making and determine accomplishments
- Success, in terms of both results and recognition

HAMMER LITHOGRAPH

North America has about 80,000 printers, most of which are classified as small businesses. Because the industry is so fragmented, it is difficult to regulate. Fragmentation also makes it difficult to provide training on new pollution prevention methods and technologies. Despite this, many printers have already adapted to the need for prevention-based change. Inks have been reformulated to remove heavy metals. Alcohol and other volatile chemicals have been removed from some solutions, lowering worker exposure and emissions. The volume of waste streams has also been reduced by recycling and reusing solutions.

Hammer Lithograph, located in a small industrial park in Rochester, New York, is the largest producer of seed packets in the United States—over 200 million each year. It also makes labels for toys and for food and beverage containers. By most printing industry standards, it is a large company with its 160 employees; most employ 20 or fewer. Four family generations have run the firm since 1912, but much of its growth has come only in the last nine years. Hammer's many quality awards at least partially explain the reason for its growth.

Hart Swisher, the company's Quality Technical Coordinator, is also responsible for environmental management. Such an arrangement gives a small company an edge over its competitors, since customer specifications for quality also include environmental and health requirements. Hammer's toy and food labels, including wrappers for McDonald's Happy Meals, must meet strict requirements for heavy metal content. Their seed packets are made from recycled paper, which costs more, but customers choose to pay this premium in order to buy a "greener" product.

Like other printers, Hammer is facing increasing regulatory pressures. Its prevention-based response has been to substitute less toxic chemicals where possible. Air emissions from presses have been reduced by using less volatile chemicals; for example, petroleum naphtha was substituted for toluene, a chemical on EPA's voluntary 33/50 emission reduction list. The company expects to easily surpass EPA's 50 percent reduction goal set for 1995; its emission reductions will total nearly 90 percent.

New equipment is selected based not only on traditional customer needs, such as volume, delivery, and image quality, but also on the need to improve EHS management. A more automated press installed in 1993, for example, is equipped with automatic cleaning equipment and temperature-controlled ink rollers to allow waterless silicon plates to be used. Hammer uses aqueous-developable plates and alcohol-free fountain solutions on its other presses, thus minimizing VOC emissions. Inks are a real challenge. Many that Hammer uses tend to form a surface skin, which produces image defects when the ink is reused. Hart Swisher is experimenting with a process that mixes used and virgin inks, then filters them, to try to meet image quality specifications.

Just-in-time delivery requirements also present environmental challenges. Customers are constantly shaving suppliers' delivery times to get their product out to market faster, however, more frequent setup changes generate more cleanup wastes. Swisher's solution to this is to schedule printing runs so that ink color sequences are matched, thus minimizing changeover, cleanups, and waste volumes—both a quality and a prevention approach. Small companies like Hammer continue to be transformed by their customers' demands for performance, challenging them to be aggressive in linking operational improvements with environmental quality.

ROGER'S BODY SHOP

Auto body shops tend to be small businesses with ten or fewer employees. Most operate on a small margin, which is hard to maintain when new equipment needs, changes in time and rate requirements from insurance companies, and new environmental regulations appear. Outreach from state pollution prevention agencies and from local chambers of commerce is one route to get information to such shops on more efficient equipment and operational changes that will help them comply with EHS regulations, as well as remain viable.

Roger's Body Shop is an interesting success story. Like many youngsters, Roger Lindeman loved to work on cars; he learned the body repair business from his father, an instructor at a local trade school. Roger set up his first shop in 1961; the present one has been in its current location in Bloomington, Minnesota, since 1979. Today, it employs 55 people, and is one of the ten largest in the country. As business grew, so did the shop's wastes, which typically include scrap metal, used paint thinner, paint cans, and filters from spray booths. In 1984, Roger Lindeman decided to get serious about reducing waste. The first step was to install distilling equipment to reclaim solvents. Thinner consumption dropped dramatically, from 100 barrels a year to 3; so did costs associated with material purchases, transportation, and disposal. Since then, the shop has upgraded its processes four times to accommodate increased business, as well as improve its reclamation process.

Other changes were also made. High-volume low-pressure spray equipment was utilized, which puts 70 percent of the product on the car, significantly reducing wayward spray in the spray booth. It also cut paint use by 50 percent. Using low VOC paint with high solids content in these spray guns further reduced the volume of thinner used, and reduced emissions. Computerized mixing systems that mix paint to the exact quantity needed for each vehicle were installed. These systems track paint use as well as VOC levels (the latter information will be used to meet future air quality permit requirements). Reusable plastic paint containers were adopted in 1989; these are recyclable when no longer useful. The shop also sorts wastes such as tires, sheet metal, composite bumper materials, cardboard, and batteries for recycling and reuse by outside vendors.

While Roger Lindeman has been the driving force behind these changes, his employees have really taken ownership. Most of the improvements made are the result of their suggestions, such as installation of Freon recycling equipment a year before it was required, as well as the use of reusable paint containers. In fact the shop's basic philosophy is to anticipate future requirements, and be the leader in the field. The shop is also unusual in the level of participation by employees in outside organizations over the years, such as the local school board and a state planning commission. Ed Nelson, charged with environmental responsibilities, reviews proposed regulations and submits comments to the Minnesota Pollution Control Agency. The shop also provides tours to representatives from state environmental agencies, insurance companies, and helps other body shops that need advice on compliance and problem-solving.

Lindeman points out that the shop's investments in equipment have paid off. Material cost savings were $22,000 in 1993 alone. The shop also saved in waste disposal costs, and significantly reduced its waste volume. Thinner use was reduced by 97 percent.

Roger's Body Shop's efforts have not gone unnoticed. In 1994, the Governor of Minnesota conferred the state's Pollution Prevention award on the shop. Evidence that top management has a commitment to prevention and continuous improvement is clear from the shop's application for that award:

> A weekly walk-through by top management inside and around our property and buildings assures that existing policies are remaining in force. This enables us to head off any problems and to change any policies that can be improved upon.

WEGMANS FOOD MARKETS

During the "solid waste crisis" of the 1980s, many companies found their bottom line eroding as waste disposal costs skyrocketed. Municipal managers panicked as overflowing landfills were closed, and some states began to balk at interstate waste shipments. Retailers were particularly hard hit at rapidly growing locations, where packaging and shipping wastes began to pile up.

Wegmans Food Markets in Rochester, New York, recognized these trends and realized that reducing wastes to landfills should also equate with dollars saved, if the right solutions could be found. Expert at tracking product sales, Wegmans corporate and store managers applied that same energy to the area of solid waste. Its recycling programs began in 1970 in their meat operations with the replacement of reusable lugs for disposable meat containers and the recycling of fat and bone waste. In 1983, they began chain-wide baling of cardboard for recycling. New recycling streams were added each year, as the result of individual employee and team suggestions. Recycled materials tracked include, for example, corrugated cardboard (53 million pounds in 1994), grease and oil, bakery scrap, photo lab waste, metals, Freon, pallets, and plastic wrap. The chain was able to convince some mills to also accept waxed corrugated cardboard for recycling, once tests had been completed to demonstrate compatibility with the recycling stream. This marks the company as a national leader in this area, in convincing its supply chain to accept the blending of composite materials into waste streams where performance is not affected.

By 1994, Wegmans overall recycling reached 62 percent, in comparison with national averages of about 20 percent for other businesses. Wegmans encourages progress by publishing a report tracking recycling streams by individual stores. Peer pressure and friendly competition encourages lagging performers onward. Recognition comes in the form of awards to the top five stores, presented by a corporate vice president.

Today, a team of three manages the program and coordinates communications: Mike Lloyd, director of purchasing; Mary Ellen Burris, director of consumer affairs, who nursed the program through infancy, and Joe Marron, former store manager and present resource recovery manager. Despite their successful performance record, Marron and Lloyd agree in a spirit of continuous improvement: "We're still not there. We have a way to go."

HERMAN MILLER, INC.

Like most furniture manufacturers, Herman Miller's operations generate a wide variety of wastes—solvents used to finish fine wood surfaces, sawdust, wood, metal, plastic and fabric scrap from construction operations, pallets, and packaging materials. These wastes were traditionally landfilled or sent to hazardous waste disposal sites, but growing disposal costs and shrinking landfill space provided strong incentives to reduce these wastes through a variety of approaches. CEO Kerm Campbell's challenge to employees was to eliminate all landfilled wastes by the end of 1995. This required not only mobilizing the workforce to find alternate uses for wastes, but also also an infusion of capital into modernization of certain facilities.

One approach the company took was to upgrade its waste-to-energy facility. Although this step will cost $1.5 million, there are a number of benefits. Future landfill disposal cost savings will significantly reduce operating costs. Natural gas consumption and costs will also be lower, since the waste-to-energy system produces 10 percent of the energy used at the site. The redesign of the system also reduces the amount of ash generated by 93 percent (which also reduces landfill disposal). In total, annual overall cost savings are expected to be $200,000.

Another step the company's management made was to adopt source reduction as a strategy to eliminate wastes before they were created. For example, paint spraying typically generates air emissions as well as solid waste. The company's new subsidiary, Powder Technology, Inc., was created to convert traditional solvent-based spray systems to newer powder coating techniques. Finely ground resin is dry-sprayed onto electrically charged parts, which are then oven-heated to melt the powder into a smooth finish. This finish is much harder and more resistant to damage than solvent-based finishes, and leftover powder can be reclaimed, cleaned, and reused. This benefits the user, the manufacturer, and the environment as well.

The company also set goals to use natural resources in a sustainable way. For example, specialists in the design and development group have been working since early 1989 to find alternative woods and finishes to replace the use of wood veneers from nonsustainably managed rain forest sources. The company's famous Eames lounge chair, traditionally made from South American rosewood, will only be offered in walnut and cherry in the future, unless a sustained-yield source for rosewood is located.

In 1993, Herman Miller received the National Wildlife Federation's Environmental Achievement Award in recognition of its "exemplary private sector achievements." Some of its other awards include the President's Environmental and Conservation Challenge Award Citation, and America's Corporate Conscience Award for Environmental Responsibility from the Council on Economic Priorities.

KODAK PARK'S SYNTHETIC CHEMICALS DIVISION

Making film is as rigorous as pharmaceutical manufacture. Multiple process steps and chemical solutions are involved, and the product, as well as the process, needs to be recertified for its quality against rigorous specifications when anything is altered. The same game rules also apply to suppliers of photographic chemicals when they want to alter a manufacturing step, or a raw material used in the synthesis of those chemicals.

Much of Kodak's film is made at Kodak Park, as are many of the specialty chemicals used in film and paper manufacture. In 1990, the Synthetic Chemicals division, the largest generator of hazardous waste at the facility, began efforts to reduce the volume and toxicity of its largest waste streams. It began by prioritizing its most promising synthetic processes. A multidisciplinary team, led by a process chemist, Matthew Cook, decided to focus on a chemical hardener for gelatine. (Without hardening agents, gelatine remains, so to speak, very "Jello"-like, and can melt or wash right off the film substrate.) The synthetic process that existed at that time for hardener manufacture produced over a million pounds of solvent waste per year, 90 percent of which went to the facility's hazardous waste incinerator. The remaining 10 percent was evaporated from the manufacturing process in a highly dilute air stream during drying. After a lot of effort, the team came up with the idea of preparing the final product not as a solid powder, but as a "melt" that could be cast into blocks. The new process was a success; not only did it eliminate over a million pounds of waste, it also made a product that was a lot easier and safer to handle. And finally, it realized cost savings of over $380,000 per year. In 1995, the project and the team won the prestigious New York State Governor's Award for Pollution Prevention.

Today, the division continues to use source reduction and other options to minimize "design waste"—the pounds of waste per pound of product. This approach is time-consuming because many existing products are made infrequently and often in small quantities. In addition, any manufacturing change requires a full process safety review. Despite this, the division continues to make progress; its goals are fully supported by division management. Neil Connon, the division's EHS manager, continues to look at innovative technologies, investing capital into biological treatment in the belief that use of immobilized microbes to treat air emissions will enable the division to meet impending Clean Air Act and other regulatory requirements.

UPJOHN

Designing out process waste is a real challenge for the pharmaceutical industry. Its products are complicated to make, often the end product of many synthetic steps. They also need to be ultrapure. Processes can use as much as 30 pounds of raw materials to generate a single pound of product. Process change is not simple, however, once FDA approval has been obtained. Despite these difficulties, Upjohn has been highly successful in creating a more efficient production process for corticosteroids (which are used in anti-itch medications and in prescription products to treat skin, allergy, respiratory, and eye disorders.)

Corticosteroids are made from the humble soybean, using a process that generates a major by-product, sitosterol, which was normally landfilled. Upjohn scientists believed that sitosterol had potential as a starting material for a number of related corticosteroid products. With management support, resources were allocated to support research on improving a number of biologically based synthetic steps, as well as a number of process steps dependent on straight chemistry. The resulting process has fewer manufacturing steps, 20 percent lower production costs, and less raw material usage. Upjohn moved production to a new state-of-the-art facility with the most modern emission-control systems available today. This project was a "win-win" story for all involved.

OXYCHEM

Finding suitable replacement solvents for ozone-depleting chemicals continues to be a challenge. Solvents traditionally used by industry are highly efficient, and for years, were regarded as safe, until their effects on the ozone layer were confirmed. One popular solvent, 1,1,1-trichloroethane, is used in electronics, paint, coating, inks, electrical, sealant, aerosols, caulking, and metal cleaning applications. Replacements were needed by 1995, since its manufacture was targeted to cease in that year. Its use was also taxed in recent years, making it increasingly expensive to use.

Recognizing this, technical leaders at Occidental Chemical Corporation, a subsidiary of Occidental Petroleum, worked with users and environmental specialists to develop suitable replacements for this formerly ubiquitous solvent, and funded research on the physical and other properties of these replacement formulations. The outcome was the a new line of solvents tailored to users' needs, none of which were ozone depleters, hazardous air pollutants, or VOCs. Each solvent in this line, also by design, had superior performance characteristics in the areas of inherent stability, lower flammability, and excellent solvency. A number of positive benefits have been realized with respect to both pollution prevention and compliance with environmental regulations. For example, a major motorcycle manufacturer and a specialty paint manufacturer have both been able to meet state and federal VOC limits, while minimizing equipment expense of waterborne or ultraviolet-curable systems.

CN RAIL

Recognizing that environmental protection, as well as safety, are major ingredients in successful rail operations, the North American rail industry is involved in a number of programs designed to minimize damages and reduce injuries from rail incidents. CN Rail, which operates approximately 20,000 miles of track in Canada and the United States, is in the forefront of these efforts. Management and technical leadership, as well as cross-industry cooperation, has been a key to the success of these programs. The Association of American Railroads works with chemical producers and other shippers in conducting training sessions. In Lansing, Michigan, a training center uses industry and state agency personnel to train emergency responders. This unique training center was developed through contributions from Michigan manufacturers and the transportation industry.

An intra-industry rail task force has developed and implemented a program to identify and monitor trains carrying certain hazardous materials in order to provide special handling beyond the safeguards mandated by law. Industry-wide standards have been set for routes with concentrations of hazardous materials. The industry also has new standards for training employees. Within the industry, Grand Trunk Western Railroad pioneered a rail tank training car outfitted with several valves and fittings found on most tank cars. The car is used to train local emergency responders.

TransCAER, a national program involving shippers and manufacturers, works closely with local governments to ensure community awareness in the transportation of hazardous materials, and proper response mechanisms in the event of an incident. In 1993 and 1994, this program contacted more than 1500 public safety officials at meetings across the State of Michigan.

PART III

PRACTICAL TOOLS FOR IMPLEMENTING TQEM

CHAPTER 16

THE TQEM MATRIX AND ITS USE

BACKGROUND

Until recently, most published materials on TQEM were highly anecdotal. To fill the need for a more structured approach to implementation, the Council of Great Lakes Industries (CGLI) began the task of developing a Quality-based approach to environmental management in 1991. The original version of its TQEM Matrix was published in 1992, and a Primer on its use followed in 1993. The Matrix was revised in 1995, incorporating concepts drawn from the 1995 Malcolm Baldrige National Quality Award criteria, as well as elements of ISO 14001.

Case studies of TQEM Matrix use are underway by the Management Institute for Environment and Business (MEB) and Carnegie-Mellon University, funded by the Great Lakes Protection Fund. Business participants in the case studies include Occidental Chemical's Niagara Falls facility and Kodak Park's Utilities Division. The National Institute for Standards and Technology (NIST) also supported the project through its recruitment of two former Baldrige Examiners as participants, Nicholas Leifeld of Serigraph, and David Crowell, then of EG&G.

The matrix has also been used for benchmarking by a CGLI TQEM Benchmarking workgroup, including business representatives as well as the Air Force Combat Command. Educators have incorporated the TQEM Matrix and concepts into their programs (e.g., Canada's Great Lakes Pollution Prevention Centre, a Canada-wide training center for business and government). Schools such as Yale, DePaul, Renssalaer Polytechnic Institute, the University of Michigan, Stanford, and the State University of New York have included TQEM concepts as well as the Matrix in courses for students in business, engineering, environmental policy, and science. The Washington, D.C., Naval District put a computerized version of the TQEM Matrix on-line for its environmental self-assessments.

THE BALDRIGE FRAMEWORK

The framework for the TQEM Matrix is based on Baldrige categories and criteria. Although the Baldrige Award annually recognizes U.S. corporations that excel in Quality achievement and Quality management, the process that underlies the award can be applied globally to measure and guide continuous improvement in all business areas, including environmental management. The Baldrige Award, administered by the U.S. Department of Commerce, is designed to promote:

■ Awareness of quality as increasingly important for competitiveness
■ Understanding the requirements for Quality excellence
■ Sharing of information on successful Quality strategies and on the benefits derived from implementation of these strategies

The Quality-based approach described here was also designed to help you conform with new international environmental management system standards; thus it also incorporates concepts drawn from the ISO 14000 environmental management standards. Like TQEM, ISO 14001 depends on senior management commitment, sound information, prevention, trained and competent employees, and the systematic integration of environmental needs into strategic and business plans and programs. Thus organizations with a sound TQEM program should encounter little difficulty in implementing ISO 14001.

EXPLORING THE MATRIX

The TQEM Matrix is both an implementation guide and a self-assessment tool. It provides:

■ A building block system or a road map that serves as guide to implementing TQEM
■ An evaluation tool to identify gaps in performance and management
■ A measurement tool that allows a unit to quantify its performance and document progress
■ A benchmarking guide

Once you assess your unit against the criteria in the Matrix and determine where gaps exist, you can develop a plan to improve management and performance, using the continuous improvement process to progressively move up the Matrix to higher levels.

The Matrix builds from the ground level (cell 1) to a "sound system" (cell 5) at the midpoint of the Matrix, toward Best-in-Class performance (cell 10).

The lower level cells (cells 1–5) are the most fundamental activities, and should be implemented earliest in the life of a unit's EHS management system. Together they constitute the elements of a "sound system." Cells above the mid-point (cells 6–10) move a unit toward EHS management excellence and eventually to Best-in-Class.

Your goal should be to progress from cell 1 in the Leadership category, where you define the EHS vision of your unit, to cell 10 in the category of Customer/Stakeholder Satisfaction, where benchmarking provides evidence that you have achieved that vision. Some units will strive to achieve Best-in-Class status in all seven categories, paralleling their Quality efforts in other business areas.

The Matrix headings correspond to individual Baldrige categories. Figure 16-1 shows how these categories are related:

■ TQEM begins and ends with customers and stakeholders. Understanding their needs and expectations is essential for a unit to improve its performance.

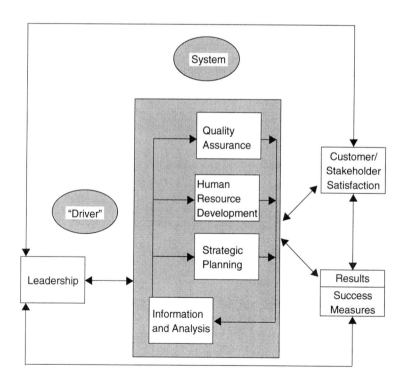

■ **FIGURE 16-1.** Quality-based management framework, adapted from Baldrige.

■ Leadership at a high level then sets the unit's course and culture.

■ Once commitment has been obtained, then information about risks, requirements, expectations, and other parameters is gathered, and options are determined.

■ Through planning, priorities are set, goals and measures developed, resources allocated, and action plans developed.

■ People, fundamental to success, are engaged and involved through an empowerment framework.

■ Quality-based processes and systems are implemented to manage and continuously improve the overall system.

■ The results obtained through such a management process should then satisfy the needs of both customers and stakeholders; benchmarking will demonstrate that the organization is Best-in-Class.

The following sections provide a brief discussion of the key criteria for each of the seven TQEM categories, as well as the type of evidence that might be presented to verify that criteria have been met. For convenience, you may want to make a copy of the Matrix and refer to it while reading the material below (Figure 16-2).

LEADERSHIP

Leadership   This category looks at senior managers' personal leadership and involvement in creating the unit's EHS expectations, and a leadership system that promotes EHS excellence in the areas of public responsibilities and corporate stewardship of natural resources.

The Matrix lists ten criteria for this category that demonstrate the effectiveness of senior manager leadership in shaping and driving the implementation of sound EHS policy and integrating it into the unit's and business' strategic plans.

Cells 1–4 of the Matrix focus inwardly on the unit's EHS management system framework. An EHS vision, principles, and values are created, documented, and communicated to the unit's workforce. That these are understood is reflected by the consistency that exists between the unit's EHS principles and the unit's strategic and action plans.

Senior managers provide leadership as role models. This is evidenced, for example, by their personal involvement in activities such as town meetings with employees, their participation in the unit's EHS council, and their adoption of EHS performance measures in their own compensation packages.

Senior managers demonstrate commitment by building an effective EHS management system that includes: (1) an effective organizational structure; (2) strategic plans and objectives that focus on both business and societal values;

(3) resource allocations that are consistent with EHS needs; (4) participation in reviews of plans and progress.

As the unit progresses upward in the Matrix, requirements move from dialogue toward more action-oriented requirements. For example, management makes environmental considerations a part of its decision-making, showing that it "walks the talk."

By level 5, the Matrix elements begin looking outward. Senior managers communicate with the public and others on EHS issues, and in some instances, create partnerships with key customers, suppliers, and other relevant parties that create value for the organization. Highly visible senior managers participate visibly and effectively in the public policy process. (For managers in smaller companies, this might mean providing public comment on proposed laws and regulations, or participating in a local environmental advisory council.)

Senior management improves its leadership effectiveness through benchmarking activities that examine the EHS leadership strategies of peers and competitors. It uses information about the perceptions and attitudes of employees as an indicator of the quality of its leadership (this is also addressed in the category on Human Resource Development).

INFORMATION AND ANALYSIS

Information and Analysis   This category looks at the effectiveness of management and use of EHS data and information to support customer/stakeholder-driven EHS performance excellence and marketplace success.

Matrix cells 1–4 in this category focus on the process of gathering EHS data and managing its delivery to users. The unit is required to determine its data and information needs, as well as the data/information quality needs of users. It gathers data/information strategically about:

- The needs, expectations, and concerns of the organization's customers and stakeholders
- Its competitors' EHS strategies
- Its own competencies and status

This includes, for example, the organization's legal, regulatory, and other requirements, such as voluntary commitments; and the EHS impacts and risks associated with its operations, products, and services.

The unit also puts processes and systems in place to assure the quality of data it collects, and designs data quality, and effective information management systems to meet users' needs for accessibility, timeliness, and other quality measures. It also gathers relevant baseline and trend data.

Level	Rank	Category: Weighing	Leadership 15%	Information & Analysis 7.5%	Strategic Planning 7.5%
Maturing	10		Benchmarking indicates unit is "Best-in-Class" in leadership and senior management commitment.	Benchmarking indicates unit is Best-in-Class in use of EHS info management strategies.	Unit's EHS strategies position unit as "Best-in-Class" in EHS stewardship.
	9		Senior management strategies for customer/ stakeholder dialog/partnership contribute to achievement of units' EHS and business objectives.	EHS cost-tracking systems in place; data widely available; life-cycle data used where appropriate to improve EHS performance.	Information on competitors' EHS strategies used to improve units' strategies and performance.
	8		Senior management proactively participates in EHS public policy process; communicates plans/ accomplishments externally as appropriate.	EHS information systems integrated with higher-level systems and used to support strategic planning.	EHS integrated into long and short-term business plans for all of unit's products, processes and services.
	7		Continuous improvement used by senior management to improve EHS management, strategies and objectives in response to changing needs.	EHS data/info analyzed and correlated with other data to support decision-making.	Strategies/objectives consistent with EHS principles and values
Growing	6		Senior management uses reward/ consequence systems to reinforce responsible EHS performance.	EHS data/info used to plan and design new products, services, processes.	EHS plans and deployment consistently aligned at all levels of the unit.
	5		Senior management communicates unit's EHS values and principles externally to key customers and other relevant parties.	EHS data/info routinely used to improve existing processes, products, services; EHS information management systems in place.	Action plans, responsibilities, timelines to implement key EHS objectives in place. Key EHS objectives communicated throughout unit.
	4		Senior management committed to unit's key strategies, plans, measures, and resource commitments. Management regularly reviews/ improves EHS management system.	External EHS data gathered, including key customers' EHS needs and interested parties views.	Long and short-term plans that include EHS objectives are reviewed and improved at least annually. Key measures include EHS measures.
	3		Senior management integrates EHS into decision-making; organizational structure contributes to realizing EHS objectives.	Processes in place to assure and improve data quality; baseline internal EHS data gathered and trends identified.	Resource allocation consistent with EHS commitments; EHS priorities integrated with other business, technical, operations priorities to create unit's strategies & goals.
	2		Senior management acts as role model & mentor. Framework to enable effective employee involvement in EHS programs in place.	EHS legal, regulatory and other internal requirements defined; key EHS risks, hazards determined.	Key EHS data on customer needs, risks, compliance, views of relevant parties, EHS impacts, used to create EHS priorities.
Beginning	1		Unit-level EHS vision, principles, values and ethics in place; communicated and understood throughout unit.	Process in place to identify EHS data needs in support of unit's key business needs; data quality needs defined.	A long-term (3-5yr) and short-term (1-2yr) planning process used that addresses EHS needs; annual operating plan includes EHS management needs.

Note: Ratings should be verifiable through available data

■ **FIGURE 16-2.** TQEM Matrix. The matrix and the self-assessment questions in Chapter 17 are also available on the diskette in the back of the book. (Reprinted with permission of CGLI.)

Management Matrix

Human Resource Development 10.0%	Process Management 15.0%	Environmental Health & Safety Results 30.0%	Customer/ Stakeholder Satisfaction 15.0%
Benchmarking indicates unit is Best-in-Class in effective involvement of workforce in EHS management	Benchmarking indicates unit is "Best-in-Class" in area of process management.	Benchmarking shows unit in "Best-in- Class" in EHS performance.	Benchmarking shows unit is "Best-in-Class" for customer stakeholder satisfaction with unit's EHS performance.
EHS needs fully integrated into unit's human resource development plan. Training/education programs for EHS staff include key business knowledge.	Continuous improvement used unit-wide for all EHS activities.	Benchmarking results used to improve EHS performance.	Customer/stakeholder-focused EHS improvements correlated with financial improvements, market share, public opinion of EHS performance.
Career opportunities providing EHS experience are widely available Employee EHS involvement improves both EHS and business performance.	Evidence exists that early inclusion of EHS considerations into product/process design cycle improves delivery, productivity, and customer/stakeholder acceptance.	Benchmarking measures identified; benchmarking initiated. External communication of EHS results to relevant external parties.	EHS data/information correlated with other data to predict future market direction opportunities.
Employees proactively initiate activities to improve EHS performance.	Processes in place to ensure suppliers and contractors meet unit's EHS requirements.	EHS improvements contribute to financial and business improvements.	EHS training/education/ communications for customers and other relevant parties improves satisfaction.
Unit's reward/recognition systems reinforce responsible EHS behavior. Measures/ trends exist for employee attitudes/ perceptions of EHS leadership and performance.	Processes in place to incorporate customer/other EHS requirements in design/development cycle for new products, processes and services.	Supplier/contractor EHS performance meets unit's requirements.	Customer/stakeholder EHS data and information managed and communicated effectively and used to improve performance and satisfaction.
Measures of EHS training effectiveness in place; employees with potential to impact EHS are competent to perform EHS responsibilities.	Prevention focus in place. Root cause analysis used for preventive/corrective action. Cross-functional EHS expertise in place. Operational controls in place.	Positive improvement trends in unit's key EHS measures.	Positive improvement trends in customer/stakeholder satisfaction.
Employees aware of risk/potential impacts of individual behavior. Employees trained to respond to emergency and other non-routine situations.	Unit-wide EHS audits used to evaluate/improve EHS management system and to determine conformance with regulatory requirements&other commitments.	EHS measures reviewed and improved at least annually.	Customer/stakeholder satisfaction measures identified.
All employees have received appropriate EHS training; employees aware of EHS compliance requirements.	EHS documentation meets regulatory and internal requirements. Records retention and document control process in place.	EHS results compared with objectives and targets and used to improve effectiveness of management systems and performance.	Effective processes used to learn, anticipate, and respond to long-term customer/stakeholder EHS requirements.
Appropriate EHS training/education programs developed and scheduled. Systems in place for periodic retraining, and for new employees.	Monitoring and measurement in place for all operations that can have significant EHS impacts. Process exists to translate EHS principles into standards/practices.	EHS results communicated internally.	Effective processes used to receive/ resolve EHS questions and concerns from customers and stakeholders; data used to anticipate and prevent problems.
EHS training/education needs identified; resources committed. EHS roles, responsibilities, authorities assigned, documented.	Monitoring and measurement needs defined. Processes in place to ensure measurement data quality; Emergency preparedness/response procedures in place.	EHS performance measures identified. Baseline data and trends collected.	Effective processes used to provide required EHS regulatory information to customers and relevant parties.

© Council of Great Lakes Industries

213

Matrix cells from level 5 upward focus on *how* information is used, and how integration and analysis at a high level add value. Information is used, for instance, to improve existing and new processes, products, or services, and to influence strategic decision-making as well as behavior and results. Resources, allocated during Strategic Planning and during other planning processes, are allocated to fill data/information gaps. In some cases, partnerships (e.g., joint R&D) will be needed to provide key scientific and technical data to guide decision-making.

Matrix cells 7 and 9 describe requirements for higher level analysis and integration of data to support decision-making. (As an example, a unit might want to examine the links between chemical exposures and health effects for individual employees, thus it might link databases for personnel assignments, chemical use, exposure data, and certain medical records. Spatial (GIS) and EHS databases might be linked in order to track groundwater contamination and cleanup, as well as manage costs.)

Integration of databases at an even higher level will allow managers, auditors, and others to access and correlate a wide variety of information, as well as to eliminate duplicate electronic records. Life-cycle assessment and full cost data, where available, can also be used to support decision-making for new products, products, or services.

Finally, benchmarking comparisons on competitors' use of EHS data and information can also be used to influence strategic direction, planning, and performance.

STRATEGIC PLANNING

Strategic Planning This category defines how the unit incorporates EHS needs and priorities into its strategic directions, and how it effectively implements plans that include EHS improvements.

Matrix cells 1–5 define requirements for EHS integration into the unit's strategic plans. EHS data and information from a wide variety of sources (e.g., regulatory needs, customer/stakeholder requirements, key risks, potential benefits) are used to create the unit's EHS priorities. In the planning process, these priorities are integrated with others from business, operational, and technical sources, and used to create strategies, goals, and objectives. The unit's "sound system" for planning also includes:

■ Allocating resources consistent with commitments
■ Defining success measures
■ Assigning responsibilities and creating action plans to deploy the unit's strategies
■ Formalizing a review process

Above level 5, the unit aligns its plans and communicates plans and objectives broadly to create consistency at all levels. It also expands its programs to include and implement the full range of expectations expressed in its EHS principles (including the "prevention of pollution," as specified in ISO 14000). It ensures that EHS considerations are integrated into all long- and short-term business plans that relate to its products, processes, and services.

Finally, it uses results from the benchmarking of competitors' EHS and business strategies to further improve its planning and its overall business performance. These efforts bring the unit to Best-in-Class performance, leading to a strengthened position on the marketplace, as well as environmental leadership.

HUMAN RESOURCE DEVELOPMENT

Human Resource Development This category defines how an organization's workforce is enabled to use its full potential in attaining the unit's EHS objectives. It also defines how an organization encourages EHS responsibility, and fosters individual and team behavior that lead to EHS and overall business improvements.

The first five Matrix cells focus on the fundamentals of a sound framework that enables the workforce to contribute productively to EHS performance improvements. Units clearly assign responsibilities and authorities, as well as provide training, knowledge, and experience that ensures awareness and competency. The workforce is aware of risks associated with their assignments, as well as potential impacts on EHS of their individual behaviors. They are trained to respond to and control emergency and other nonroutine situations.

The upper five Matrix cells focus on expanding individual and team contributions. For example, the unit encourages employees to use a prevention mindset and to proactively contribute to the design of procedures and processes, as well as products and services. Employees also contribute ideas that conserve resources (material, energy, financial, and human) and are life-cycle based.

Cells 8 and 9 further expand workforce potential through personal development plans that provide needed cross-training and experience so that EHS managers and staff gain broader appreciation of key business, financial, and operations issues, strategies, and objectives. Career development and education opportunities in EHS management are also made widely available; for example, interim EHS assignments for business/operations managers are encouraged.

Managers who have had practical experience with environmental management will have a different mind-set toward those issues, a greater ability to recognize and manage risk, and greater willingness to integrate environmental priorities into business plans.

QUALITY ASSURANCE/PROCESS MANAGEMENT

Quality Assurance/Process Management This category defines key processes that ensure the unit's regulatory, customer, and stakeholder-driven needs will be effectively met for the development and functioning of its operational processes, products, and services.

The Matrix describes a number of fundamental processes that must be in place to ensure that a unit's EHS needs are met. Cells in the lower half emphasize monitoring, measurement, and documentation. While a number of these requirements are regulatory in nature, others are internally driven (e.g., development of internal performance standards based on environmental principles, audit systems, and a prevention focus. Both preventive and corrective action processes are required, including root-cause analysis for problem-solving. Active involvement of workers in work design leads to error-proofing, minimizing EHS incidents.

Above level 5, formal processes are required to incorporate customer/stakeholder and internal requirements into the design cycle for new and existing processes, products, and services, as well as to ensure that suppliers and contractors meet the unit's EHS requirements. In some cases, this may mean training and assistance is needed.

At the "mature" phase of EHS management system development, the unit should also be able to demonstrate that the early introduction of EHS considerations into the design cycle leads to improvements in cycle time, productivity, customer/stakeholder acceptance and satisfaction, and other business improvements. It should also ensure that life-cycle and cost-risk-benefit data, where appropriate, are used to support design and modification of products, processes, and services.

EHS RESULTS

EHS Results This category looks at the organization's EHS performance in key areas associated with its products, processes, services, and EHS management systems, as well as financial performance indicators linked to these areas.

The lower five Matrix cells require that units track EHS performance measures, communicate data broadly throughout the unit, and use data to improve management systems and performance, where this is needed. The unit will schedule formal reviews to compare performance data with expectations, and determine where additional effort is needed. It will also use the process of continuous improvement to move more effectively toward its goals.

As the unit progresses upward in the Matrix, improvements in performance will become visible in each targeted area. Management will reinforce those improvements through appropriate reward and recognition systems. The unit will also measure the EHS performance of suppliers and contractors against its expectations.

Its EHS improvements will be designed to drive financial improvements. The unit will examine performance information and determine how to effectively communicate it externally to its customers and other relevant parties. As the unit reaches the highest levels of the Matrix, its performance will be comparable to other World-Class performers. Benchmarking will then be initiated with peers and competitors, and should be highly focused, rather than broad (i.e., a rifle rather than a shotgun).

CUSTOMER AND STAKEHOLDER FOCUS AND SATISFACTION

Customer and Stakeholder Focus and Satisfaction   This category defines the unit's systems for customer focus, learning, and relationship-building. It also looks at key measures such as customer/stakeholder satisfaction with the unit's EHS performance, competitors' performance in this area, and the impact of EHS considerations on the unit's market share.

The Matrix cells in this category progress from a reactive stance to a proactive and anticipatory response to the EHS needs and expectations expressed by customers and other relevant parties.

A unit first ensures that it provides regulatory information to its customers and others as required by law. It then ensures that effective processes are in place to receive and resolve any EHS concerns and questions. This information is used to proactively anticipate and prevent future problems, and to predict future trends and requirements.

The unit also measures the extent to which it has satisfied its customer/stakeholders expectations. This data is incorporated into the improvement process for its existing products, processes and services, as well as future ones. It also provides EHS training, education, and communications to its customers and other relevant stakeholders.

The unit also correlates its EHS customer/stakeholder satisfaction data with other data (e.g., technology innovations, competitors' strategies) to predict future market direction opportunities. At higher levels, its improvements in customer/stakeholder satisfaction should also be correlated with improved financial performance, market share, and public opinion.

Benchmarking then demonstrates that the unit is Best-in-Class in customer and stakeholder satisfaction with the unit's EHS performance.

SCORING THE MATRIX

How to Develop and Track Your Score

You first need to become familiar with the layout of the Matrix (Figure 16-2) before you begin the scoring process. The seven categories of the matrix are labeled as columns across the top of the Matrix. Each category or column, in turn, has ten "ranks" or cells. Notice that the numbering system for the cells is shown on the left-hand margin of the Matrix, and progresses from 1 at the bottom to 10 at the top.

The Matrix is designed to serve as a building block system that lets you systematically examine each of these categories. Some areas of your unit may currently be operating at a Beginning level (or cells 1–3) on the Matrix, while others may be more advanced units operating at a a high, or Mature level (cells 7–10), approaching World-Class or Best-in- Class performance.

The criteria described in individual Matrix cells (Baldrige calls them ranks) are the major "areas to address" in developing excellence in environmental or EHS management.

The weighting of each of the seven major categories is shown at the top. You will learn how to use weightings, if you so desire, in a later section.

The terms "approach, deployment, and results" are used in Malcolm Baldrige National Quality Award assessments. These terms are also defined later in the Glossary. In general terms, "approach" is most important at the Beginning stage of a continuous improvement journey. As you move up the Matrix into the Growing range (ranks 4–6), the cells tend to include characteristics that are more oriented to deployment. Finally, as deployment of TQEM becomes pervasive and you are in the Maturing stage (ranks 7–10), cells more frequently include results-oriented characteristics.

Since your task is to develop a score that describes the current EHS management level for your unit, it is important to recognize that you may not have all the information you need. You will thus need to involve others in this process and develop consensus on both the score as well as the improvement process to follow.

To arrive at a self-assessment score for each category in the Matrix, you may find the following process useful:

1. Define an assessment team. This team should be a cross-functional team with representatives from relevant areas such as EHS management, manufacturing, distribution, legal, information management, business units, financial services, maintenance, and R&D.

2. Provide all team members with a copy of the Matrix and the scoring instructions, and ask them to review both before the first team meeting. Ask them to consider what each cell means, in terms of "evidence" that would indicate that the cell is deployed, or in place, in the unit.

3. At the first scoring session, review the scoring instructions. Begin discussion of Matrix cell elements and develop consensus on acceptable "evidence" of deployment. More than one meeting may be needed to complete this discussion.

4. When agreement is reached, then begin the scoring process as follows. Starting in the lower left-hand corner of the Matrix (Leadership, rank 1), each team member individually rates every cell in the matrix using the following rating system:

   ■ D, or Deployed, means that the characteristic in the cell is fully in place.
   ■ P, or Partially Deployed, means that some effort has been initiated.
   ■ N, or Not Deployed, means that no activity has been initiated.

5. You should also determine a numerical score for each cell. To do this, assign scores as follows:

   ■ Cells rated D receive a score of 1.0.
   ■ Cells rated P receive a score of 0.5.
   ■ Cells rated N receive a score of 0.

   The convention recommended for scoring in this book also includes the following rule: for any column where there is an N rating, cells above the N-rated cell receive a score of 0, whether they are rated D, P, or N. This is because the Matrix is a building block system; the characteristics in lower level cells provide a sound foundation for higher level cells. (Not all organizations rigorously follow this rule.)

6. You should be able to verify the ratings you assign to each cell through information available within the unit.

7. If a particular cell in the Matrix isn't applicable, don't score the cell. Instead proceed to the next cell.

8. To determine a consensus rating for each cell, the meeting facilitator should use a consensus process. The easiest and most systematic way to handle this is to focus on only one category at a time and work your way up from rank 1 to rank 10. Also check that ratings for any similar cells in other categories are consistent. If they are not consistent, resolve any differences using the consensus process, and adjust the rating.

9. Add up the score for each category (or column).

10. Record consensus ratings (and/or scores) of individual cells on a working copy of the Matrix.

11. Repeat these steps for each category in the Matrix.

Some organizations also find a colored-dot system useful for scoring, since it provides colorful and visible evidence of where the unit's performance currently is. When the Matrix is displayed, the unit's performance is instantly apparent to those who understand the color dot system. The convention used is to assign:

- A green dot to cells that are fully deployed
- A yellow dot to cells that are partially deployed
- A red dot to cells where no activity has yet been initiated

From a distance, the presence of red dots will signal where the unit's major gaps are. This activity is highly effective in a group setting, and has been used in many workshop settings with both large and smaller organizations.

Determining an Overall Weighted Score

Now that your team has determined a score for each Matrix category, your next step is to determine the overall weighted score for the total Matrix. Using a copy of the scoring form (make a copy of Figure 16-3):

1. Enter the total score for each Matrix category in the box labeled "Total Category Score." In the sample scoring form (Figure 16-4), for example, the assessment team assigned a score of 4 to the Leadership category.
2. Multiply the score for each category by its weighting factor. Enter this result in the Weighted Category Score box for that category. In the sample scoring form, the weighting factor 15 for Leadership is multiplied by the score of 4, and the weighted score is then 60.
3. Repeat steps 1 and 2 for each of the seven categories.
4. Add the seven Weighted Category Scores to get your Total Matrix Score.
5. Date the scoring form, and save it to compare with subsequent scores.
6. To get a clear picture of how your unit stacks up, and to monitor your progress over time, plot the total score for each category next to the maximum score possible for each category on a scoring summary chart (such as in Figure 16-5).

USING THE MATRIX TO IMPLEMENT TQEM, CLOSE GAPS, AND IMPROVE PERFORMANCE

Determining your numerical score for the first time provides a baseline for future measurements. Since this self-assessment process aims at continuous improvement, you should repeat it at least annually. The difference between where your unit is performing and where you would like to be represents a gap that you need to close. If your goal is to be Best-in-Class for EHS performance, then your long-term goal should be to fully deploy every cell in all seven categories of the matrix.

Before you can begin this process, however, be sure that you have the level of commitment needed to reach your goal. In the event that top management is not fully committed to a high level of EHS leadership, some progress

Scoring Form   Date:_____

	Total Category Score	Weighting Factor	Weighted Category Score
1. Leadership	☐	X15 =	☐
2. Info. & Analysis	☐	X7.5 =	☐
3. Strategic Planning	☐	X7.5 =	☐
4. Human Resource Dev.	☐	X10 =	☐
5. QA of Env. Performance	☐	X15 =	☐
6. Environmental Results	☐	X30 =	☐
7. Customer Satisfaction	☐	X15 =	☐
Total Matrix Score			☐

Scoring Form   Date:_____

	Total Category Score	Weighting Factor	Weighted Category Score
1. Leadership	☐	X15 =	☐
2. Info. & Analysis	☐	X7.5 =	☐
3. Strategic Planning	☐	X7.5 =	☐
4. Human Resource Dev.	☐	X10 =	☐
5. QA of Env. Performance	☐	X15 =	☐
6. Environmental Results	☐	X30 =	☐
7. Customer Satisfaction	☐	X15 =	☐
Total Matrix Score			☐

■ **FIGURE 16-3.** Scoring forms for TQEM matrix.

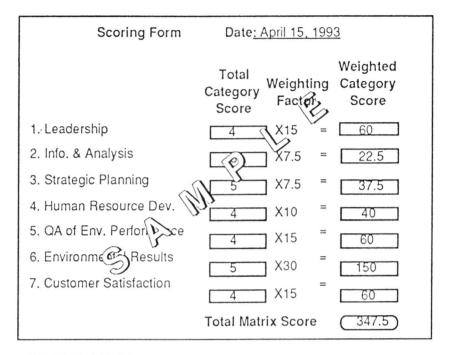

■ FIGURE 16-4. Sample completed scoring form for TQEM matrix.

can be made by engaging management at a lower level of the organization. Your goal, however, should be to win consistent support from all levels. Grassroots efforts can take you only so far. If this is the major stumbling block to your progress, review what Chapter 3 has to say about gaining greater management commitment.

When you are ready to move forward, you will need to engage the right participants. Remember the need for cross-functional involvement, and include in your team representatives from operations, EHS, and all other areas that will have an impact on your success. Recognize that the improvement process will require long-term commitment of attention and resources. Those who began the Quality journey in the mid 1980s in the United States found that five years was the norm for full implementation. If you have a Quality program in place, this should significantly shorten your start-up time for your own program. You should also remember that documenting what you do is a key activity. Both outsiders and insiders will require evidence that your program is in place.

The process described below draws from the experience of two units that used the Matrix for self-assessment and management, Occidental Chemical Corporation's Niagara Falls facility, and Kodak Park's Utilities Division. Their experience is documented in two case studies funded by the Great Lakes Protection Fund, and prepared in collaboration with the Management Institute for Environment and Business (MEB) and Carnegie Mellon University's Green Design Pro-

Initial Self-Assessment of Your Unit

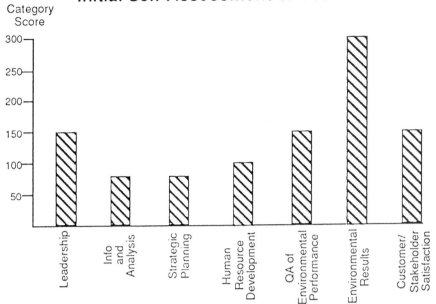

Subsequent Self-Assessment of Your Unit

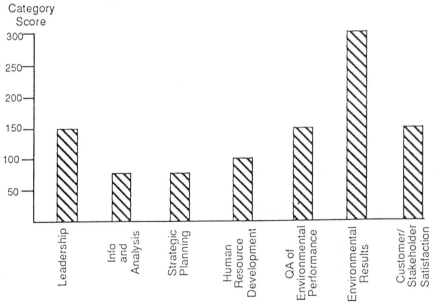

☐ Your unit's self-assessment score (plot on figure using results obtained in self-assessment).

▨ Maximum Possible Score

■ **FIGURE 16-5.** Scoring Summary Charts. (Reprinted with permission of CGLI.)

gram. Also participating in this process were two former Baldrige Examiners, Nicholas Leifeld of Serigraph, and David Crowell, formerly of EG&G.

Closing Gaps

The following process, or a variation on it, will enable your team to systematically close gaps. Remember that the Matrix is a building block system, and the lowest cells form a foundation for cells above. Therefore, this process focuses first on cells rated as "Not Deployed" in the lower areas of the Matrix, and next on "Partially Deployed" cells, before it addresses cells higher up in the Matrix.

1. First, determine who is responsible for leading the improvement effort. Make sure that some member of the original team remains involved, if possible, or have oversight.
2. Decide which category, or categories, the unit should begin working on first, and then prioritize the remaining categories. It may be necessary to address several categories at the same time, if their key gaps are closely related, or if they are equally high priorities. Alternatively, it may be important to make improvements in one category before you can address a dependent category; that is, the root cause of a deficiency may be associated with another category. For example, it may be necessary to determine the potential impacts of environmental regulations (Information and Analysis Category), before senior management becomes fully committed to allocating resources to environmental improvements (Leadership Category).
3. In the Matrix categories that the unit decides to tackle first, begin with the lowest cell rated either N or P, and develop an improvement plan that will move the unit toward deployment. You can use the Deming P–D–C–A continuous improvement cycle for this purpose. Searching out the root cause of deficiencies that underlie either an N or P rating will help the unit develop the best improvement plan.
4. Define specific obstacles to deployment and state precisely what action the unit will take to overcome them. Be certain that improvement plans include timelines, responsibilities, and method for measuring improvement.
5. Continue this process, addressing each cell rated N or P.
6. Repeat this process for each category, addressing categories in the order in which you prioritized them.

A list of questions based specifically on individual Matrix cells is given in Chapter 17. These questions, which focus on EHS management systems, can also be incorporated into the unit's internal compliance/conformance audit program.

Remember that your long-term goal should be to improve your unit's management and performance to a level consistent with its stated objectives. In many instances, this will require a significant effort in implementing improvement. Many units will find *that they do not need to create a new management system, but simply identify and correct gaps in their existing system, and bring about the cultural change that is needed for this decade and beyond.*

With time, the changes made as a result of this process should become part of the unit's culture. And, with a well-defined road map in place, the time to make significant improvements should be reduced.

CHAPTER 17

ASSESSING THE QUALITY OF YOUR TQEM PROGRAM

ASSESSMENT QUESTIONS COMPLEMENTING THE TQEM MATRIX

Many organizations routinely audit or assess conformance with legal and regulatory requirements. Some have extended this to include their EHS policies, standards, and practices, as well as other elements of their environmental management systems and processes. There is little consistency, however, in such assessments at this point.

While the elements of the ISO 14001 conformance standard provide a baseline that may be useful for management systems assessments, not all elements of a mature program may be captured. Performance and customer/stakeholder satisfaction, for example, would not be included, and these are clearly of interest to organizations that have mature programs aimed at a leadership or Best-in-Class position in all aspects of the business.

The list of self-assessment questions provided below was developed to fill the need for a more comprehensive approach. The questions were stimulated by the TQEM Matrix criteria, which are based on Baldrige areas most relevant to EHS management. But the questions also include material drawn from the ISO 14001 environmental management system conformance standard.

The questions were constructed using a yes/no format, so that a numerical score can be developed, if desired. In any case, the assessment team has much to gain by going beyond a simple yes/no response. It should require supporting data, and also ask questions that are "how" or "why"-based, in order to evaluate the unit's underlying management and operating philosophy. This probing will allow assessors to discover whether the unit's management systems are superficial and focus on a "quick fix," or are soundly based and centered on continuous improvement and a prevention ethic. They can also pinpoint key areas for improvement, and, through this, add value.

Assessors should also remember that, when they review assessment results with the unit's management and employees, they should provide positive reinforcement wherever it is clear that the management approach is sound.

TQEM SELF-ASSESSMENT QUESTIONS

Questions shown in italics relate specifically to ISO 14001 requirements.

	YES	PARTIALLY	NO

Leadership

EHS Vision, Policy, and Principles

	YES	PARTIALLY	NO
Has top management of the unit established a documented EHS vision and *policy/principles?*	☐	☐	☐
Were these developed using a consensus process, with input from lower levels of the organization as appropriate?	☐	☐	☐
Does the unit have a statement of ethical practices?	☐	☐	☐
If the unit is part of a larger organization, are its EHS vision, and policy/principles consistent with its parent organization's?	☐	☐	☐
Are the policy/principles appropriate considering the nature, scale, and EHS impacts of the unit's products, services, and activities?	☐	☐	☐
Do the unit's policy/principles include a commitment to continuous improvement?	☐	☐	☐
Do they include a commitment to comply with relevant regulations, legislation, and other external and internal requirements?	☐	☐	☐
Have the unit's EHS policy/principles been implemented?	☐	☐	☐
Are they regularly reviewed and updated?	☐	☐	☐
Have they been communicated internally?	☐	☐	☐
Are they available to the public?	☐	☐	☐

	YES	PARTIALLY	NO
Are they understood by management and other employees?	☐	☐	☐
Is understanding evaluated and used to improve both understanding and commitment?	☐	☐	☐
Do the policy/principles provide a framework for setting and reviewing objectives and targets?	☐	☐	☐
Have the unit's EHS policy/principles been translated into performance standards, goals, and action plans?	☐	☐	☐
Is there an effective organizational structure in the unit to support the EHS program?	☐	☐	☐
Is there a senior or high-level manager (or managers) who has responsibility and authority for EHS management, including the EHS management system requirements?	☐	☐	☐

Does this manager regularly report to top management on:

	YES	PARTIALLY	NO
■ *The effectiveness of the unit's EHS management system, and opportunities for improvement?*	☐	☐	☐
■ Performance against the unit's key EHS measures?	☐	☐	☐
Has senior management put an internal EHS communication process in place that extends throughout the unit?	☐	☐	☐
Is there an effective process for senior management to communicate with and respond to external customers and stakeholders on their significant EHS issues, as appropriate to the business?	☐	☐	☐
Does the unit have an annual EHS report?	☐	☐	☐
Does it have a process to deal with feedback on it?	☐	☐	☐

	YES	PARTIALLY	NO

Visible Personal Commitment

	YES	PARTIALLY	NO
Does the most senior EHS manager within the unit have ready access to, or report to, senior management (e.g., the CEO)?	☐	☐	☐
Is senior management EHS leadership an expectation?	☐	☐	☐
Does senior management demonstrate EHS leadership and serve as a leader/role model in this area?	☐	☐	☐
Does senior management communicate the unit's policy/principles to customers and other stakeholders?	☐	☐	☐
Does senior management participate in the public policy process?	☐	☐	☐
Are senior management strategies for dialogue and partnership with key customers and stakeholders reflected positively in the unit's financial performance?	☐	☐	☐

Commitment to Integration of EHS into Business Planning

	YES	PARTIALLY	NO
Has senior management approved a unit-wide plan to address its EHS issues?	☐	☐	☐
Is management committed to providing the needed resources to implement the plan?	☐	☐	☐
Is the plan integrated into the unit's overall business plan?	☐	☐	☐
Do managers at all levels use EHS considerations as an integral part of decision-making?	☐	☐	☐
Is the continuous improvement process used in EHS management?	☐	☐	☐
Is a reward/consequence system used by senior management to reinforce commitment to EHS management and performance throughout the unit?	☐	☐	☐
Is this system effective?	☐	☐	☐

YES   PARTIALLY   NO

Commitment to Framework to Empower/Enable Employees

Is there a framework in place to empower/enable employees in the area of EHS management? ☐ ☐ ☐

Are employees encouraged to communicate the unit's EHS policy/principles externally? ☐ ☐ ☐

Is there a process to determine if employees view senior management as role models and leaders with respect to EHS management? ☐ ☐ ☐

Was this information provided to senior management and used to improve their performance? ☐ ☐ ☐

Did this change employee perceptions toward senior management EHS leadership? ☐ ☐ ☐

Benchmarking

Have you benchmarked the area of EHS Leadership? ☐ ☐ ☐

Did the use of results from benchmarking help the unit improve its leadership in this area? ☐ ☐ ☐

Information and Analysis

Types of Data Collected

Is there a process in place to identify data/information and analyses needed for responsible EHS management? ☐ ☐ ☐

Does the data/information gathered include:

- *Applicable laws, regulations, and other internal commitments?* ☐ ☐ ☐
- *Compliance/conformance with laws, regulations, and other external commitments?* ☐ ☐ ☐
- *Conformance with internal unit EHS standards, policies?* ☐ ☐ ☐
- *Risks and hazards associated with the units' products, operations, and services, including their impacts on environment, health, and safety?* ☐ ☐ ☐

	YES	PARTIALLY	NO
■ Other government needs (e.g., public policy input)	☐	☐	☐
■ Shareholder and Board of Director expectations?	☐	☐	☐
■ Customer needs?	☐	☐	☐
■ Supplier and contractor needs?	☐	☐	☐
■ Community expectations?	☐	☐	☐
■ Employee issues and concerns?	☐	☐	☐
■ General public issues, perceptions?	☐	☐	☐
■ Advocacy group concerns?	☐	☐	☐
■ Industry group issues (trade, technical associations)?	☐	☐	☐
■ Internal unit needs (e.g., EHS reporting, communications)?	☐	☐	☐
■ Costs associated with EHS management?	☐	☐	☐
■ EHS training and education needs?	☐	☐	☐
■ Performance trends for selected EHS indicators?	☐	☐	☐
■ EHS assessment and audit results?	☐	☐	☐
■ Process safety review results?	☐	☐	☐
■ Competitor's EHS policies and strategies?	☐	☐	☐
■ Permit requirements and issues?	☐	☐	☐
■ Peformance data for EHS control and measurement equipment?	☐	☐	☐
■ Unit's capabilities to meet future EHS needs (e.g., technology and other expertise)?	☐	☐	☐

You can add other types of EHS information gathered in the space below:

YES **PARTIALLY** **NO**

Quality of Data/Information

Is there a process to determine EHS data users quality needs? ☐ ☐ ☐

Are these needs documented? ☐ ☐ ☐

Is there a process to ensure that EHS data collection and dissemination meet users' needs for scope, validity, accessibility, timeliness, clarity relevance, and other important parameters? ☐ ☐ ☐

Does the extent of computerization of EHS data/information meet users' needs (e.g., for accessibility, reliability)? ☐ ☐ ☐

Are EHS databases integrated with each other, where this would add value? ☐ ☐ ☐

Are EHS information management systems appropriately integrated with other systems at a higher level (e.g., with financial, quality, production)? ☐ ☐ ☐

Is there a process to anticipate and meet future EHS information management needs? ☐ ☐ ☐

Management and Use of Data/Information

Are EHS information management systems designed to facilitate internal and external EHS reporting? ☐ ☐ ☐

How Data Is Used

Is EHS data/information a key element of decision-making and planning for new products, processes, and services, and improving existing ones? ☐ ☐ ☐

Is it used to support decision-making at all levels? ☐ ☐ ☐

Is it used to continuously improve environmental management and performance, as appropriate to the unit's policy and goals? ☐ ☐ ☐

	YES	PARTIALLY	NO
Are results of risk assessments conveyed to management and other individuals involved in planning and decision-making, and used to appropriately manage risk?	☐	☐	☐
Have you identified impediments to successful data use, and methods to overcome these impediments?	☐	☐	☐
Has access to relevant EHS data/information changed behaviors of senior managers and other employees?	☐	☐	☐
Has access to EHS data contributed to employee empowerment (e.g., enabled employees to more effectively carry out their EHS responsibilities)?	☐	☐	☐
Are EHS cost-tracking systems in place?	☐	☐	☐
Is life-cycle analysis data available?	☐	☐	☐
Is it used where appropriate to improve EHS performance?	☐	☐	☐
Is there evidence that appropriate use of data contributes positively to financial performance, as well as leads to environmental or health/safety benefits?	☐	☐	☐

Benchmarking

Have you benchmarked how you collect, manage, and use EHS data/information?	☐	☐	☐
Did you use this information to improve your data management and use?	☐	☐	☐

Strategic Planning

Planning Processes

Is there a long- and short-term planning process to address EHS issues?	☐	☐	☐
Is it linked to the corporate or unit business planning process?	☐	☐	☐

	YES	PARTIALLY	NO
Does the annual operating plan (annual budget) address EHS needs, resource commitments, and an implementation framework?	☐	☐	☐
Are the unit's key EHS impacts used to create its EHS priorities?	☐	☐	☐
Are EHS issues integrated with others when resource needs are prioritized during strategic planning (e.g., does strategic planning include EHS issues/impacts and alternative solutions, including technological, as well as financial, operational, and other business requirements)?	☐	☐	☐
Are there unit-wide EHS goals and objectives?	☐	☐	☐
Are the unit's resource commitments sufficient to support its EHS plans, including the implementation of its EHS management system?	☐	☐	☐
If not, is the unit prepared to deal with the consequences?	☐	☐	☐
Do resource commitments include appropriate human resources and skills, as well as technology and financial resources?	☐	☐	☐
Are plans, goals, and resource commitments communicated throughout the unit?	☐	☐	☐
Is there a process to create consistent goals, objectives, and targets at all appropriate levels of the unit?	☐	☐	☐
Are these documented?	☐	☐	☐
Are the unit's EHS goals, objectives, and targets consistent with its EHS policies and principles?	☐	☐	☐
Are plans in place at all relevant levels that include timelines, resources, responsibilities, and authorities?	☐	☐	☐
Are these documented?	☐	☐	☐

	YES	PARTIALLY	NO
Are they reviewed and updated regularly (e.g., at least annually)?	☐	☐	☐
Are key EHS milestones established at all levels of the unit?	☐	☐	☐
Do they include a commitment to preventing pollution of the environment, as well as preventing adverse effects on safety and health?	☐	☐	☐
Does the planning process also include future EHS needs?	☐	☐	☐
Does it proactively address needs that go beyond regulatory compliance?	☐	☐	☐
Are improvement plans long-term oriented?	☐	☐	☐
Does the planning process provide sufficient short-term flexibility, ensuring that EHS considerations will be reviewed for any new project, product, or service introductions?	☐	☐	☐
Is the planning process itself continuously improved?	☐	☐	☐

Input to Planning

	YES	PARTIALLY	NO
Is customer/stakeholder EHS information used as input to the planning process?	☐	☐	☐
Is the process for this input formally documented?	☐	☐	☐

Reinforcing EHS Commitment

	YES	PARTIALLY	NO
Is there a process to reinforce/reward the integration of EHS issues into strategic planning?	☐	☐	☐
Is this process effective?	☐	☐	☐

Human Resource Development

Clear Assignment of Responsibility

	YES	PARTIALLY	NO
Are all employees aware of their EHS roles, responsibilities, and authorities?	☐	☐	☐

	YES	PARTIALLY	NO
Are EHS responsibilities documented?	☐	☐	☐
Are they effectively communicated?	☐	☐	☐
Are EHS responsibilities understood?	☐	☐	☐
Is there a process to measure and improve understanding?	☐	☐	☐
Are managers and others held accountable for EHS performance?	☐	☐	☐

Training and Education

	YES	PARTIALLY	NO
Is there a process to identify the unit's EHS training and education needs?	☐	☐	☐
Is the scope and depth of EHS training and education appropriate to the level of the unit's EHS potential external and internal EHS impacts?	☐	☐	☐
Have sufficient resources been committed to develop and deliver EHS training?	☐	☐	☐
Is training regularly reviewed and improved?	☐	☐	☐
Is there a process to measure training effectiveness?	☐	☐	☐
Is this information used to improve EHS training?	☐	☐	☐
Have all employees whose work may have a significant impact on EHS received appropriate training?	☐	☐	☐

Are procedures in place to ensure that they are aware of:

	YES	PARTIALLY	NO
■ *The need to conform with EHS laws, regulations, internal procedures, and requirements of the EHS management system?*	☐	☐	☐
■ *Significant impacts (actual or potential) of work activities, and EHS benefits of improved individual performance?*	☐	☐	☐

	YES	PARTIALLY	NO
■ *Emergency preparedness and response requirements?*	☐	☐	☐
Are employees that perform tasks that can cause significant environmental impacts competent on the basis of their education, training, and/or experience?	☐	☐	☐
Does the unit have a process to identify training needs associated with its customers and other stakeholders?	☐	☐	☐

Career Development and Integration with EHS Goals

	YES	PARTIALLY	NO
Do the unit's human resource development programs for employees support the unit's EHS as well as its business priorities?	☐	☐	☐
Do training/education programs for EHS staff also include key business knowledge?	☐	☐	☐
Are opportunities widely available for all employees in the area of EHS management?	☐	☐	☐

Employees Attitudes Toward EHS Management

	YES	PARTIALLY	NO
Are processes in place to determine employee attitudes toward EHS issues?	☐	☐	☐
Are employee attitudes and perceptions positive about unit's EHS performance?	☐	☐	☐
Are these attitudes/perceptions consistent with senior management's perceptions?	☐	☐	☐
Is information about employee perceptions communicated to senior management?	☐	☐	☐
Is this information used effectively to improve senior management's leadership in the area of EHS management?	☐	☐	☐
Do employees proactively initiate activities to improve EHS performance?	☐	☐	☐
Do employees voluntarily participate externally in EHS programs in the community and elsewhere?	☐	☐	☐

	YES	PARTIALLY	NO

Are reward/consequence systems used to reinforce employees contributions to EHS management/performance? ☐ ☐ ☐

Do employees view themselves as enabled/empowered in the area of EHS management? ☐ ☐ ☐

If not, is there a process to improve this? ☐ ☐ ☐

Process Management

QA Processes and Systems

Are monitoring and measurement needs defined? ☐ ☐ ☐

Are measurement data quality needs defined? ☐ ☐ ☐

Are internal standards in place? ☐ ☐ ☐

Are processes in place throughout the unit for effective internal EHS communications? ☐ ☐ ☐

Is the EHS management system documented, including its core elements and how these interact or interrelate? ☐ ☐ ☐

Is related documentation clearly referenced so that it can be readily found and accessed? ☐ ☐ ☐

Is documentation in place for all procedures that can affect EHS performance? ☐ ☐ ☐

Where measurements are performed by external contractors or suppliers, are processes in place to ensure that the quality of data/information generated meets the unit's specifications? ☐ ☐ ☐

Is there a documented process to determine risks and hazards associated with operations, products, and services? ☐ ☐ ☐

Are EHS objectives for new products, processes, and services documented? ☐ ☐ ☐

Are processes in place to ensure that EHS objectives are followed within operations, as well as to develop and modify new and existing products, processes, services? ☐ ☐ ☐

	YES	PARTIALLY	NO

Are effective document control procedures in place, including referencing, so that:

- ■ *Documents can be located?* ☐ ☐ ☐
- ■ *Documents are periodically reviewed, revised, and approved as required by authorized personnel?* ☐ ☐ ☐
- ■ *Current versions are available at all locations where their accessibility is essential to the effective functioning of the EHS management system?* ☐ ☐ ☐
- ■ *Obsolete documents are removed to avoid unintended use?* ☐ ☐ ☐
- ■ *Any obsolete document retained for legal and/or other purposes is so identified?* ☐ ☐ ☐

Are EHS documents legible, dated, and readily identifiable? ☐ ☐ ☐

Are they maintained in an orderly manner and retained for specified time periods? ☐ ☐ ☐

Are procedures in place defining how EHS documents are created and modified? ☐ ☐ ☐

Are procedures in place to identify, maintain, and dispose of EHS records, including training, audit, and review records? ☐ ☐ ☐

Are EHS records legible, identifiable, and traceable to the activity, product, or service involved? ☐ ☐ ☐

Are EHS records stored and maintained so that they are readily retrievable and protected against damage, deterioration, or loss? ☐ ☐ ☐

Are retention times for EHS records established and recorded? ☐ ☐ ☐

Are records maintained to show conformance with the unit's EHS management system? ☐ ☐ ☐

For processes, products, and services that can potentially have adverse EHS effects, are there documented procedures to prevent negative consequences? ☐ ☐ ☐

YES PARTIALLY NO

*Are these procedures also designed to avoid
deviations from the organization's policy,
objectives, and targets?* ☐ ☐ ☐

*Do these procedures stipulate operating
criteria?* ☐ ☐ ☐

*Are processes/activities that can have a
significant EHS impact regularly monitored
and measured, by:*

   ■ *Recording needed performance-related
    information?* ☐ ☐ ☐
   ■ *Creating operational controls?* ☐ ☐ ☐

*Is monitoring equipment suitably calibrated
and maintained?* ☐ ☐ ☐

   ■ *Are processes in place to ensure the
    precision and accuracy of EHS
    measurement systems?* ☐ ☐ ☐
   ■ *Are internal calibration standards for
    measurement systems in place?* ☐ ☐ ☐

*Are records for calibration and maintenance
retained according to the unit's procedures?* ☐ ☐ ☐

*Have you created procedures relevant to the
EHS aspects of goods and services purchased
from outside contractors and suppliers?* ☐ ☐ ☐

*Have relevant EHS procedures also been
communicated to contractors and suppliers?* ☐ ☐ ☐

*Is a process in place to identify and respond to
potential accident and emergency situations,
and to prevent and mitigate the EHS impacts
associated with them?* ☐ ☐ ☐

*Is a process in place to review and improve
these procedures, including using information
derived from accidents and emergency
situations?* ☐ ☐ ☐

Are these procedures periodically tested? ☐ ☐ ☐

Is there a prevention focus throughout the unit? ☐ ☐ ☐

Is pollution prevention an established practice? ☐ ☐ ☐

	YES	PARTIALLY	NO
Is there a documented procedure for unit-wide audit or assessments of conformance with applicable laws and regulations?	☐	☐	☐
Does it cover the unit's principles, practices, standards, commitments (e.g., goals/targets) and environmental management system requirements?	☐	☐	☐
Is the audit program, including its schedule, appropriately designed, based on the nature of the unit's activities, as well as results of past audits/assessments?	☐	☐	☐
Do audit/assessment procedures cover scope, frequency, and methods, as well as responsibilites and requirements for conducting audits and reporting results?	☐	☐	☐
Are internal self-assessments in place in all units?	☐	☐	☐
Are third party assessments used to independently verify conformance with the unit's management system requirements, and compliance with external requirements?	☐	☐	☐
Is information from all assessments communicated and reviewed by management and others who need it?	☐	☐	☐
Is it used to improve EHS management and performance?	☐	☐	☐

Corrective and Preventive Action

	YES	PARTIALLY	NO
Are documented procedures in place to effectively address nonconformances?	☐	☐	☐
Are responsibilities and authorities for this defined?	☐	☐	☐
Do the procedures include actions to mitigate impacts associated with nonconformances?	☐	☐	☐
Does they include corrective as well as preventive action?	☐	☐	☐

	YES	PARTIALLY	NO
Is root-cause analysis used to ensure that corrective action prevents recurrence of existing problems or occurrence of new ones?	☐	☐	☐
Are changes in procedures required by corrective/ preventive action documented and effectively implemented?	☐	☐	☐
Do quantitative measures extend throughout the entire unit?	☐	☐	☐
Is cross-functional expertise, including EHS expertise, used to develop or modify products, processes, and services?	☐	☐	☐
Is there an effective EHS review/approval process in place to develop new products, processes, and services, or to modify existing ones?	☐	☐	☐
Is the continuous improvement approach in place for EHS management at all levels of the unit?	☐	☐	☐
Is there a formal process to ensure that input from all relevant customer/stakeholders is collected, communicated, and used to improve EHS performance?	☐	☐	☐

Management Review

	YES	PARTIALLY	NO
Does top management periodically review the EHS management system to ensure its suitability, adequacy, and effectiveness?	☐	☐	☐
Is sufficient information provided to allow management to carry out this evaluation?	☐	☐	☐
Is this review documented?	☐	☐	☐
Does the review process also include EHS policy, objectives, and the EHS management systems, considering audit/assessment results, changing circumstances affecting the business, and the unit's commitment to continuous improvement?	☐	☐	☐

	YES	PARTIALLY	NO

Benchmarking

	YES	PARTIALLY	NO
Was any benchmarking done in the area of EHS process management?	☐	☐	☐
Were benchmarking results used to improve EHS process management?	☐	☐	☐

Results

Establishing and Communicating Measures and Results

	YES	PARTIALLY	NO
Is there a process in place to create measures for EHS performance?	☐	☐	☐
Are measures in place for EHS performance?	☐	☐	☐
Are these measures updated at least annually?	☐	☐	☐
Was input from customers/stakeholders used to select and update measures?	☐	☐	☐
Have baselines been established for EHS measures?	☐	☐	☐
Are trends positive for EHS measures?	☐	☐	☐

Evaluating and Using Results

	YES	PARTIALLY	NO
Does EHS performance meet the goals/targets and timelines specified in the unit's plans?	☐	☐	☐
If not, are processes in place to bring performance in line with expectations?	☐	☐	☐
Are processes in place to communicate measures, results, and trend data/information to those who need it?	☐	☐	☐
Is there a system in place to reinforce positive EHS improvements?	☐	☐	☐
Is there a process in place to use results and trend data to identify opportunities for continuous improvement of EHS management and performance?	☐	☐	☐
Are there improvements in both EHS and financial measures?	☐	☐	☐

	YES	PARTIALLY	NO
Does supplier/contractor EHs performance meet the unit's requirements?	☐	☐	☐

Benchmarking

| Has the unit benchmarked its EHS performance? | ☐ | ☐ | ☐ |
| Were benchmarking results used to improve EHS performance? | ☐ | ☐ | ☐ |

Customer/Stakeholder Satisfaction

Management Processes and Measures

Are processes in place to effectively receive, document, and respond to relevant communications from external customers and stakeholders?	☐	☐	☐
Are processes in place to identify and meet existing EHS compliance requirements for customer/stakeholder information about the unit's products, services, and operations?	☐	☐	☐
Are these processes effective?	☐	☐	☐
Are processes in place to respond to customer/stakeholder EHS questions and concerns?	☐	☐	☐
Are they effective?	☐	☐	☐
Are processes in place to proactively identify customer and stakeholder concerns?	☐	☐	☐
Are measures in place to measure customer/stakeholder satisfaction with the unit's EHS performance?	☐	☐	☐
Is there a process in place to update these measures?	☐	☐	☐
Is customer/stakeholder satisfaction improving?	☐	☐	☐
Are processes in place to improve satisfaction, using this information?	☐	☐	☐

	YES	PARTIALLY	NO
Are processes in place to obtain customer/stakeholder input?	☐	☐	☐
Is information about customer/stakeholder satisfaction with EHS aspects of the unit's business integrated into the unit's continuous improvement cycle for all aspects of operations, products, and services?	☐	☐	☐
Do EHS training/education programs for customers/stakeholders improve their satisfaction with the unit's EHS performance?	☐	☐	☐
Is customer/stakeholder satisfaction data integrated with other data to predict future market directions?	☐	☐	☐
Is customer/stakeholder satisfaction data correlated with financial improvements, market share?	☐	☐	☐

Benchmarking

	YES	PARTIALLY	NO
Did you benchmark the area of customer/stakeholder satisfaction?	☐	☐	☐
Was information from benchmarking used to improve customer/stakeholder satisfaction?	☐	☐	☐

CHAPTER
18

LEARNING FROM A CASE STUDY OF A MODEL COMPANY

BACKGROUND ON THE CASE STUDY

The case study below was developed using the contributions and knowledge of a number of industry participants in a TQEM workgroup, as part of the Council of Great Lakes Industries' (CGLI) initial program in this area. It reflects real practices in place in the business world within manufacturing and service industries. Participants represented chemicals, rubber, consumer products, auto, forestry and paper, rail, utilities, steel, R&D, imaging and office products, and telecommunications sectors. They are personally recognized in the acknowledgement section of this book. When we first took on the challenge of integrating the many excellent practices in place in their organizations into this case study, we were not sure it would work. Time proved that this was possible, and we all learned from the experience and from each other, and enriched our own and our organization's capabilities in the process.

THE CASE STUDY

Overview

Kem-Tek is a chemical manufacturing unit established in Ohio during the early 1900s. In 1982, we became a subsidiary of XYZ Company. Our facility, spread over 400 acres, includes 30 major buildings, most of which were constructed between 1940 and 1960. We employ a workforce of 1500, including 900 union, 400 exempt, and 200 nonexempt personnel. The site underwent a secondary expansion in the late 1980s, including the construction of a state-of-the-art manufacturing plant for a new product for industrial use. A high level of process control is in place in all our high volume production areas.

As a manufacturer of plastics, industrial chemicals, and specialty chemicals, we are an integral part of the supply chain for chemical, automotive, appliance, and other durable and nondurable goods manufacturers. About 255 of our products are internally used by our parent company, and 5 percent are marketed to consumers and municipalities.

In response to the needs of our major customers, we have significantly expanded our technical services, particularly in the area of environmental support, to provide greater value-added, and to discourage backward integration. We have also simplified our management structure to increase our responsiveness to customers.

In 1990, environmental management was expanded and integrated into an Environment, Health, and Safety (EHS) Department. Paula Smithe is the vice president responsible for the department; she reports directly to Douglas Brown, the division vice president and general manager of the site. Our EHS Department includes a centralized technical staff of twelve, as well as fifteen coordinators located within production and development departments. Our corporate headquarters, including its EHS Department, is located approximately 250 miles away, and provides us with a broad base of technical support.

Faced with economic pressures and increased domestic and foreign competition, our site has placed a high priority on integrating its productivity-driven projects with environmentally driven ones. For example, Just-In-Time (JIT) manufacturing has had a major impact on our productivity, reducing cycle times through shortened production runs to meet customer needs. As we developed new technologies and equipment to implement JIT, we also resolved potential environmental concerns such as increased waste levels. We were also able to improve the effectiveness of recycling/recovery technologies operations in areas where frequent product changeovers were affecting waste volumes, thus improving both profitability and environmental performance.

Critical to the success of such programs was our adoption in the late 1980s of Total Quality Management (TQM), which included identifying major customer and stakeholder environmental needs. Our plant's responsiveness to those needs has been shown by our success in integrating these needs, including the concept of sustainability, into our business planning, and by the successful partnerships we have developed.

In dealing with suppliers, for example, our site's Research and Development (R&D) personnel are working on joint projects, tailoring formulations to meet site-level objectives for source reduction. In dealing with customers, we have been working with both automotive and appliance manufacturers to improve recyclability of their products. To support this, we are also participating in life-cycle analysis studies on plastics with a university-based technology center and the U.S. Environmental Protection Agency (EPA). In 1992, we signed on to EPA's Auto Industry Initiative, focusing on reducing the impact of toxic chemicals on the environment.

Recognizing that our spectrum of potential competitors could expand to include customers interested in improving profitability through backward integration, we convinced our major customers of the added value of superior service and technical support we offer in the environmental area.

The site is also participating in a regional Center for Waste Reduction project to improve the efficiency of postproduction waste treatment, which will minimize releases to the environment. This technology is not proprietary, and is shared with others within industry. Through a trade association, we also cosponsored a study on innovative soil remediation technologies to be carried out by our State University-based Environmental Technology Development Center.

As a responsible manufacturer of chemical products, we recognize the need to improve communications with the public on environmental issues; hence we publish an external annual environmental report that describes our progress in developing products and processes that support sustainability, as well as our commitment to sound EHS management systems, based on TQM.

Our leadership and achievements have been recognized in a number of ways. For example, in 1986 and 1988, we received community and state-based awards for our Greenbelt program, which beautified the surroundings of our site, including developing a park for employee and public recreation, and also preserved an extensive wildlife and wetlands area. In 1991, we were the recipient of a Ford Q1 Supplier award, which evaluates a variety of parameters including environmental and community involvement.

In 1992, we received a state-level pollution prevention award for two major projects: reduction of chemical emissions through innovative membrane technologies, and the introduction of new technologies to eliminate heavy metal additives as stabilizers for plastics, which significantly reduced emissions to water.

To remain a leader in the area of EHS management, we will need to aggressively improve our productivity in a way that is environmentally responsible, as well as to continue to reinforce those partnerships that allow us to do this. The following account, while only a snapshot in time, also provides a window on how we plan to reach our future vision.

Leadership Category

Vision and Principles Kem-Tek's vision is to become a world-class facility in the eyes of our customers and other stakeholders with respect to our operations, our products, and our values and operating principles.

Our site's EHS mission is to become the highest value manufacturer of chemicals for the global marketplace in a way that promotes pollution prevention and sustainability, in order to achieve our vision.

To accomplish our mission, we created a site-level EHS Committee in 1989 chaired by our site general manager, Douglas Brown, division vice president, and cochaired by Paula Smithe, vice president of EHS management.

Our unit and our parent company adopted the Chemical Manufacturers Association's Responsible Care program and principles in 1989. The site's mission, vision, and policies, as well as Responsible Care principles, were communicated to all line managers for review with other employees. Copies of these are displayed in all departments.

Douglas Brown sent a personal letter to all employees, customers, and suppliers explaining the Responsible Care program and principles, and emphasizing commitment to EHS stewardship and sustainability.

Visible Personal Commitment

The leadership of our senior management is outstanding. Douglas Brown, our general manager, is well-known by our employees and the community alike for his personal commitment to responsible environmental management. In talks with employees and the public, he describes our Quality Improvement Process (QIP, Figure 18-1), and its success in improving the environmental performance of our products, processes, and services. He personally reviews the site's QIP programs, including those focused on environmental improvement. Paula Smithe, our vice president for EHS management, is widely recognized for her role in fostering environmental R&D partnerships, and locally recognized for initiating a program to interest promising students in science and technology fields.

In 1990, they laid the groundwork for a framework to enable workers to participate actively in the environmental area, which now includes expanded training, delega-

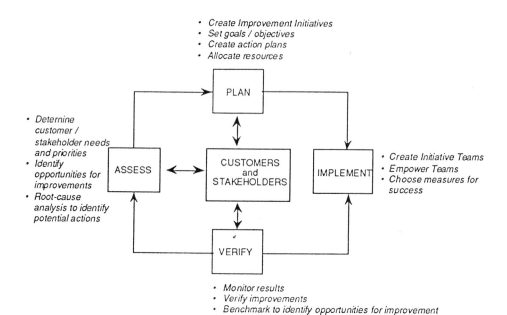

■ **FIGURE 18-1.** Case Study: Quality improvement process model to effect continuous improvement. (Reprinted with permission of CGLI.)

tion of decision-making downward, and addition of EHS staff to worker teams and quality circles. Douglas Brown, the general manager, personally presents the site's annual awards to department teams and individuals.

Both managers are highly visible during yearly site EHS assessments. Douglas Brown also requires a personal report from management on any noncompliance matter or significant EHS incident, including follow-up corrective action.

Doug Brown and other senior site managers place a high priority on communicating with customers and stakeholders on EHS issues. For example, a Community Advisory Committee was created that meets quarterly at the plant. At the first meeting, site managers presented the site's EHS principles and its environmental improvement accomplishments. Both Douglas Brown and other senior managers host quarterly town meetings with employees to answer questions and provide open dialogue on all issues, including EHS. Paula Smithe also presented the site's goals, pollution prevention plans, and accomplishments at several national and regional forums.

Senior managers interact externally with a number of stakeholder groups. Douglas Brown is a member of the local community environmental advisory committee, and an active participant in the community and site's Earth Day celebration. He sponsored a Greenbelt project in the late 1980s that created permanent green space, including a recreational park and forest/wetlands conservation areas, surrounding the site. In 1994, Paula Smithe initiated a science and environment-focused program for local students and teachers. She works with other companies on regional issues through two regional councils, and initiated publication of the site's annual environmental report for external distribution. This report reviews the site's major goals and describes its accomplishments. The site's EHS and public affairs staff participate in the public policy process through trade and technical association activities.

Commitment to Integration of EHS into Overall Business Plans In 1990, the new vice president of EHS became a formal member of the site's strategic planning team. Improvement goals and programs were proposed, based on an assessment of EHS improvement needs determined by plant teams, EHS staff, business units, and other support areas. A Pareto process was used to determine which approaches would return the most value to operations, business units, the community, and the environment. Resources were committed to top-ranked projects and included in the short- and long-term plans for the site.

Douglas Brown holds line managers accountable for including EHS considerations in all their decision-making. Approval of long- and short-term plans requires that these issues be addressed and sign-offs obtained from designated site EHS staff. At all levels, EHS issues are included in planning and decision-making through a TQM process, which is now in place throughout all departments.

Reward/consequence systems are widely used throughout the site to reinforce responsible EHS management. For example, we have incorporated EHS as a separate element of annual performance ratings. Gain-sharing is in place; that is, pay reflects gains in EHS performance, among other parameters. We make yearly awards to departments or teams meeting the unit's environmental performance improvement goals. Our site newsletter regularly reports on successful projects and celebrates individual and team achievements. A process is being formalized to include input from all stakeholders to strategic planning.

Benchmarking   Although no formal process is in place, EHS staff interacts with counterparts through trade and technical associations, and uses an ongoing computerized literature search to compare the plant's EHS programs with those at other facilities.

Information and Analysis Category

Types of Data Collected   We gather a wide range of basic EHS data. For example:

- We document regulatory EHS compliance data needs and maintain a matrix chart showing required reports, types of data, reporting timelines, and responsibilities.
- We maintain environmental data needed for such reports, all analyses performed to derive data, and a chemical emissions inventory to facilitate such reporting. The latter is also used to track waste reduction progress.
- We gather other types of data that support our proactive programs such as chemical exposure reduction, spill reduction and prevention, waste reduction, accident prevention and reduction. Many of these programs are required by our commitment to the Responsible Care program. A computerized system maintains training requirements, schedules, and records.
- We identify risks through ongoing assessment. Operations and on-site EHS staff review existing and new operations to determine risk levels, prioritize concerns, and recommend corrective action. Risks associated with products are determined in cooperation with corporate EHS staff (including toxicologists and other specialists). Teams determine toxicity and safety concerns with respect to customer use, supplier concerns, needs for testing, labeling, and communications. The teams also factor into their recommendations current and anticipated requirements, as well as company standards.
- We conduct department-run assessments on compliance as well as EHS management. Team leaders and department heads review results of corrective action, as well as determine whether a prevention-approach has been adopted.

The site also collects a significant amount of external EHS data, such as:

- Customer and supplier environmental requirements, collected by business units through direct interactions
- Community concerns, gathered by the local advisory committee or from direct complaints to our public relations staff

- Public and advocacy group issues, for example third party surveys gathered by our own or our corporate EHS staff, or by trade associations
- Government requirements and expectations, determined by site and corporate EHS staff that monitor regulations and anticipate future requirements
- Other formal and informal interactions and programs including industry, trade, and technical associations, government panels and committees, and academic institutions (sponsored research programs)

Quality of Data   The site purchases environmental analytical services externally from An-Elite Services Corporation, located in the same city. The quality of basic environmental data is ensured through their rigorous Quality Assurance/Quality Control (QA/QC) program. EPA and other government agency-approved methodologies are used wherever required. The company has a well-documented program in place for all analytical equipment and standards, including lab recertifications as required. Procedures are reviewed and revised regularly. A documented training program is in place for new and current lab personnel. Experienced personnel receive training as equipment is upgraded or new technologies implemented. Data is transmitted to our plant electronically; we have common, shared software packages to collect and manipulate data. Our EHS staff visit An-Elite Services' facility regularly to review results, procedures, and resolve any questions or concerns.

Data user needs are determined by our internal EHS staff before data collection is begun. A representative from An-Elite Services is also included in initial meetings. Data users are regularly surveyed to determine level of satisfaction and needed improvements with respect to validity, relevance, frequency, scope, completeness, and clearness of reports, as well as the timeliness and adequacy of their dissemination.

Data Management Systems   On-site data management systems are in place for all regulatory and company-required EHS data, and are well documented, including responsibilities, procedures, and retention and storage requirements. We have adopted computerized systems; most are PC-based, although some mainframe and manual systems also exist. Our long-term goals is to:

- Improve the site-wide integration linking production, financial, and EHS data
- Improve access of operations and other staff to EHS data
- Have consistent reporting formats to facilitate reporting to corporate offices and to regulatory agencies

How Data Is Used   Trend data is available in a number of areas, for example, records of accidents, spills, and emissions to air. Data users specify where maintaining trend data is relevant. In 1989, trend data was broadened to include: all quantified emissions and discharges; waste reduction data (including TRI chemicals and a number of other toxic materials prioritized by EHS staff); employee attitudes toward EHS performance; customer satisfaction data on EHS performance of products and services. Examples of such data are shown in Figures 18-2 through 18-10.

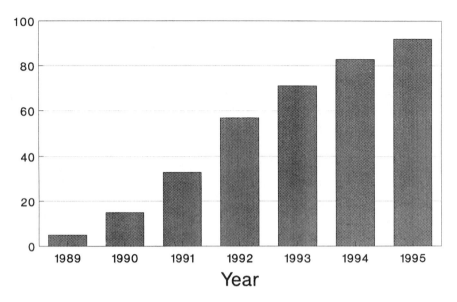

■ FIGURE 18-2. Case Study: Percent teams with EHS representation. (Reprinted with permission of CGLI.)

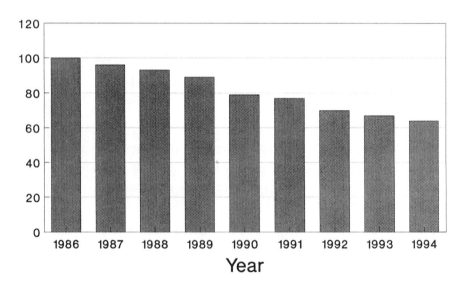

■ FIGURE 18-3. Case Study: Energy use normalized to production. (Reprinted with permission of CGLI.)

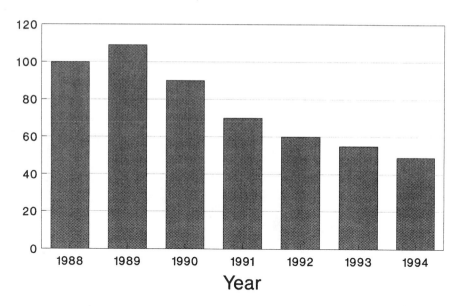

■ **FIGURE 18-4.** Case Study: TRI emissions, percent of 1988 volume. (Reprinted with permission of CGLI.)

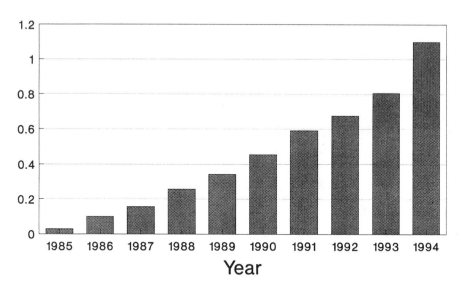

■ **FIGURE 18-5.** Case Study: Pollution prevention savings (Reprinted with permission of CGLI.)

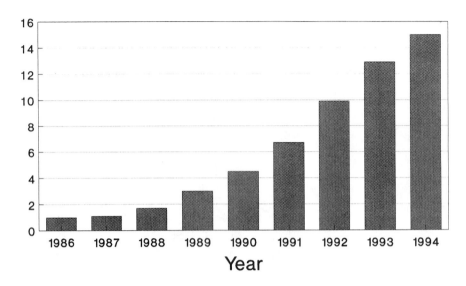

■ FIGURE 18-6. Case Study: Number of EHS calls received (Reprinted with permission of CGLI.)

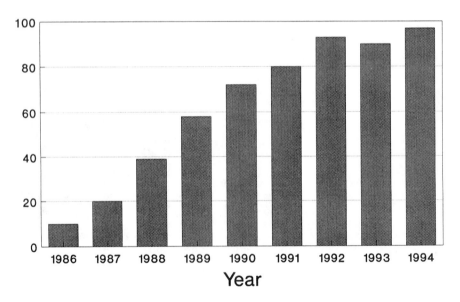

■ FIGURE 18-7. Case Study: Percent calls responded to in 24 hours. (Reprinted with permission of CGLI.)

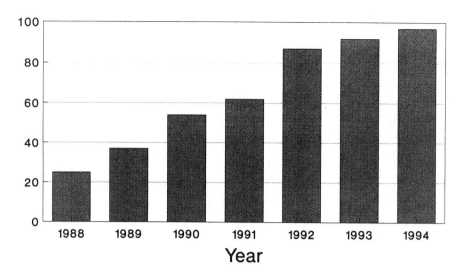

■ FIGURE 18-8. Case Study: Percent new products/processes on-time meeting customer EHS needs. (Reprinted with permission of CGLI.)

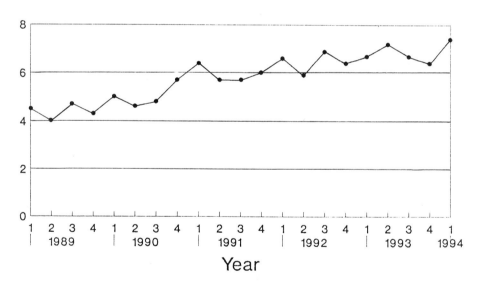

■ FIGURE 18-9. Case Study: Customer satisfaction rating. (Reprinted with permission of CGLI.)

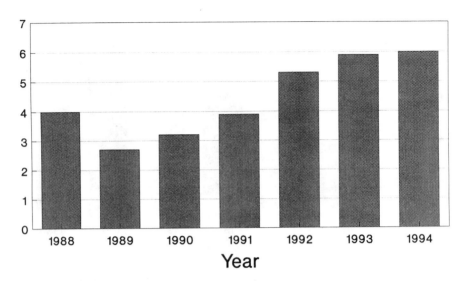

■ **FIGURE 18-10.** Case Study: Community rating of EHS performance. (Reprinted with permission of CGLI.)

EHS trend data are now routinely used to prioritize improvement efforts for both operations and products. Operations and EHS staff regularly review data on spills, chemical exposure levels, waste levels, waste reduction programs, community concerns, and employee attitude surveys. Business unit and EHS staff review customer inquiries and responses. Specific examples where trend data was instrumental in improving performance in existing operations and products include the following:

■ Spill data trends are charted monthly and reviewed by line management and by operations-level teams. Root-cause analysis is used in a number of departments to identify and correct problems. Over the past three years, the number of spill incidents for a major department has been reduced by 80 percent and spill severity (toxicity/volume)was significantly diminished.

■ Customer concerns are trended by business units for each product to set priorities for action. As a result, we have improved labeling, customer information, documentation, packaging, shipping, and formulations.

■ Where an improved analytical procedure was adopted to obtain better worker exposure data, an existing process was redesigned and new procedures established and documented to improve worker safety.

EHS information is used to design and develop new products/processes, for example:

■ Based on new information provided by our corporate EHS department on toxicity of a chemical projected for use in a new synthetic chemical manufacturing process, we developed and constructed a substitute process.

- Based on information provided by our industrial customers, we are developing a new line of aqueous-based cleaning solvents that will reduce wastes from our own site as well as customer facilities.
- We are developing specifications for levels of specific toxic contaminants in certain raw materials obtained from external suppliers to minimize customer concerns with product use.

The site collects and uses EHS data/analyses in its strategic decision-making. For example, based on community and worker concerns, and on spill data trends, as well as on potentially more stringent regulations, we committed to a major upgrade of chemical storage facilities over the next four years. This commitment also includes expanded hydrogeological studies for the site, as well as an investigation of innovative remediation technologies at a local university R&D center.

As the result of increased dissemination and understanding of the significance of EHS data, there has been a noticeable change in the attitude and awareness of line managers, as well as other employees. This is evidenced, for example, by a 50 percent increase in implementation of EHS-related suggestions over the past two years. These include changes in operating procedures, improved documentation, substitute material for maintenance, and recycling and reuse projects. Teams worked with EHS and R&D staff to initiate and complete major process improvements. This increase in worker involvement began within a single department. Successful projects initiated by this department were then communicated to other site departments at team meetings and through the site's newsletter.

Benchmarking   Although no formal benchmarking was initiated, individuals responsible for developing information management systems collaborate with peers within a technical association to compare effectiveness of various information management software/hardware packages.

Strategic Planning Category

Planning Process   Through the site's long- and short-term planning processes, we develop goals, performance measures, strategies, and an implementation framework. While goals set through this process reinforce corporate goals, they are locally driven by business unit, department, and site needs. EHS priorities are set by each of these, and integrated with other business needs. Overall site priorities are then set during our yearly planning retreat.

Once priorities are assigned, a senior level team from management, operations, business units, and support areas (including EHS) develops consensus on where resources should be allocated so that all of the plan's key objectives can be met. Although we revise all such plans annually, the size and relative autonomy of the site gives us enough flexibility to adjust short-term plans as needed.

Following the annual planning process, we communicate the goals and objectives we set (including EHS objectives) to all of our department and team leaders. They in turn develop consistent department/team-level plans. Douglas Brown also takes the lead to communicate the site's major priorities and goals to employees at town meetings, so that a consistent message is heard at all levels. We review all department-level plans for consistency before they are approved.

Our EHS improvement programs underway are for the most part well-integrated into both long- and short-term plans. For example, plans that included adoption of JIT to increase productivity also included development funding to minimize increased waste levels due to more frequent product changeovers. Changes included improved recycling equipment and cleaning formulations. Plans to increase sales included expansion of our environmental support services to provide added value to customers.

Input to Planning We use a variety of processes to obtain customer/stakeholder input before we begin planning. We get input from customers, suppliers, advocacy groups, the public, employees, community, and government sources. We have found these direct interactions invaluable. They help us develop a strategy that accommodates both short- and long-term needs. These interactions have also been effective in changing the culture of the site, setting performance expectations, and matching these expectations with resources.

Reinforcement of Commitment to Environmental Excellence Managers' performance is evaluated through a formal appraisal process that rates their ability to identify and anticipate EHS needs as well as their ability to integrate them into long- and short-term plans in a way that strengthens the bottom line.

Human Resource Development Category

Clear Assignment of Responsibility We document the more general EHS responsibilities of our managers and other employees in our site standards and policies. Specific responsibilities are documented within department assignment-related procedures. Supervisors are required to review these with employees and to document this review process using a checklist, before employees' assignments changes or when new employees begin a work assignment.

Training/Education In 1990, we began to rebuild our EHS training program in consultation with our corporate EHS staff and an external consulting firm. We expanded our training programs and contracted with corporate staff to review and update these programs yearly. In mid-1992, we added two dedicated on-site trainers and increased our travel and training budget for all on-site EHS staff.

We completed revising our training program in mid-1992 and are now using a site-side computerized system to schedule and track training.

We identified three critical elements in our site's employee empowerment framework. All are relevant to EHS management and performance:

- An expanded training and competency program
- Expanded cross-functional expertise in all site teams (Figure 18-2)
- Downward delegation of decision-making (documented in guidance to all site managers/team leaders)

By year-end 1993, all employees had completed the first round of training requirements. This training was geared to the employee's responsibility level and capabilities. For example:

- All our managers participated in a one-time eight-hour EHS management training session. In 1994, each participated in a four-hour course on high profile issues. Shorter presentations on new regulations, changing customer needs, or EHS performance trends are included in the agenda of monthly operations meetings.
- Employees in operations, R&D, maintenance, transportation, utilities, and other staff areas completed assignment-specific EHS training. A checklist was used to document that all critical performance and management areas had been covered.
- All new employees on the site received a general two-hour EHS orientation that includes an overview on Right-to-Know, Responsible Care, and the site's EHS principles. A fifteen-minute videotape on the site goals and accomplishments was also shown at team meetings in all departments.
- Other training programs were made available to employees as required or requested, for example, presentations or tapes on specific regulations, waste minimization, site and corporate principles and goals. A listing of programs is available on the site's electronic mail system.

Career Development/Integration with EHS Goals   In our experience, cross-functional training is an indispensable tool in improving environmental performance. This applies to our on-site EHS staff as well as to other employees. All of our EHS staff have had some operations experience. Two plant supervisors were formerly EHS coordinators. One managed the waste reduction program in a major production area. Although this program is not yet formalized, in the future we will make such opportunities more available through a job-posting system. We also plan to increase the level of training and education opportunities to those who may never have EHS staff positions, but would benefit from more in-depth EHS knowledge. We also plan to expand our EHS staff training program to include business and financial training.

Employee Attitudes   For the past three years, we have been monitoring employee attitudes toward EHS management and performance through a general purpose employee survey. This survey is being redesigned to include more EHS questions. We also evaluate individual attitudes, and receive individual feedback, during annual performance appraisals.

In the first two years of the survey, we noted no improvement in attitude toward site performance against EHS goals. We also found a slight increase in concern about EHS issues. This year's survey was more positive. We attribute this to our aggressive communications approach where we focus on our accomplishments and the breadth of projects underway. Employees also expressed greater satisfaction with the site's EHS leadership this past year.

Reward and Consequence Systems   All of our departments have celebrations that recognize teams that reach milestones. Teams are given a discretionary celebration budget for this purpose. Personal recognition by team leaders and other plant managers is an essential part of the celebration process and improved morale. Other tangible recognition processes for EHS accomplishments include gain-sharing, performance appraisals, yearly awards, and site and the community's Earth Day celebration. We also recognize employee successes through stories in our site newsletter.

Process Management

Test Data Quality   We selected our external contract EHS analytical laboratory using a number of criteria:

- High quality analytical data (a documented QA/QC program)
- Reputation for reliability with other customers
- Responsiveness to our turnaround needs
- Compatibility with our reporting and documentation system needs
- Reasonable service price
- Although their price is about 20 percent above competitors, in our experience their QA/QC management and service record is far superior. Our parent firm and several large local firms also routinely purchase their service.

Our EHS staff regularly visit the contract lab to review their program and performance. The lab's test reports routinely include precision data. Analytical standards purchased from accredited external suppliers are cross-checked according to protocol against standards from other suppliers. Standards made internally are checked against purchase standards. The lab also participates in annual round-robin testing programs with other major laboratories.

Management Processes for the Development of Products, Processes, and Services   Our business success depends on building successful linkages with our major suppliers and customers, as well as key stakeholders. In turn, we need to link their needs with our development community.

The systems we use for this include our Customer Action Teams and other such vehicles that help us to:

- Define current and future EHS/customer/stakeholder concerns, needs for new products, services, processes, and potential impacts of changes in existing ones.
- Evaluate impacts of current and future regulatory requirements on our site operations and on product use.
- Determine future training needs, labeling needs, and transportation impacts
- Integrate these requirements formally into the overall objectives set during the planning cycle
- Translate these objectives into product specifications during the development cycle

Our development cycle is a formally documented process (Quality Assurance of Manufacturability) that includes:

- Cross-functional representation, including EHS staff
- Development of design parameters that are fully customer/stakeholder-driven
- Formal review of designs against specifications
- Sign-off by development teams, management, and EHS staff at appropriate development checkpoints
- Feedback from selected customers, before final release

The design, development, and review teams all include a member of our Alert, Team (comprised of R&D and EHS staff) who identifies potential showstoppers relating to manufacture or use. Similar review processes determine whether to release new or modified equipment for installation. Follow-up performance reviews are also scheduled for these installations.

Our documentation system builds on an EHS manual that covers our policies, responsibilities, organizational structure, and requirements. The manual also cross-references all related documentation, and defines responsible entities for maintaining procedures, data, and tracking performance. We have a document control process that allows us to retrieve both original and revised EHS documents. The type of storage medium and the frequency of creating new files are determined by the retention requirements of the data.

Continuous Improvement   A continuous improvement process is used for development and modification of all products, processes, and services. It is also used to improve our EHS management systems. Our teams use root-cause analysis to determine probable causes of problems, then develop and implement practical solutions. We verify improvements. We also follow up with preventive/corrective action where the improvement program is not on track. We track continuous improvement efforts in a number of areas, such as spill prevention, compliance (discharge exceedences), repeat audit findings, and waste reduction.

We also measure the effectiveness of our improvements through customer/stakeholder feedback. Our continuous improvement efforts focus on incremental improvements as well as breakthroughs.

We adopted department-run safety inspections several decades ago. These were expanded in 1988 to environmental and health areas. Our corporate-level audit process complements our local assessments. Results of the former, as well as follow-up action, are shared with senior management as well as with department managers.

When we adopted JIT to meet changing customer delivery requirements, we were then faced with increased waste levels. A department team used the continuous improvement process to identify waste reduction opportunities, including exploring and adopting several breakthrough technologies.

Quantitative Measures   Quantitative measures are in place in virtually all departments; these include, for example:

- Recycling office paper, reducing paper use
- Energy conservation
- Packaging reduction
- Waste reduction
- Incident reduction
- Cycle time reduction

Environmental Results Category

Key Measures   We track a number of key environmental performance measures, each of which is critical to the quality of our EHS management and performance, as well as to our customers and stakeholders. We review these measures annually, basing any changes on input from both external and internal sources. Our measures currently include:

- Energy use (Figure 18-3)
- TRI emissions (Figure 18-4)
- Pollution prevention savings (Figure 18-5)
- Number of EHS calls (Figure 18-6)
- EHS calls responded to within 24 hours (Figure 18-7)
- Meeting delivery dates for new products and services that relate to customer EHS requirements (Figure 18-8)
- Customer/stakeholder satisfaction with respect to EHS-related complaints or concerns (Figure 18-9)
- A third party survey on the community's rating of our EHS performance (Figure 18-10)
- Implementation of prevention-based corrective action of EHS assessments
- Incident frequency (accidents, spills, safety concerns)
- Progress on Responsible Care commitments

Beside these current measures, we also track a number of key initiatives (Table 18-1). Baseline and trend data has been gathered for our key measures, and it shows improvements with time.

■ TABLE 18-1 Environmental Initiatives

Initiative	Objective	Metric (Indicator)	Results
Pollution Prevention			
EPA's Auto Initiative	Substitutes for heavy metals by June 1995	Quantity of heavy metals used	Initiated December 1992
EPA 33/50 Program	50% reduction by 1992; 75% by 1995	Monthly report	Met 1992 goal
Aqueous cleaning solvents	Transition complete by 1995	Quantity of solvents used	Transition completed
Accidental release elimination	Reduce 30% by 1993; 70% by 1994; eliminate 100% to groundwater by 1994	Monthly Report	Ahead of target
CFC phaseout	Meet/exceed 1995 compliance goal (100% phaseout of use)	Complete compliance	70% phaseout in 1992
Responsible Care			
Implementation	Complete implementation by December 1996.	Annual report to CMA	Progressed from Level II (evaluation stage) to Level IV (implementing action plan)
Life-Cycle Analysis/Sustainability			
Joint research program	Foster design of products for recyclability	Percent of appliances that are recyclable.	Initiated March 1993
Buy-back program for plastics	Foster integrated recycling systems		Projected for 1994
EHS Management Systems			
Fully computerized EHS information system	Needs analysis by April 1993; complete design by March 1994	Cross-section of customers surveyed; successful design review	Complete
Corporate system link	Install/debug	Alpha/beta testing	
Local PC network	Periodic upgrade	Audit of current needs	
Computerized cost-savings-system	System in place by 1994	Cost analysis report available	
Cycle Time Reduction			
Meet customer environmental requirement for new plastics	Reduce time for design/delivery by 50%	Actual customer delivery date	Underway March 1993

Preprinted with permission of CGLI.

Improving Trends Although the number of EHS-related questions has rapidly risen over the past five years as public awareness has grown, our ability to meet our aim of a 24-hour response time is improving. As a result, customer/stakeholder satisfaction with response time is also improving.

We have also been successful in meeting customer requirements for new or improved products and services, including eliminating heavy metal additives as stabilizers for plastics, improved packaging for industrial and consumer products, introduction of a buy-back program for plastics from appliance manufacturers, and installation of an on-line system to share chemical information with customers and transporters.

Waste reduction programs show positive trends. We were able to meet all of our targeted goals, including reducing hazardous waste levels and reducing energy consumption. We also exceeded our targeted goals for reducing SARA/TRI chemical emissions by 1992. Our cost savings from our overall pollution prevention programs have been significant.

Our performance has been improving in implementing prevention-based corrective action identified during EHS assessments of our site, using our quality improvement process. We have also significantly reduced the number of aggregated site incidents over the past four years, and are among the industry leaders in the area of minimum days lost due to accidents. We track this through a daily on-line reporting system. We also track corrections at the department level.

Since implementing Responsible Care in 1989, our average performance has improved from Phase II (evaluating practices against Responsible Care codes) to Phase IV (implementing an action plan).

Improvement Systems We review all trend data with senior management and department heads at monthly staff meetings. We use QIP to identify opportunities to improve our performance as well as our management system. All changes made are reviewed and approved by our on-site EHS staff to ensure they are prevention-based.

We also provide environmental reports to corporate headquarters. We benchmark our performance against results reported in the company's aggregated corporate-level report, and review these results at monthly site, department, and team meetings. Key results are also widely posted for employee review.

Corrective action plans for major incidents are provided to the site's general manager and EHS manager within 24 hours.

We update our choice of measures annually, using input from customers and other stakeholders.

The site managers reinforce performance by personally recognizing departments and teams that have met or exceeded their targets. The team selects the type of recognition or activity (for example, a celebration, purchase of new recreation equipment or upgraded computer equipment, or a community-based outreach program).

Customer/Stakeholder Satisfaction Category

Meeting Basic Requirements   Kem-Tek's customers and stakeholders are very diverse. It has a large base of industrial suppliers as well as customers. Because the latter have a long history with us, and our business strategies and capabilities are well-matched, we have been very successful in anticipating their EHS concerns and needs. Our programs go far beyond what is required.

However, we also provide high quality support in meeting existing customer, community, and employee-based regulatory requirements, such as Material Safety Data Sheets (MSDS), labeling, packaging, transportation documentation, Right-to-Know information on chemicals, and emergency planning data. We participate in a community EHS training program through our local industrial council.

We maintain two toll-free hot lines. One is related to customer information on chemicals, and the second is for community and employee concerns. Our written policy specifies same-day turnaround response to hot-line questions. Questions of a less urgent nature from the general public, are referred to our Site Communications office, where the requirement is for a maximum three-day turnaround. We track the reason for the complaint on concern, and the effectiveness of our response system, such as: number of calls received; calls responded to within the required time frame; degree of customer satisfaction with our response; and the courtesy, responsiveness, and efficiency of staff responding to requests.

We have a formal method to resolve complaints/concerns. It includes:

- Classifying the type of complaint and concern, and verifying it
- Assigning responsibility for follow-up
- Formally acknowledging the concern and providing at least an interim response or corrective measure within 24 hours
- Beginning corrective action using root-cause analysis and continuous improvement
- Follow-up action with the customer directly, if value is added
- Documenting action

Proactive Programs to Measure Satisfaction   We have a number of effective ways to track customer EHS issues beyond complaints or concerns, as well as customer satisfaction, for example:

- We track the number of product/process changes delivered on time.
- Our Customer Action Teams meet regularly with larger customers and record results and concerns in a site database.
- Our marketing representatives also conduct semiannual senior management level interviews with key customers that include EHS issues.
- We conduct a third party survey of customers.
- We have direct electronic connections with a number of our suppliers

and customers in response to their need for faster turnaround on EHS information.

This customer-related data is regularly reviewed by business unit managers, operations, and service staff, and used as input to improvement programs.

We track our employees' EHS concerns as well as their satisfaction with the site's EHS performance through our opinion surveys, and also through open town meetings.

Our Annual Report to Shareholders includes a report on our EHS accomplishments, including progress against the site's major goals. Our annual environmental report also invites readers to contact us directly on any product or operational EHS concern.

We use a third party survey of the community by a local industrial council to trend community satisfaction with local industry's EHS performance.

Satisfaction Trends   Satisfaction trends are positive in some areas:

- Industrial customer satisfaction shows positive trends since support/service programs were expanded in mid-1990.
- Some employee satisfaction trends are positive in areas where we have strong communications programs. In areas where trends are flat, departments have organized employee focus groups, the results of which should lead to employee initiated continuous improvement projects.
- Community surveys are also mixed. We have received good reviews on communicating our EHS accomplishments and receive recognition for our science and education outreach programs in the school system. However, there is some community concern about chemical risks. We believe that our community would benefit from a lay-level course on the benefits and risks associated with chemicals and are working with our local industrial council and Parent/Teacher Association to develop such a program.

As an indicator of increasing customer and public recognition of our EHS performance, we have received several external awards. In 1991, we received a Ford Q1 Supplier Award in recognition of the proactive programs we initiated over a five year period, several of which related to EHS-related modifications in products, as well as proactive community-oriented programs such as the Greenbelt program, and our high school teacher/student training programs.

Active Involvement of Stakeholders in Problem-Solving   Our EHS staff is working cooperatively with state agencies and trade associations to develop rational prioritization methods that include risk, cost, benefit, emission levels, volume/toxicity. This information will be used to determine where resources should be focused in areas such as waste reduction, plant modifications, and end-of-pipe treatment improvements. We also directly involve employees from operations through department teams in defining and implementing EHS improvement opportunities.

QUESTIONS TO ASK ABOUT THE CASE STUDY

- In what ways does the EHS management system of Kem-Tek resemble your own?
- Where specifically do differences exist?
- How did Kem-Tek's senior management demonstrate its commitment to EHS management and high-level performance?
- How did it identify and gather data and information of significance to its EHS needs?
- What EHS strategies were key to its success?
- What key management processes and systems did it put in place for EHS management?
- How did it mobilize and motivate its workforce?
- Were its results in alignment with its objectives?
- What were its key success measures, and were these aligned with what its customers and stakeholders expected?
- Did it effectively consider and involve customers and stakeholders in resolving key issues or concerns?
- Compare its performance to the criteria in the TQEM matrix, then develop a score for its EHS management and performance, and determine:
  - What were its strengths?
  - Where were the major gaps in each category?
  - What gaps should be attacked first to improve its management and performance?
- Does the case study give you any clues to root causes of problems?
- If not, propose likely root causes for each gap you identified, as well as appropriate corrective action to address each, based on your own knowledge and experience.

CHAPTER NOTES

CHAPTER 1

1-1. A study by General Systems Company, Inc., a Quality management consulting firm, showed that companies with TQM systems consistently exceeded the industry average for return on investment by improving product quality and reducing costs associated with inspection and other activities. They also increased market share through improved quality and productivity. A PMS Associates study also found a link between Quality, market share, return on investment, and profitability. A study of Deming Prize winners between 1961 and 1980 by the Japanese Union of Scientists and Engineers also found stable or improved financial and safety performance, exceeding the industry average.

1-2. Interestingly, the Japanese were first to apply TQM systematically to pollution control. In 1971, a study group was formed in Japan to create rational, scientific methods for sampling, analysis, and measurement techniques, based on QC concepts. In the mid to late 1970s, the EPA also began focusing its attention on Quality assurance of sampling and other aspects of environmental monitoring.

CHAPTER 5

5-1. In addition, you should also be aware that the 1994 version of ISO 9000 includes considerations such as "protection of the environment, health, safety, security, and conservation of energy and natural resources."

5-2. GEMI's primer on cost-effective pollution prevention initiatives is actually an introduction to the concepts of full cost and total cost assessments. It provides useful lists and definitions of direct, hidden, contingent liability, and "less tangible" costs, and shows how these relate to pollution prevention projects. The primer emphasizes incorporating environmental costs into business decision-making processes, noting that the purpose is to "raise the economic valuation of pollution prevention projects to a level that is equal to, not greater than, other alternative investments."

CHAPTER 6

6-1. GIS tools, originally developed for use by space and defense agencies, are widely used by policy-makers, planners, and regulators for planning and decision-making within the space, defense, health, natural resource, environmental, and economic development communities. Spatial (aerial and satellite) maps have been linked with databases of demographics, zoning, biological species, and wetlands, in order to determine where to site new transportation corridors. GIS is widely used for commercial applications such as market research, urban development planning, real estate and utility rights-of-way (Douglas, 1995). GIS has already become an essential tool in emergency planning and response (e.g., flood, hurricane, earthquake, catastrophic accidents). The availability of historical data also allows planners to evaluate the impact of past changes and predict potential future effects.

6-2. "Moore's law" (the source of which is Gordon Moore, a cofounder of Intel) states that the performance of chip technology, as measured against its price, doubles every eighteen months or so. Technologies are outdated sometimes even before introduction.

6-3. A joint Dutch government and chemical industry study (Association of the Dutch Chemical Industry, 1991) however, does include economic costs, and Graedel and Allenby (1995) feel that some version of their approach could be useful for decision-making in areas such as industrial ecology.

6-4. The four smaller companies participating in the World Resources Institute's study companies were in Washington state, which requires companies to submit with their pollution prevention reports a description of the environmental cost accounting methods used to estimate cost savings for each project.

CHAPTER 7

7-1. In his classic publication, Management: Tasks, Responsibilities, Practices, Peter Drucker (1985, p. 125) defines strategic planning as "the continuous process of making present entrepreneurial (risk-taking) decisions systematically and with the greatest knowledge of their future; organizing systematically the efforts needed to carry out these decisions; and measuring the results of these decisions against the expectations through organized, systematic feedback."

7-2. McDonald's adopted a three-layered sandwich wrap to replace its foam clamshells, which resulted in a 90 percent waste volume reduction, less air emissions and water discharge, and significantly less energy consumption. The joint Environmental Defense Fund/McDonald's Corporation (1991) final report on this project notes that:

> [T]he decision to phase out polystyrene packaging and substitute paper-based wraps cannot be evaluated as a generic "paper vs. plastic" issue. Rather the considerable source reduction merits of the decision emerge only by closely examining the packages involved. Not all plastics or paper materials are created equal, therefore the specific nature of the materials involved—their mode of production, their current rate of recycling, and so on—dramatically affects their relative environmental consequences and must be carefully taken into account in any comparison.

7-3. Environmental technologies are one of the fastest growing industry segments today, amounting to more than $350 billion worldwide in 1994. The United States dominates this market with $134 billion in revenues, but only exports about 10 percent. The environmental technology segment includes about 45,000 companies ranging in size from small consulting companies to large multinationals. The latter account for about half of the overall revenues. That leaves nearly 45,000 firms competing for the remainder of the pie, companies that average fewer than 50 employees. The technologies offered by these companies cover four major categories: monitoring and assessment; remediation; restoration (to improve damaged ecosystems); and avoidance (e.g., pollution prevention). Much of the product or service mix is not "high technology" oriented. The product mix includes items such as filters, containers, liners, and pipes. Products with a higher "technology content" include pollution control equipment for air or water, and laboratory and field instrumentation.

7-4. The U.S.-based Chemical Manufacturers' Association (CMA) has begun annual reporting on its Responsible Care program, as well as the success of its membership in meeting EPA's voluntary "33/50" program commitments (this program committed companies to voluntary reduction in TRI emissions of 33 percent by 1992 and 50 percent by 1995.) CMA's members met their 33 percent reduction goal for 1992 a full year early. Its survey of member companies also uncovered a number of management systems areas where improvement was needed, such as:

■ Independent external evaluation of its performance
■ Standardized public reporting

■ More effective methods to reach the workforce to catalyze cultural change

CHAPTER 8

8-1. The term "empowerment" is often used to describe a number of vehicles used to mobilize human potential in a positive way; however, in some circles the term provokes dissent. The term "enabling" is less controversial, equally persuasive, and is used by many in place of "empowerment."

CHAPTER 10

10-1. Process mapping is used in combination with continuous improvement at companies such as Texas Instruments to drive products to six sigma quality (approximately 3.4 defects per million opportunities).

10-2. Both ISO 14000 and the 1995 revision of ISO 9000 will forever institutionalize the link between corrective and preventive action. Thus procedures and practices themselves must now be scrutinized for their potential to create nonconformances or other undesirable outcomes, and must be redesigned to remove this potential.

CHAPTER 11

11-1. A joint KPMG/Wharton School benchmarking study was initiated in 1995 to examine the performance areas that companies are tracking and the tools they are using. The study is also expected to shed light on the relationship between long-term profitability and environmental performance.

11-2. Measures reflect the bias, perspective, and values of individuals/groups involved in the selection process. With respect to perspective alone, for example, different stakeholder groups may be most concerned with issues/impacts that occur on different temporal or management scales, or those that reflect a geographic versus a political, or social system perspective. Measure selection also tends to evolve with time. When issues are first emerging, measures tend to be confined to human activities and their effects (lagging indicators), and only later evolve toward management activities, outcomes, and management effectiveness measures (leading indicators). Measures also tend to "cascade" across systems boundaries. That is, the same measure (e.g., waste levels) can serve as a stressor to the environment or natural resource base, but it can also serve as a performance indicator for an industry-based pollution prevention program. (Wever, 1994a).

CHAPTER 12

12-1. Perhaps you know that you have arrived when recognition also extends to the media. *Forbes Magazine's* 1993 survey of 10,000 executives and analysts resulted in a top ten list of U.S. environmental leaders: AT&T, Apple Computer, Church & Dwight, Clorox, Digital Equipment, Dow Chemical, Herman Miller, HB Fuller, IBM, and Xerox. On its 1995 list, disclosed through the Green Newsletter, were Rubbermaid, Levi Strauss, Coca-Cola, DuPont, Dow, Dayton Hudson, Henry Miller, 3M, Corning, and Johnson & Johnson. Both Dow and Herman Miller are on both lists.

CHAPTER 13

13-1. Integrated Logistics Support is a collection of analytical, planning, and management tools. While it uses a life-cycle approach, it differs from traditional LCAs in that it also incorporates costs. Both LCA and Integrated Logistics Support are analytical tools, however, rather than decision tools. The data they generate can be plugged into a design-decision framework such as DFE (or Design for Quality, Design for Cost, Design for Manufacturability, etc.). Reverse logistics applies traditional logistics tools to activities associated with waste streams, focusing on their reintegration through either closed-loop or open-loop systems.)

13-2. Although these examples illustrate the business gains and the implied environmental benefits of logistics management improvements, it is difficult to quantify the latter. A 1993 study published by the Great Lakes Commission evaluated the potential EHS impacts of a macro-level shift from waterborne to truck or rail transportation of cargo in the region. It examined potential risks from oil and hazardous materials spills and from dredging and dredged materials disposal; it also compared energy use and fuel efficiency, air pollution and emissions, as well as safety, noise, and congestion effects. The study examined movement scenarios for a variety of commodities (potash, coal, taconite, cement, petroleum and petrochemical products, grain, paper, wood pulp, iron ore, and steel) over selected routes (e.g., Sarnia, Ontario to Chicago, Illinois; northern Europe to Cleveland, Ohio) including comparisons with truck/rail alternatives through other inland routes, where useful). The study concluded that vessel transport had clear benefits over train or truck for the case studies, finding that it was safer, used less fuel, and produced less emissions when compared with equivalent commodity hauls by rail or truck. Higher fuel efficiency for vessel movements were also determined, compared with other modes. While this information should be useful to individual businesses dealing in commodity shipments, they will need to look at their own individual transportation scenarios. The study is a useful model for businesses that ship other types of materials.

BIBLIOGRAPHY

Ankers, Ray. 1992. "Measuring Safety and Environmental Performance and Risk." GEMI Conference proceedings, pp. 131–132.

Association of the Dutch Chemical Industry, Integrated Substance Chain Management, December 1991.

Barnes, George. 1993. "Case Study: Xerox's Waste Free Initiatives." Executive Enterprises conference: *Successfullly Utilizing Environmental Measurement, Benchmarking and Employee Empowerment.* Washington, DC

Bartlett, Christopher A. and S. Ghoshal. 1995. "Changing the Role of Top Management: Beyond Systems to People." *Harvard Business Review* 73: 132–143.

Blackburn, James B. 1994. "Ethics, Science and Envirionmental Decision-Making." *Environmental Toxicology and Chemistry* 13: 679–681.

Bober, Maria M., J. W. Mitchell, R. Hays Bell, and W. L. Hart. 1993–1994. "Corporate Performance Standards at Kodak." *Total Quality Environmental Management* 3: 177–180.

Bounds, Wendy. 1994. "Grocery Glitz, As Big as Kodak Is in Rochester, NY., It Still Isn't Wegmans." *Wall Street Journal* (December 27) 224: 1.

Bowles, Jerry and Joshua Hammond. 1991. *Beyond Quality.* New York: G.P. Putnam's Sons.

Camp, Robert C. 1989. *Benchmarking: The Search for Industry Best Practices that Lead to Superior Performance.* Milwaukee: ASQC Quality Press.

Canadian Standards Association. 1994. *Life Cycle Assessment: Environmental Technology,* Z760-94. Rexdale, Ontario.

The Conference Board. 1995. *TQM and Environmental Management*. Quality Research Panel Number 4, Spring.

Council of Great Lakes Industries, 1993. *Total Quality Environmental Management Primer.* Ann Arbor, MI.

Dambach, Barry F. and B. R. Allenby. 1995. "Implementing Design for Environment at AT&T." *Total Quality Environmental Management* 4: 51–62.

Davidson, Hilary S. 1994. "Growing an Environmental Leadership Strategy at Duke Power Company," *Total Quality Environmental Management* 3: 439–455.

DePree, Max. 1989. *Leadership Is an Art.* New York: Doubleday.

Diamond, Craig. 1995. "Demonstrating the Implementation of Environmental Management Systems Using Consensus Standards as Benchmarks." American Institute of Chemical Engineers Summer Meeting, Boston.

Ditz, D., Z. J. Ranganathan, and R. D. Banks. 1995. *Green Ledgers: Case Studies in Corporate Environmental Accounting.* World Resources Institute. Wash. DC.

Douglas, William J. 1995. *Environmental GIS: Applications to Industrial Facilities*, Boca Raton, FL: CRC Press, Inc.

Drucker, Peter F. 1985. *Management: Tasks, Responsibilities, Practices.* New York: Harper and Row.

The Economist. 1995. "Can Republicans Fix It?" (March 11–17) 334: 25–26.

Edwards, Scott, T. Yonkers, B. Moore, B. Briesmaster, P. Dappen, M. Haecker, and S. Cuttino. 1994. "Meeting the Environmental Management Challenge at U.S. Air Force Bases." 20th Environmental Symposium and Exhibition of the American Defense Preparedness Association.

Environmental Defense Fund and McDonald's Corporation. 1991. *Waste Reduction Task Force Final Report.*

Ferguson, William C. 1993. "Building a Solid Ethical Foundation in Business." *Business Ethics: Generating Trust in the 1990s and Beyond*, The Conference Board, Report 1057-94-CH, pp. 9–10.

File, K. M. 1989. "The 1989 *Business Ethics Awards.*" *Business Ethics* (November/December), 20–25.

Fortune, 1994. "Delivering the Goods" (November 28), 64–78.

Fortune, 1993. "The National Business Hall of Fame," April 5, vol. 127, pp. 108–112.

General Accounting Office (GAO). 1991. "Management Practices: U.S. Companies Improve Performance Through Quality Efforts." United States General Accounting Office Report to the Honorable Donald Ritter, House of Representatives, Report Number: GAO/NS1AD-91-190, May.

Global Environmental Management Initiative (GEMI). 1992. *Environmental Self-Assessment Program.* Washington DC.

Global Environmental Management Initiative (GEMI). 1994. *Finding Cost-Effective Pollution Prevention Initiatives: Incorporating Environmental Costs into Business Decision Making, A Primer.* Washington DC.

Gloria, Thomas, T. Saad, M. Breville, and M. O'Connell. 1995. "Life Cycle Assessment: A Survey of Current Implementation." *Total Quality Environmental Management* 4: 33–50.

Graedel, T. E. and B. R. Allenby. 1995. *Industrial Ecology.* Englewood Cliffs, NJ: Prentice-Hall.

Graedel, T. E., B. R. Allenby, and P. R. Comrie. 1995. "Matrix Approaches to Abridge Life Cycle Assessment." *Environmental Science and Technology* 29: 134A–139A.

Haecker, M. A., S. Edwards, B. Moore, and B. Zaruba. 1995. "Exploiting Desk-Top GIS for Effective Environmental Information Presentation and Communication at U.S. Air Force Bases." Air and Waste Management Association meeting.

Hamel, Gary, and C. K. Prahalad. 1994. *Competing for the Future: Breakthrough Strategies for Seizing Control of Your Industry and Creating the Markets of Tomorrow.* Boston: Harvard Business School Press.

Harvard Business School. 1990. *Ashland Oil Inc.: Trouble at Floreffe,* Case study: 9-390-017.

Hiatt, Arnold S. 1993. "Social Responsibility and the Bottom Line." *Business Ethics: Generating Trust in the 1990s and Beyond.* The Conference Board, Report 1057-94-CH, pp. 11–12.

Hopkins, Thomas D. 1995. "A Guide to the Regulatory Landscape." *Jobs & Capital,* Fall, Vol. 4, pp. 28–31.

Ishikawa, Kaoru. 1985. *What Is Total Quality Control? The Japanese Way.* Englewood Cliffs, NJ: Prentice-Hall.

ISO/DIS 14001, 1995. "Environmental Management System Conformance Standard." The International Organization for Standardization. Geneva, Switzerland.

ISO/DIS 14004, 1995. "Environmental Management Systems—General Guidelines on Principles, Systems, and Supporting Techniques." The International Organization for Standardization. Geneva, Switzerland

ISO 9000: International Standards for Quality Management, 3rd ed., International Organization for Standardization, Geneva, 1993.

James, Peter. 1994. "Business Environmental Performance Measurement." *Business Strategy and the Environment.* UK: ERP Environment, pp. 59–67. Shipley, West Yorkshire, UK.

Johannsen, Lynn. 1995. "If Innovation Is Important to Your Organization's Survival, How Will TQEM Help?" *Total Quality Environmental Management* 4: 135–141.

Johnson, Curtis J. 1995. "Browning-Ferris Industries' Computerized System for Managing Audit and Environmental Performance." *Auditing for Environmental Quality Leadership: Beyond Compliance to Environmental Excellence,* John T. Willig, Editor. New York: John Wiley & Sons, pp. 291–299.

Karch, Kenneth M. 1994. "Getting Organizational Buy-In for Benchmarking: Environmental Management at Weyerhaeuser." *Total Quality Environmental Management* 3: 297–308.

Klafter, Brenda A. 1992. "Case Study: AT&T and Intel Pollution Prevention Benchmarking." GEMI Conference proceedings, pp. 75–80.

Klafter, Brenda A., B. Dambach, T. McManus, J. Sekutowski, and A. Soderberg. 1993. "Environmental Benchmarking: At&T and Intel's Project to Determine the Best-in-Class Corporate Pollution Prevention Programs." GEMI Conference proceedings, pp. 37–45.

Kolluru, Rao V. 1995a. "Minimize EHS Risks and Improve the Bottom Line." *Chemical Engineering Progress* (June) 44–52.

Kolluru, Rao V. 1995b. *Environmental Strategies Handbook.* New York: McGraw-Hill.

Kristof, David S. 1992. *Digital Equipment Corporation: Benchmarking Against Standards of Excellence.* The Environmental TQM Conference. New York: Executive Enterprises.

Lash, J. and D. Buzzelli. 1995, "Beyond Old Style Regulation." *Journal of Commerce* (February 28).

Levering, Robert and Milton Moskowitz. 1993. *The 100 Best Companies to Work for in America.* New York: Doubleday.

Levin, Victoria. 1994. "Using Benchmarking to Minimize Common DOE Waste Streams." *Methodology and Liquid Photographic Waste, Vol. 1. Sandia National Laboratories,* (SAND 93-3992).

Long, Frederick J. and M. Arnold. 1995. *"The Power Of Environmental Partnerships."* The Management Institute for Environment and Business. Fort Worth TX,: Dryden Press.

Lynn, F. M. 1994. "Community Advisory Panels Within the Chemical Industry: Antecedents and Issues." *Business Strategy and the Environment.* ERP Environment, pp. 92–99. U.K. Shipley, West Yorkshire, UK.

Mulligan, William. 1993. "Demonstrating the Power of Empowerment." *Successfully Utilizing Environmental Measurement, Benchmarking and Employee Empowerment.* Executive Enterprises conference, Washington, DC.

Murphy, Patrick E. and G. Enderle. 1995. "Managerial Ethical Leadership: Examples Do Matter." *Business Ethics Quarterly* 5: 117–128.

National Institute of Standards, 1995. Malcolm Baldrige National Quality Award Criteria. Department of Commerce.

Nulty, Peter. 1993. "The National Business Hall of Fame," *Fortune* 127: 108–112.

Orlin, Judy, P. Swalwell, and C. Fitzgerald. 1993–1994. "How to Integrate Information Strategy Planning with Environmental Management Information Systems." *Total Quality Environmental Management* 3: 193–202.

Peach, Robert. W. 1990. "Creating a Pattern of Excellence," Target, Vol. 6, Winter, p. 15.

Peach, Robert W. 1994. *The ISO 9000 Handbook*, 2nd edition. CEEM Information Services. Fairfax, VA.

Peters, Thomas and Robert Waterman. 1992. *In Search of Excellence: Lessons from America's Best-Run Companies.* New York: Harper & Row.

Porter, Michael. 1985. *Competitive Advantage: Creating and Sustaining Superior Performance.* New York: The Free Press.

Porter, Michael and Claas van der Linde. 1995. "Green and Competitive." *Harvard Business Review* 73: 120–133.

Price Waterhouse. 1994. "Progress on the Environmental Challenge."

Reimann, Curt W. and H. Hertz. 1993. "The Malcolm Baldrige National Quality Award and ISO 9000 Registration: Understanding Their Many Important Differences." *ASTM Standardization News* (November), 42–51.

Ruble, Barbara Jo, 1995. "Supporting Auditing Programs with Automated Tools." *Auditing for Environmental Quality Leadership: Beyond Compliance to Environmental Excellence,* John T. Willig, Editor. New York: John Wiley & Sons, pp. 281–290.

Schmidheiny, Stephan. 1992. Changing Course, Cambridge, MA: MIT Press.

Schrum, Roger. 1991. "Challenge in Crisis Management: A Case Study of the Pittsburgh Diesel Fuel Spill. GEMI Conference proceedings pp 181–185.

Scott, Mary and Howard Rothman. 1994. *Companies with a Conscience: Intimate Portraits of Twelve Firms that Make a Difference.* New York: Citadel Press.

Secor, J. D. 1992. "Rooting for America: The Bonding of an Environmental Initiative with Community Relations." GEMI Conference proceedings, pp. 165–168.

Skooglund, Carl M. 1993. "Using Peer Companies to Audit Ethics Programs." *Business Ethics: Generating Trust in the 1990's and Beyond,* The Conference Board, Report 1057-94-CH, pp. 19–20.

Smart, Bruce. 1992. *Beyond Compliance, A New Industry View of the Environment.* World Resources Institute.

Thomas, Dave. 1994. *Well Done!: The Common Guy's Guide to Everyday Success.* New York: Harper.

Uttal, Bro. 1987. "Companies that Serve You Best." *Fortune* (December 7), 98–116.

Weitz, Keith A., J. K. Smith, and J. L. Warren. 1994. Developing a Decision Support Tool for Life-Cycle Cost Assessments. *Total Quality Environmental Management* 4: 23–36.

Weld, Royal F. 1993. "How CEO's See It." *ECO Magazine* 1: 6–14.

Wells, Richard. 1995. "Auditing for Compliance Is Only the Beginning: Lessons from Leading Companies." *Auditing for Environmental Quality Leadership,* John T. Willig, Editor. New York: John Wiley & Sons, pp. 11–21.

Wells, Richard, P. M. N. Hochman, S. D. Hochman, and P. A. O'Connell. 1992. "Measuring Environmental Success." *Total Quality Environmental Management* 1: 315–327.

Wever, Grace. 1991. "The Impact of Voluntary and Regulatory Approaches on Net Present Value." Economics and Environmental Regulation Session, Canadian Chemical Conference and Exhibition, Toronto.

Wever, Grace. 1993. "Using TQEM as a Management Framework for Sustainability." Water Environment Federation Conference, Los Angeles, AC93-045-004.

Wever, Grace. 1994a. "The Need for Ecosystem-Based Performance Indicators to Drive Responsible Policy and Management Strategies." *Indicators of Environmental Performance and Ecosystem Condition,* National Academy of Engineering conference, Woods Hole, MA.

Wever, Grace. 1994b. "Applying TQM to the Public Policy Process: A Case Study of Great Lakes Regional Environmental Issues." Annual Environmental Excellence course. Government Institutes, Orlando, FL.

Wever, Grace. 1995a. "Applying a Total Quality Management Framework to the Public Policy Process, Part I: The Framework." *Total Quality Environmental Management* 4: 63–73.

Wever, Grace. 1995b. "Applying a Total Quality Management Framework to the Public Policy Process, Part II: A Case Study of the Great Lakes." *Total Quality Environmental Management.* 4: 75–91.

Wever, Grace and G. Vorhauer. 1991. "Development of a Baldrige-type Total Quality Environmental Management Award for the Great Lakes Region." GEMI Conference proceedings, pp. 195–200.

Woods, Sandra K. 1994. "Making Pollution Prevention Part of the Coors Culture." *Total Quality Environmental Management* 3: 31–38.

Wise, Glenn L. 1995. "Ciba Geigy Develops New Regional Remediation Teams to Manage Superfund Programs." *Total Quality Environmental Management* 4: 21–32.

Wolf, Hans A. 1993. "Ethics by Example." *Business Ethics: Generating Trust in the 1990s and Beyond*, The Conference Board, Report 1057-94-CH, pp. 18–19.

GLOSSARY

AOP Annual Operating Plan, a document that describes programs and funding for one fiscal year.

Approach Methods, including philosophy, used to implement a requirement shown in a given cell. Criteria for Approach include:

- Degree to which the approach is prevention-based
- Appropriateness of tools and techniques used to meet the requirement
- Degree to which the approach is systematic, integrated, and consistently applied
- Degree to which the approach embodies effective self-evaluation feedback and adaptation cycles to sustain continuous improvement
- Degree to which the approach is based on quantitative information that is objective and reliable
- Indicators of unique and innovative approaches, including significant and new adaptations of tools and techniques used in other applications or types of businesses

Assessment/Audit Process that systematically verifies/determines performance as well as management system deficiencies and proficiencies (strengths and weaknesses).

Baseline Data collected initially (often before improvement efforts) that provides a reference point to evaluate effectiveness of improvement efforts.

Benchmarking The search for those best practices that will lead to superior performance of a unit.

Best-in-Class   The best known performer for the characteristics being measured. A commonly used process to determine this is benchmarking.

Business Plan   A document that details methodology, strategy, funding, and so on, used to attain business goals. This document normally covers at least five fiscal years, and more often, the life of a product or project.

Consensus   Reaching agreement, or developing a common opinion, among all or most members of a group.

Continuous Improvement Cycle   Systematic process that elevates performance to higher level by identifying improvement opportunities, developing and implementing plans, verifying improvements, and corrective/preventive action. Deals with both breakthrough as well as incremental types of improvements.

Cross-Functional Team   Team that includes expertise and/or representation from all areas required to reach group's goals and objectives (e.g., could include management, employees from operations, financial, business unit, maintenance, EHS, legal, information systems, and R&D).

Customer/Stakeholder   The current or future recipient of the many and diverse outputs (products, processes, services) of an organization, team, or individual. This includes customers (current, former, internal, external), government, shareholders, senior management, suppliers, employees, community, media, academia, and the public.

Deployment   Refers to the extent to which approaches are applied. The criteria used to evaluate Deployment include the following:

- Appropriate and effective application to all product, operations, and service characteristics
- Appropriate and effective application to all transactions and interactions with customers and stakeholders
- Appropriate and effective application to all internal processes, activities, facilities, and employees

Key Result Areas   Broad-based areas of performance that, when measured, give a unit an evaluation of its critical customer/stakeholder-driven processes.

Mission   Charge given to unit, organization, or other entity that defines its role, purpose, product, scope, and customer/stakeholder base.

Mistake-Proofing   A process that examines possible failure modes and takes action to prevent their occurrence.

Pareto Process   Process used to compare and prioritize issues/actions, and so on. Quantitates, where possible, potential outcomes, consequences, costs, frequencies of occurrence, and so on.

Principles   Guiding elements or directives that govern a unit's decision-making, development, planning, and implementation activities.

Process   A group or series of activities or events that transform materials or ideas into a useful product or service.

Result   Refers to outcomes or effects produced by successfully implementing a TQM system. Criteria for Result include:

- Extent of improvement achieved in quality of management processes and systems, as well as performance
- Rate and breadth of improvement
- Demonstration of sustained improvement
- Significance of improvements from the unit's business perspective
- Comparison with industry and world leaders
- Ability to show that improvements are derived from Quality management systems/processes

Root-Cause Analysis   Process that systematically determines the fundamental reason behind a problem or concern so that corrective and/or preventive action can be applied.

Stakeholder   One with a share or interest in the unit, such as employees, customers, shareholders, suppliers, management, community, government, public interest groups, and academics.

Strategic Plan   A broad long-term action plan designed to lead a unit to its goals.

TQM   Total Quality Management, a systematic, pervasive approach to constantly improving the quality of products, processes, and services of a unit.

Trend Line   Line on a graph that shows overall direction of data. The line is drawn in such a way that approximately half the data points lie on either side of the line.

Unit   A company, organization, division, department, subsidiary, work center, and so on.

APPENDIX

Students may want to compare elements of environmental principles published by individual companies, business associations, and advocacy groups. Some are provided here; others can be found in the general literature or obtained from individual trade associations, companies, and other organizations on request.

RESPONSIBLE CARE GUIDING PRINCIPLES*

To recognize and respond to community concerns about chemicals and our operations.

To develop and produce chemicals that can be manufactured, transported, used, and disposed of safely.

To make health, safety, and environmental considerations a priority in our planning for all existing and new products and processes.

To report promptly to officials, employees, customers, and the public, information on chemical-related health or environmental hazards and to recommend protective measures.

To counsel customers on the safe use, transportation, and disposal of chemical products.

To operate our plants and facilities in a manner that protects the environment and the health and safety of our employees and the public.

To extend knowledge by conducting or supporting research on the health, safety, and environmental effects of our products, processes, and waste materials.

*Source: Chemical Manufacturers Association.

To work with others to resolve problems created by past handling and disposal of hazardous substances.

To participate with government and others in creating responsible laws, regulations and standards to safeguard the community, workplace, and environment.

To promote the principles and practices of Responsible Care by sharing experiences and offering assistance to others who produce, handle, use, transport or dispose of chemicals.

A number of business organizations have created environmental principles, including national trade associations and international bodies. The International Chamber of Commerce's Business Charter for Sustainable Development, consisting of a set of sixteen principles, is given below. Several other organizations (e.g., the Chemical Manufacturer's Association and the American Forest and Paper Association) have also developed such lists. Companies that adopt such principles must go beyond rhetoric to practices, developing standards and practices that are consistent with the underlying values and ethics.

International Chamber of Commerce Business Charter for Sustainable Development

1. *Corporate Priority* To recognize environmental management as among the highest corporate priorities and as a key determinant to sustainable development; to establish policies, programs, and practices for conducting operations in an environmentally sound manner.

2. *Integrated Management* To integrate these policies, programs, and practices fully into each business as an essential element of management in all its functions.

3. *Process of Improvement* To continue to improve policies, programs, and environmental performance, taking into account technical developments, scientific understanding, consumer needs, and community expectations, with legal regulations as starting point; and to apply the same environmental criteria internationally.

4. *Employee Education* To educate, train, and motivate employees to conduct their activities in an environmentally responsible manner.

5. *Prior Assessment* To assess environmental impacts before starting a new activity or project and before decommissioning a facility or leaving a site.

6. *Products and Services* To develop and provide products or services that have no undue environmental impact and are safe in their intended use, that are efficient in their consumption of energy and natural resources, and that can be recycled, reused, or disposed of safety.

7. *Customer Advice*   To advise, and where relevant, educate customers, distributors, and the public in the safe use, transportation, storage, and disposal of products provided; and to apply similar considerations to the provisions of services.

8. *Facilities and Operations*   To develop, design, and operate facilities and conduct activities, taking into consideration the efficient use of energy and materials, the sustainable use of renewable resources, the minimization of adverse environmental impact and waste generation, and the safe and responsible disposal of residual wastes.

9. *Research*   To conduct or support research on the environmental impacts of raw materials, products, processes, emissions, and wastes associated with the enterprise and on the means of minimizing such adverse impacts.

10. *Precautionary Approach*   To modify the manufacture, marketing, or use of products or services or the conduct of activities, consistent with scientific and technical understanding, to prevent serious or irreversible environmental degradation.

11. *Contractors and Suppliers*   To promote the adoption of these principles by contractors acting on behalf of the enterprise, encouraging and where appropriate, requiring improvements in their practices to make them consistent with those of the enterprise; and to encourage the wider adoption of these principles by suppliers.

12. *Emergency Preparedness*   To develop and maintain, where significant hazards exist, emergency preparedness plans in conjunction with the emergency services, relevant authorities and the local community, recognizing potential transboundary impacts.

13. *Transfer of Technology*   To contribute to the transfer of environmentally sound technology and management methods throughout the industrial and public sectors.

14. *Contributing to the Common Effect*   To contribute to the development of public policy and to business, governmental and intergovernmental programs and educational initiatives that will enhance environmental awareness and protection.

15. *Openness to Concerns*   To foster openness and dialogue with employees and the public, anticipating and responding to their concerns about potential hazards and impacts of operations, products, wastes, or services, including those of transboundary or global significance.

16. *Compliance and Reporting*   To measure environmental performance; to conduct regular environmental audits and assessments of compliance with company requirements, legal requirements, and these principles; and periodically to provide appropriate information to the Board of Directors, shareholders, employees, the authorities, and the public.

INDEX